The Open Circle
Peter Brook's Theatre Environments

THE OPEN CIRCLE
Peter Brook's Theatre Environments

ANDREW TODD AND JEAN-GUY LECAT

faber and faber

First published in 2003
by Faber and Faber Limited
3 Queen Square London WC1N 3AU

Published in the United States by Faber and Faber Inc.,
an affiliate of Farrar, Straus and Giroux LLC, New York

Designed and typeset by Faber and Faber Limited

Printed in and bound in Malta by Gutenberg Press Ltd

All photographs were taken by Jean-Guy Lecat except for the following:
Andrew Todd, pages 3r, 5, 221 (2 photos); Béatrice Heyligers, 7, 8, 36, 54, 57;
Gilles Abegg, 22, 124, 125 *top l&r*, 182, 183, 186, 211, 223; Jean-Charruyer, 39; Nicolas
Tikhomiroff, 42 (3 photos), 45; Mary Ellen Mark, 48, 49; Mark Enguerand, 70;
Agnès Patrix, 73; Philippe Mulon, 76l; Bernand, 80; Nicolas Treatt, 83;
George Méran, 131; Philippe Mulon, 138 (2 photos), 140 *top l&r*; Matthias Horn, 205 *top*;
Rosa Frank, 205 *bottom*; Philippe Vialatte, 217 (2 photos); P. Victor/Maxppp, 227.
Page 120: plan after drawing by Toshiya Kusaka. Page 197: picture of Convento
do Beato António courtesy of Companhia Industrial de Portugal.

A CIP record for this book
is available from the British Library
ISBN 0–571–21490–8

10 9 8 7 6 5 4 3 2 1

Contents

Preface and Acknowledgements

The title of this book goes some way towards describing a configuration of theatre space which Peter Brook has used for over thirty years: a three-quarters embrace of an acting area by an audience, with the other quarter left open to a background surface or volume. This acting area is not necessarily a literal circle (although it often has been), but metaphorically speaking, whether the environment is a rectilinear modern theatre, a horseshoe-shaped *théâtre à l'italienne* or a haphazard village square in Africa, the audience forms a *circle of community*, a society in microcosm momentarily assembled around the action, in full awareness of itself and the space it occupies. Contrary to the frontal, image-driven configuration of most 'two-room' or proscenium theatres, this form opens itself to possibilities of chance interaction, inviting a subtle destabilization of the dichotomy of 'us' – audience – versus 'them' – performers. Furthermore, the selection of the spaces themselves denotes an openness to the independent reality of *things*: the mud walls of Africa, the tombs of Persepolis and the background environments in dozens of 'found' spaces in Europe and America which form the 'fourth wall' of these circles are allowed to retain their identity: they are not presented in a self-consciously 'theatrical' manner.

'The Open Circle' could also serve to describe the nature of the collaboration which has brought about both the performance spaces themselves and this text. Peter Brook's group – the Centre International de Creations Théâtrales (CICT) – is fundamentally based on the notion of *sharing* – responsibility, ideas, roles, activities. Actors have washed down marketplaces in order to perform there, have arranged audience members in city streets, learned how to rake sand for the 'Zen garden' setting of *The Tempest*, and put out backstage electrical fires in Australia; 'technical' staff have provided ideas for the *mise-en-*

scène, stolen branches from the Bois de Boulogne, and dug up countless samples of earth around the world; musicians have become actors, and actors have become musicians.

The spaces described in this book depended for their creation on the *disciplined freedom* of this collaboration – particularly that between Brook, technical director Jean-Guy Lecat and designer Chloé Obolensky. The book, likewise, has developed as a group activity: in the first instance a dialogue between myself (a curious outsider, a putative 'audience member') and Jean-Guy, always guided and provoked by Peter Brook, and also drawing upon the differing insights of Yoshi Oida, Bruce Myers, Natasha Parry, Maurice Bénichou, Jean-Claude Carrière, Sotigui Kouyaté, Chloé Obolensky and Marie-Hélène Estienne (whose idea it was originally to compile this work). The aforementioned are long-standing members of the Centre's circle of collaborators; their varied (and sometimes contradictory) impressions, together with Brook's, are presented throughout the book by way of illustration of and counterpoint to the narrative text. Rather than presenting a homogeneous account, the aim has been to show the diversity – perhaps even chaos – which can be necessary for successful collective creation. It is hoped that some overall sense of how the Centre has produced its work will emerge from between the lines.

The book's structure is largely narrative, beginning with the turning-point discovery of the Théâtre des Bouffes du Nord and an examination of the reasons for this theatre's appropriateness for the Centre's activities in the light of Brook's preceding quarter-century of work; the story is then continued chronologically at the Bouffes and on tour, describing the unpredictable, passionate and inventive search the Centre has undertaken to find a temporary home for its work in a world which typically offers little in the way of inspiring theatre spaces. The aim of this search has been to create a community refounded every night in constantly changing circumstances, and through this to eke out a sense of what might turn *universally* between vastly different peoples and places.

The theatrical worlds described in this book depend on sharply defined environments and on a powerful sense of enclosure and threshold. The search behind them, however, begins by setting aside all boundaries and definitions, to start with a blank slate and an open mind. One of the first principles of this search is that the more one respects and attempts to communicate with a public, the more worthwhile the shared experience is likely to be. The Centre's journey of discovery in the realm of theatre space is uniquely broad and rich; it is perhaps the most comprehensive experiment of such a kind since the time of Shakespeare and Molière.

Information which, for want of a better word, I shall call 'technical' – dimensions, materials, etc. – has been included in the text at a certain risk of encumbering the narrative. It is included because it is dangerous to present these quantitative factors in isolation from the theatrical *qualities* they have engendered, which themselves are inseparable from a much broader story of culture and place. If the specific forms of the Centre's spaces are to be of use to others (which is an important aim of the present volume), the particular, concrete circumstances behind their creation need to be understood in order to draw any lessons of general value.

This book has benefited from the support, participation and insight of many people and institutions. The Graham Foundation for Advanced Studies in the Visual Arts generously funded research, documentation and design during work on the second draft. Neil Wallace's precedent study on this subject, which included interviews with Mel Gussow, Michael Billington and some of the company members, and studies he commissioned from Iain Mackintosh and David Williams contain many thoughts which have helped us in our work. Deborah Warner, Declan Donnellan, Biel Moll, Hugh Hardy, Jack Martin, Rose Fenton, Robert Palmer, Roy Somlyo and Harvey Lichstenstein have recounted their involvement – whether direct or tangential – with the Centre's work; some of them are quoted in the text. Nina Soufy has shown exemplary patience and generosity in the tracking down and supplying of documentary material, as has Micheline Rozan. Members of the Bouffes du Nord's staff, especially Sophie Darragui, have provided much support. (The book was largely written at the theatre in the Centre's archives; the majority of the 30,000 photographs in the collection – and therefore of those in this volume – were taken by Jean-Guy Lecat.) David Bradby, Elizabeth Kubany of Hardy Holzman Pfeiffer Associates, Beth Emelson of the Vivian Beaumont Theatre, Klaus Nasedand of the Deutsches Schauspielhaus, Hamburg, and Bill Murray and Elena Park at BAM have also been helpful with documents and details.

In addition to the continual review of the book undertaken

within the Centre (especially by Peter Brook), the text has been reviewed by Alex Anderson, David Williams, Antoni Ramon and Amedeo Petrilli (who deserves particular recognition for sustained support and encouragement). Their comments have had a positive influence on both details and general form, but they themselves should be excused from any faults that remain, which are entirely our own responsibility. Others who have provided encouragement, inspiration and practical support – whether direct or indirect – include David Leatherbarrow, John Dixon Hunt, the late Ivan Illich, Giancarlo de Carlo (who published an article of mine in his review *Spazio e società* which formed the germ of the present volume), Maddalena Ferarra, David Mayernik, Maria Delogu, Laurence Forbin and especially my wife, Bridget O'Rourke, whose well-judged patience and impatience have been key ingredients in the process of producing this book.

Ruggero Pierantoni graciously engaged with a series of questions we raised related to the perception of space, providing a thorough insight into the responses that contemporary biophysics might have concerning phenomena which have had a determining influence on the form of the spaces in this book. While it is impossible in this context to reproduce the entirety of his contribution, it is hoped that a collaboration of this nature between scientists and artists might point the way towards a richer consideration (in a subsequent volume) of the nature of theatre space – a domain which has become victim to a somewhat ossified, uncomprehending relationship between 'artistic' architectural 'decorators', pseudo-scientific scenographic consultants, and *very* scientific technical directors.

Laia Escribà, Sara Palomares, Kerstin Follenius, Anne Pollock and Jan Bluhm endured the stifling heat and cramped conditions in Jean-Guy's office (not to mention the noise from a clothing factory in the space above) to produce the superb architectural drawings which are essential to this book.

Particular thanks are due to Michael Earley, who was intimately involved in the genesis of this book; to Peggy Paterson and Ron Costley at Faber for their fortitude, patience and good humour; and to Peter Brook, self-described 'godfather' of the project, whose wit, generosity, criticism and – above all – common sense lie at the still centre of this circle.

Andrew Todd

Paris, 2003

The Open Circle

1: Home: The Bouffes du Nord

> What is finding? Finding is *recognizing* that what you are
> looking for suddenly is there.
> PETER BROOK

Discovery

In the evening rush hour the rue du Faubourg Saint-Denis is
clogged with traffic leaving Paris for the northern suburbs.
Indian men chatter in groups on the pavement at the end of a
day's work; up towards Montmartre there are African women
in beautiful dresses, their babies tucked into the back. The
shops are not what you'd find on the *Grands Boulevards*:
Varaspathy Textiles, Sakhti Emporium (with plastic Ganeshas
and Gandhis in the window), a halal butcher whose skinned
lambs' heads stare out on to the street. A noisy elevated Métro
crosses at the boulevard de la Chapelle, running along the line
of the eighteenth-century city wall.

On the south-west corner of the intersection, where an
entrance to the city used to stand, there is a perfectly ordinary
glazed café *terrasse*. A modest plastic sign indicates an affilia-
tion with a theatre, but there is no evidence of such a space visible from the street. Inside there are the *zinc*, wooden chairs
and marble-topped tables of a typical Parisian café. These
familiar objects mingle with details which heighten the atmosphere: hand-painted signs for *Le Mahabharata*, *La Cerisaie*
and *Ubu aux Bouffes*; a chef's station which spills out through
the door of a tiny kitchen into the room, so that the finishing

The café of the Bouffes
du Nord

touches to his dishes are performed in the bosom of the restaurant. The ochre walls rise to a generous height and are adorned with two ageing mirrors. But the most unusual charge comes from the customers themselves: there is a higher level of energy than one would find in another café at the end of a day, a buzz of anticipation. The large volume fills with a gradual crescendo of conversation; some people linger near the door, waiting for the moment when an unspoken consensus ends the drinking and the rush begins for returns and the theatre's last-minute stage-side cushions.

Back outside in the city, tolerating rain or cold, the crowd huddles through a doorway at the centre of the block's nineteenth-century façade. The crush continues up a short flight of stairs, through more doors, and into a curving passage whose inside wall is of exposed rubble, as if one had discovered a quarry buried deep within the city block. The curve presages a volume buried deeper still, on the other side of the rock. After a last door, this room suddenly relieves the crush, dissipates the nervous energy into its height. The eye is led around the arc of three balconies, then up slender columns to the filigreed cupola. The balconies, grey with age, gather the audience around a shaft of space which hovers above a central playing area. Opposite, two high bands of wall have a story to tell in their scars and the intermingling layers of faded and glowing paint. Between these walls there is a battered arch, and beyond that a vast rectangular volume whose back wall is smeared with the same colours as the vertical bands in the first space. Cracked moulding divides the wall's surface; there are deep pockmarks and fissures.

The audience is tightly focused around the acting area, facing inward in mutual awareness. The chamber beyond the proscenium arch opens this circle into another world which is reciprocal to it, a huge scale against which the intimacy of the arena finds relief. Its walls belong to the same world as the auditorium, but suggest the possibility of imagining oneself somewhere else: in a palace, a mosque, a vast landscape, a cave, a forest. The audience, trailing with them the memory of the outside air, the noise of the Métro and the café's smoke, are enclosed inside the mass of the city, hushed in preparation for the beginning of the performance.

Hundreds of people discover the Théâtre des Bouffes du Nord in this way each night, whether for one of Peter Brook's productions or for one of the many international companies he invites to use his theatre. Brook's is probably the only theatre which could draw a 'cultured' public to this tough corner of the 10th arrondissement. The conventional monuments of the theatrical establishment – the Odéon and the Comédie-Française, for example – fit in well with the museums, palaces and churches around them. The Bouffes du Nord, however, is literally buried in an unbroken texture of ordinary life; a visit here is made special before one steps through the door because of the reversal of expectations it entails – a kind of pilgrimage into the everyday. (Perhaps Shakespeare's audience felt a similar frisson as they crossed the Thames, leaving the City for the lawless Bankside.)

Peter Brook did not consciously intend to put this ordinary corner of Paris on the map of world theatre. He did not set out specifically to find a forgotten theatre in a multi-ethnic neighbourhood. If there was an intention in his discovery of the Bouffes du Nord, it lay in an openness to the many chance factors which made the theatre available at the right time, and in having, over years of work, prepared himself to know that its surprising and delicate blend of qualities was exactly what he was looking for.

> PETER BROOK: *One day, nearly thirty years ago, Micheline Rozan suggested that we go and look at an abandoned theatre behind the Gare du Nord. We arrived at the place de la Chapelle, but there was absolutely no evidence of the building: just a typical nineteenth-century Parisian façade turning the corner of the boulevard. We investigated further: there was some loose boarding covering a hole in the wall which we wrenched aside and then crawled into a dark tunnel. There was debris all around, and still no sign of the promised space. Suddenly a door opened and there was the Bouffes – a majestic volume with light streaming down through the dome and the dusty air on to what looked, at ground level, like a bomb site. There was a heap of rubble in the middle of the space with wires hanging everywhere, evidence of destruction in progress.*
>
> *I was immediately certain that this was the right place for us. Even in its suffering condition there was an elegance to the proportions, a dignity to the atmosphere. It was clearly a theatre, but it looked nothing like it must have done previously: the 'cultural' skin of architectural finish had been cauterized away. All the stalls seats were missing, except a few that had been smashed up and thrown to one side. It seemed obvious that all we had to do was sweep away the rubble and find a means to sit people at the ground level. The balcony seats were fine – they could be used as they were. And the walls could also stay as they were – covered in pockmarks, flayed raw by time, weather and human destruction. The owner was quickly contacted and offered to rent us just the auditorium, blocking up the proscenium so he could still use the volume behind. This might have worked – as a kind of Eliza-*

The Bouffes du Nord
at the time it was
discovered by Peter
Brook in 1974

*bethan theatre – but he then changed his mind and offered us the
whole space, including the void left where he had demolished the
former stage; we decided to leave this hole as it was, and use it as
a rather unconventional entrance to the acting space.*

*Money and time were the next problems: we absolutely want-
ed to open* Timon of Athens *in this theatre for the 1974 Festival
d'Automne, otherwise we'd be in the situation of using someone
else's space, and our group would have nowhere to go after the
production. Micheline Rozan directed her formidable powers of
persuasion at Michel Guy, an old friend who had just been*

appointed Minister of Culture by Georges Pompidou. He was doubtful at first, but Micheline insisted, and we had the money and the necessary permits in record time. The designer Georges Wakhevitch put a team of his assistants to work at phenomenal speed building seats out of wooden planks with straw cushions, making adjustments for fire safety, levelling the floor surface to make it into our new stage. The deadline was so soon upon us that some spectators on the first night were literally glued to their seats because the varnish hadn't had time to dry – we ended up paying them compensation for the bits of skirt and trouser they left behind.

Micheline and I decided that we should have the lowest ticket prices possible, the same price for every seat, and no reserved places. (We settled on 10 francs for our first few productions.) We wanted to banish any ideas of social hierarchy in the theatre, of poorer people taking a separate entrance and climbing to the 'gods'. We also wanted to open the theatre to people from the neighbourhood, inviting them free of charge to preview nights, putting on Christmas and Easter shows, and having a cheap matinee every week which could attract old people or whole families who might not think of going to the theatre after dark, or

HOME: THE BOUFFES DU NORD

because it was too expensive.

Fortunately Timon *worked very well here, and everyone who came to see it was charmed by the space. It gave us the idea to begin work immediately on several other shows: we stayed at night after the performances to rehearse* Les Ik, *and we thought further ahead to* Ubu *and* The Conference of the Birds. *After three years of travelling, playing in all manner of environments, we had suddenly found a home.*

JEAN-CLAUDE CARRIÈRE: *In the case of the Bouffes I think one can speak of love at first sight, of falling for a space. And, as when one falls in love with a woman, one had no idea what the course of the relationship would be: in the first instance it was just something natural and evident. This place is extraordinary. The first time I went there with Peter the floor was covered in rubble, and there was a curious dishevelled man sitting on a heap of broken plaster and drinking from a bottle of Pommard. (He offered us a swig, which we accepted, sitting down on blocks of cement.) There was a touch of the fairy tale about it – a space seemed to be waiting for us in a state of slumber, miraculously preserved from the demolitions of the 1970s which destroyed many sites in Paris. The Bouffes had absolutely nothing to do with any preconceived ideas we could have had of a theatre for ourselves: we were looking for a space, but we had no idea if it should be modern or old. The Bouffes was unimaginable for us:* it told *us what to do.*

The Bouffes du Nord was in danger of coming to a definite conclusion of its 100-year history when Peter Brook chanced upon it. Its owner, Narcisse Zecchinel, had little desire to use it as a theatre (a role which it had not undertaken for twenty-two years): in fact he was preparing to demolish it bit by bit in order to use the site for a car park. Fire had damaged the balconies, and he had destroyed the stalls seating; a leaking roof was allowed to continue the process of degeneration from above. It was at just this point of near-death that it awakened in Brook an answer to many of the questions about space raised during the nomadic search his group had undertaken since the late 1960s (described in the following chapter). Stripped bare of the civilizing encumbrance of upholstered chairs and a decorative finish, it was an essential theatrical form, a raw space made for gathering and sharing. The fire had scorched off the top skin which stops the imagination at a specific style or period; now the gaze was able to penetrate layers

Jean-Claude Carrière has collaborated as writer and translator on many of the Centre's productions, in particular the *Mahabharata* and *The Conference of the Birds*. He has written screenplays for Luis Buñuel (*Belle de Jour, The Discreet Charm of the Bourgeoisie*), Jean-Luc Godard, Milos Forman and Volker Schlöndorff. He has written several books, inlcuding *Un Dictionnaire Amoureux de l'Inde* and *La Force du bouddhisme* (with the Dalai Lama).

9

suspended partway between cultural definition and natural disintegration, between the here and now and the dissolution of all at the end of time.

The theatre's passage through history is etched on the walls, but these traces do not bring to mind specific events. Unlike La Fenice in Venice, whose recent degradation was very public (and tinged with politics), the Bouffes is a forgotten, inscrutable ruin, a commemoration of only a general entropy. But of course it *did* chart a very particular course in order to arrive at its 1974 nadir, and it had drawn at its creation upon a unique series of precedent forms which link it closely to the beginnings of Western theatre.

Origins

Until Peter Brook discovered and transformed it, the Bouffes du Nord had an erratic existence coloured more by failure than by success. In fact, at the beginning, it seemed possible that it would never get off the ground at all: in its first decade, from 1876 to 1885, there were no fewer than fifteen artistic directors in succession, all of whom failed to find an audience for the theatre. Olga Léaud was perhaps the worst of an unsuccessful bunch: after her production had failed, she fled the theatre with the contents of the safe, before the actors and staff had been paid; the theatre had to close briefly as a result.

The staircase between the stalls and first balcony inside the auditorium

Although the building itself received positive notices, it seems that this city-edge neighbourhood was not ready to support such a venture, in spite of the populist appeal to *opera buffa* contained in its name. The rue du Faubourg Saint-Denis was then, as it is now, a seedy part of town – 'rather deserted and dangerous, not a good place to walk through after dark', according to a contemporary observer.* Located at the inter-section of the exterior boulevard and a major artery to the northern suburbs, the building had its façade composed to take full advantage of its position of welcome at an entry point into the city. But it seems that the distance from the Gare du Nord (where the city's hackney cabs stopped) and from more prosperous Montmartre was a real handicap; the immediate neighbourhood, made up of dignified nineteenth-century Haussmannian blocks, could not provide a suitable audience by itself for its low-brow programme of 'café-concert' performances.

*Unattributed quotation in the archives of the Bibliothèque National des Arts du Spectacle.

The theatre's fortunes were revived, at least artistically

speaking, by the arrival of Abel Ballet as director in 1885. He invited Aurélien Lugné-Poë's Théâtre de l'Œuvre company to take up residence, which they did from 1893 to 1896. Lugné-Poë, one of the first modern directors of note in French theatre, put on the earliest Parisian productions of Ibsen (including *An Enemy of the People* and *The Master Builder*, which were dismissed as 'Ibsenities' by the critics). Part of the 'Nabis' circle (which included Gauguin, Maurice Denis and Pierre Bonnard, prefiguring abstraction with their fascination with pure colour and shape in painting), he was a pioneer of the darkening of the auditorium during performances (following Wagner at Bayreuth), using light and colour as almost abstract elements on the stage.

The Théâtre de l'Œuvre had aims and methods uncannily similar to those of the International Centre: it was an open-ended collaboration between actors, artists and musicians of diverse cultural origins, with a base in Paris and lengthy periods of touring abroad to bring the work into contact with an international public as broadly constituted as the group itself. Ambitious plans to set up satellite bases in London, The Hague and Berlin were not realized; there was, however, a series of return visits made by illustrious companies such as Stanislavsky's Moscow Art Theatre. Lugné-Poë's designer at the Bouffes was the painter Édouard Vuillard, who sometimes worked in the theatre's unheated atelier in collaboration with Pierre Bonnard and Odilon Redon. Alfred Jarry was his assistant director at the time; the year after the company left the Bouffes (for their permanent home at what is still known as the Théâtre de l'Œuvre) they created *Ubu Roi* – which would later be produced by the Centre in the adapted form of *Ubu aux Bouffes*. (Another echo of the theatre's past was the Centre's Christmas revue prepared in 1982, which took its name – *Ta Da Da* – from the 1876 opening production.)

Column capital on the first balcony in the theatre, pre-1952 colours

An extension of the Métro and the opening of the nearby La Chapelle station in 1904 gave the theatre a new lease of life, and the building was rejuvenated and fitted out with electricity (undergoing also a brief change of name to 'Théâtre Molière'). Aristide Bruant (whose face was made famous by Toulouse-Lautrec's portrait) made his stage debut here at this time. A fallow period followed until the end of the First World War. In 1918 producers Oscar Dufrenne and Henry Varna incorporated the theatre into their consortium of 'neighbourhood' auditoria, which recycled for a local clientele productions that had already succeeded in the Boulevard venues. The popular shows they provided (including *Yes! We Have No Bananas*) harked back to the theatre's original bawdy music-hall vocation.

More serious, though financially less successful, was the six-year tenure of Paul le Danois in the early 1930s: he hosted the Théâtre d'Art International, which presented work including *Ivanov*, Friedrich Wolf and Hans Chlumberg's *Miracle à Verdun*. Once again the theatre closed during the war (in fact it was barely active from 1935), and, despite an attempt by Jean Serge to capture the energies of post-war Paris in an ambitious programme of serious drama (including *Les Bouches inutiles* by Simone de Beauvoir), then an attempt by Charles Beal to recover a popular public, the theatre closed its doors apparently for good in 1952, unable to afford the repairs and maintenance needed for it to conform with security regulations.

If the theatre found its destiny through Peter Brook – becoming an internationally important space attracting many theatre companies, musicians, comedians and dancers, full to the rafters most nights – one might say that in this first phase of life it repeatedly, ungratefully, shrugged off attempts to inhabit it in a manner which was at odds with its latent core identity. Perhaps this had something to do with the form of the building: when used in its original proscenium format it had appalling sight lines, most of the audience on the sides being unable to see more than a sliver of the stage. What, then, were the motivations behind its design? What factors underlay its unique, curious shape?

The Origins of the Form of the Bouffes du Nord

> Instead of asking the names of the director and actors, everyone who enters the Bouffes wonders: who is the architect?
> Opening-night review, *Le Figaro*, 30 November 1876

The Théâtre des Bouffes du Nord was designed by Louis-Marie Émile Leménil, a little-known architect who also built the row of apartment buildings behind which the theatre is hidden. He was friends with Halanzier, director of the Opéra, which might help explain this commission, given that his other work was confined to the commercial (the Crédit Industriel headquarters) or the residential (beyond the rue du Faubourg Saint-Denis he had also built private villas and chateaux, and the interesting light-industrial/residential quar-

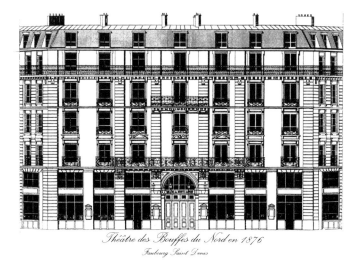

Théâtre des Bouffes du Nord en 1876
Faubourg Saint Denis

Reconstitution of the
theatre's original eleva-
tion, with cafés on both
sides of the entrance

ter of the rue des Immeubles-Industrielles near the Bastille).
He studied at the École des Beaux-Arts in Strasbourg, and
spent some time in St Petersburg. Any precise influence these
experiences may have had on the creation of the Bouffes, however, is obscure: the theatre's archives, including Leménil's
original designs and correspondence, disappeared at some
point during the fallow period of 1952–1974.

In certain respects the Bouffes drew upon well-established
precedents: the decor, the boxes on the stalls and first-balcony
levels and the plaster mouldings which used to fill the spaces
between the upper arches linking the cast-iron columns to the
dome are all similar in style to those of the Odéon and several
other Parisian theatres. But what is unusual (indeed almost
unique), and particularly clear now that the familiar red and
gold accoutrements have been scorched away, is the actual
form of the theatre.* The conventional horse-shoe/ellipse of
the *théâtre à l'italienne* has its long axis perpendicular to the
plane of the proscenium (as at the Odéon) in order to position
the central bulk of the audience at sufficient distance from the
stage to appreciate the pictorial image presented in the frame
of the proscenium. (There are also acoustic reasons for the
development of this shape.) In the Bouffes du Nord the ellipse
is turned through 90 degrees so that its long side is parallel to
the stage front, with the result that the sight lines towards the
original stage were particularly bad for a large part of the audience seated at the sides.

Leménil had only one built example of this transverse-
ellipse form to draw upon: Alexandre Dumas (the son of the
famous novelist) had used this configuration in his Théâtre

*Other theatres with a
similar form include Palladio's Teatro Olimpico at
Vicenza (described later),
Laguepierre's theatre in the
Wurttenberg Palace in
Stuttgart, and the afore-
mentioned Maly Theatre in
St Petersburg. The trans-
verse-ellipse form was used
twice by Gianlorenzo
Bernini: for the church of
Sant Andrea al Quirinale in
Rome and for the piazza in
front of St Peter's, in both
cases to give the effect of a
sudden embrace upon
entering a space, a com-
pression against the ultimate destination of altar or
basilica entrance.

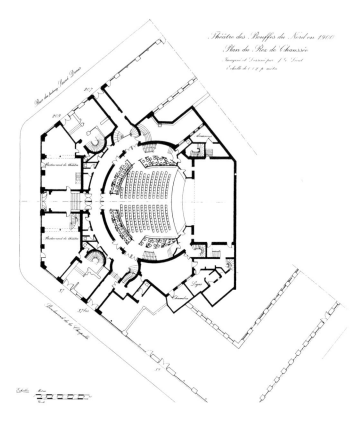

Reconstitution of the plan of the theatre at the end of the 19th century

Historique. This was demolished in the 1860s, but it was referred to in the most comprehensive and up-to-date survey of theatre architecture in French, which Leménil probably would have known. The 1860 *Parallele des principaux théâtres modernes d'Europe*, written by Joseph Filippi and illustrated by Clement Contant, contained a short commentary on the transverse-ellipse auditorium, stating presciently of the Dumas building that 'although imperfect, [it] contains the germ of a good idea, which the future will develop'.*

Also mentioned in Filippi's brief history of this form of auditorium is its key theoretical treatment, an essay on the design of a theatre published in 1765 by Charles-Nicolas Cochin.* Cochin presented drawings of a transverse-ellipse theatre together with a text explaining its virtues compared to the theatres of the day. He stresses the greater intimacy created by the bulk of the audience being positioned closer to the performer and by the advancing of the performer into the same space as the audience on an unprecedentedly large apron stage. He talks particularly of the acoustic quality of this disposition, and it is worth quoting his comments, as they foresee some of the characteristics that Peter Brook would find so

*Joseph Filippi, *Parallele des principaux théâtres modernes d'Europe*, p. 14.

*Cochin was an architectural adviser attached to the court of Louis XV. He had a hand in many of the key projects of the Enlightenment era, such as the Panthéon, the place Louis XV (now the place de la Concorde) and the church of the Madeleine. His 1765 treatise was a contribution to the lively debate

pleasing in the Bouffes du Nord two centuries later:

> To the considerable advantage of having advanced the actor into the auditorium, which prevents the voice from being lost in the wings, and which puts him – as it were – in the middle of the spectators, there joins a second, namely that the audit-orium, being circular and shallow, and ending at almost the same distance from the actor throughout, the waves of the voice promptly stopped cannot produce an echo, and are not free to distribute throughout a long space which would weaken their vibrations . . . One should desire to hear distinctly the most faint articulations, rather than having to speak more loudly . . . It seems, at least, that this is what is to be desired in a theatre where everything must be declaimed as naturally as possible, and where it is most important not to lose anything of what the actor says, rather than to be struck violently by the efforts he can make to astonish the ear.*

Cochin's plan shows features which were repeated by Leménil. The space has a complete, unified, geometrical form which was captured, as at the Bouffes, in a decorative ceiling which describes exactly the shape of the auditorium. The classic circular ceiling pattern seen at the Odéon or the Opéra Garnier never quite matches the plan, because the ellipse of the auditorium splays open to meet the proscenium arch. It is in this 'opening out' region that boxes are commonly placed facing across the apron of the stage (or the orchestra pit). Cochin and Leménil could not put boxes in this transition zone, because in the 'transverse' form this part of the ellipse faces directly back into the auditorium. Instead, Cochin transformed the two side zones into secondary proscenia with their own decor – small side spaces for short scenes or quick changes of locale. In the Bouffes du Nord the positions of these secondary proscenium arches were occupied by the blank side walls which are perhaps the most distinctive outcome of the building's transverse-ellipse form. The Bouffes is, as far as we know, the only theatre in the world with such walls. When the actors occupy the middle space the walls belong to the world of the audience *and* to the world of the play. They can be penetrated to make 'real' doors which communicate in a highly flexible way between the 'here' of the theatre – or the 'here' of the play's world – and a recognizably different place (Carmen's bedroom, for instance). They are a

concerning theatre geometry which arose at that time in France – a debate in which Victor Louis, architect of the roughly circular Grand Théâtre in Bordeaux, and Étienne-Louis Boullée, designer of a vast hemispherical theoretical opera house, were chief participants.

*Charles-Nicolas Cochin, *Projet d'une salle de spectacle pour un théâtre de comédie* (Paris, 1765), pp. 6, 9, 11 (trans. A. Todd)

Section/elevation showing the three stage openings of Cochin's project (compare drawing of the Bouffes on p. 32)

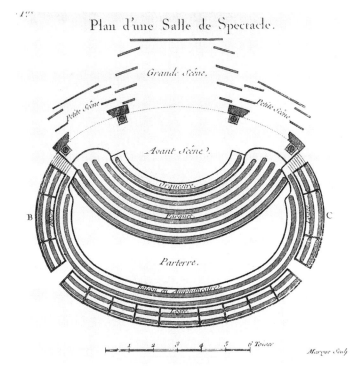

Plan d'une Salle de Spectacle.

Grande Scène.

Petite Scène

Petite Scène

Avant-Scène?

Orquestre.

B

C

Parterre.

Plan of C. N. Cochin's project for a transverse-ellipse auditorium

kind of permanent decor, smaller-scale offshoots of the vast back wall, and act superbly as acoustic diffusers.

Cochin's idea was a hybrid – he wanted a unified space with an intimate rapport between performer and audience, but he also had to satisfy the contemporary taste for illusionistic scenery and staging. His scheme was not built, perhaps precisely because this compromise required too much of a stretch. This is borne out in comments by his contemporary Pierre Patte, an architectural engraver and ally of the rationalistic Jacques-François Blondel, who was opposed to

Cochin's circle of court-favoured designers such as Jacques Germain Soufflot. In 1782 Patte published a treatise on theatre architecture which compared various existing designs and proposed a new form in the light of this analysis. He singled out Cochin's scheme for criticism, because 'the actors find themselves . . . too isolated in the middle of the audience, and too far from the decorations; there would be no illusion, the theatrical action would appear small and without effect'.* In other words, the idea was at odds with its time. It represented a desire for unity in theatre space – a desire which has surged up at various periods of history. The *théâtre à l'italienne* represents a movement towards the opposite pole: a distancing, a separation of actor and audience in the service of a fixed image on the stage – a movement which has reached its logical conclusion in the frontal, 'us–them' twentieth-century theatre.

Cochin did not create his scheme *ex nihilo*. As he takes care to note in his text, the invention of the transverse-ellipse theatre should be attributed to Andrea Palladio, the great Venetian Renaissance architect, who used this configuration in his Teatro Olimpico, built in Vicenza in 1580–5. Palladio had stud-

*Pierre Patte, *Essai sur l'architecture théâtrale* (Paris, 1782).

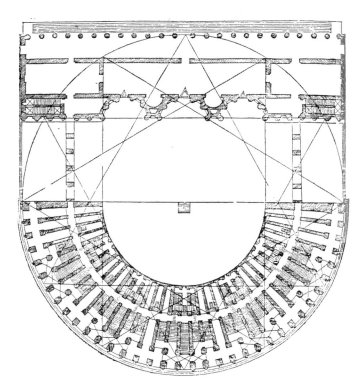

Palladio's drawing of the roman theatre made for Danile Barbaro's edition of Vitruvius' *Ten Books*

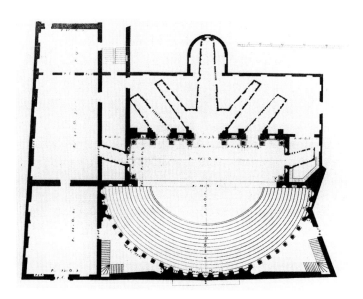

ied the only surviving architectural text of antiquity, Vitruvius's *De architectura*, in which there is a description of how to
draw the plans of Roman and Greek theatres. (It is a complicated business of a circular zodiacal diagram giving the position of the stage and the entrances through the *frons scaenae* –
a mapping of heavenly measures on to the microcosm of the
stage.) Being of a practical bent (he was a stonemason by
training), Palladio had surveyed the remains of some Roman
theatres to provide a pragmatic foundation for the illustra-
tions he engraved for Daniele Barbaro's 1556 edition of Vitruvius. These plans became reality in the form of a temporary
theatre he built in Venice (near what is now the Accademia);
soon afterwards he was asked by the Olympian Academy in
Vicenza to provide a permanent interior theatre for its rather
fusty excursions into classical drama. He was to build into an
existing masonry shell, confined by the urban fabric at the
edge of the Olympians' complex. This space was narrow, and
hence ill-suited to the Vitruvian circle. Palladio, with the
improvisational *brio* which is so characteristic of the Italian
Renaissance, therefore simply squashed the circle towards the
stage, conserving the essentials of the Roman diagram in an
ellipsoidal auditorium.

So the Bouffes du Nord, accident-prone as it always has
been (in the most productive and destructive senses), ultimately owes its unique form to an accident of site in sixteenth-
century Italy. Its form, furthermore, places the theatre only

two steps away from the ancient world – from the origins of Western theatre in the religious ceremonies of Athens and Epidauros, and the Roman theatres they inspired.

The Form of the Bouffes du Nord Today

Peter Brook took two fundamental decisions in appropriating the form of the Bouffes du Nord: actors and audience must be together in the same space, and the new 'stalls' seating should be on the same level as the acting surface, with no threshold sepa-

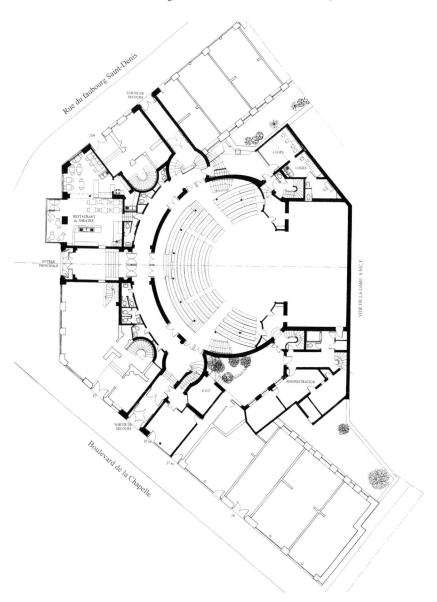

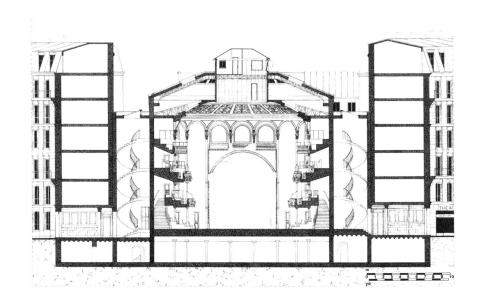

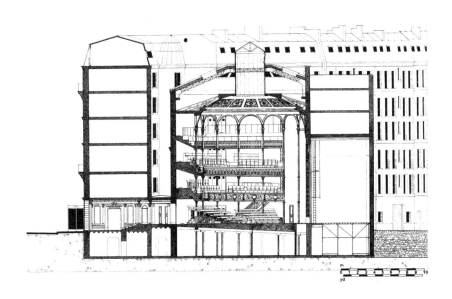

HOME: THE BOUFFES DU NORD

rating the world of the play from the world of the audience.

In the Bouffes du Nord the action takes place remarkably close to the audience: centre stage is only 10 metres away from the furthest spectator of the 250 at ground level. (There are a further 125 seats on each of the two lower balconies, making a total of 500 in a space which apparently held 1,000 in its previous life.) The acting area is defined by the arc of the front bench, which begins at the outside edges of the side walls; it runs roughly parallel to the balcony in the centre, and splays outward to achieve a width of 13 metres between extremities. The distance from the centre of the front row to the plane of the proscenium arch is 9.5 metres, so the bands of wall to either side of the proscenium feel very close, pressing in on our field of vision. The zone which they frame through a soaring 8-metre-wide opening – that of the former stage – has, as we have seen, rather poor sight lines from the auditorium. People at the sides look across the space, and see only a small triangle of the 'stage' surface. Brook's interpretation of the Bouffes – putting the actors in the middle – makes a virtue of this defect. But the usable acting zone is limited by the fact that the tiers of seating on the balconies are arranged so as to be able to see the distant original stage, not the central arena: because of this, an actor standing less than 3 metres from the front row starts to disappear for the back row of the balconies, and the same goes for the view from the sides when an actor stands too far from the central axis. This means that, of an overall acting surface of 200 square metres, only a small zone of about 40 square metres has good visibility for all the audience.

Yoshi Oida has collaborated regularly with the International Centre since the earliest experiments in 1968. He has played roles as varied as a neurological patient in *The Man Who* and Drona in *The Mahabharata*. Prior to joining the Centre he trained in the Noh theatre and collaborated with the writer Yukio Mishima.

Yoshi Oida: *The most comfortable acting place is in the centre. When you enter the stage it feels right to go straight to the middle. Sometimes I go to the side walls for a special purpose, but you can't stay there for long because people on one side can't see. The comfortable acting space is about 6 by 6 metres, and this is just about the right size to do work of quality and concentration – a good human scale. It also happens to be the same size as the stage in a smaller Noh theatre.*

Bruce Myers: *One has to move all the time so as not to obscure the view of people at the side, let's say, for too long – you're always adjusting slightly, making a fuller image, a fairer share for all the people. And at the same time this movement, in an actor with a*

HOME: THE BOUFFES DU NORD

well-trained, sensitive body, gives life to the character he is play-ing. On a proscenium stage, however, you can stand still as long as you like – a bit too long sometimes, to the point where life is driven out of the playing.

One of the theatre's most striking characteristics is the absence of a middle scale between the intimate acting area and the fuller volume of the total stage: the performers are physi-cally very close to the public, but the background against which they appear is vast and distant. The stage of the Bouffes du Nord is very deep – 17 metres – and the back wall is 11 metres high and 16 metres wide. Curiously, rather than dwarf-ing the actor, this clash of scales *reinforces* the human presence: one reads the large and the small *reciprocally*, rather than in opposition to one another. This depth also allows enormous flexibility of theatrical effect. The world of the play can be con-centrated on the space in front of the proscenium arch (very often this zone is defined with an object such as a rock or a piece of furniture); then the scale can be suddenly amplified by occupying the whole depth, or by changing the accent of the lighting in the 'back' zone. (This cinematic fluidity was used to great effect in the battle scenes of *The Mahabharata*.) The proscenium arch, rather than cutting off the world of the play, now has the role of a flexible threshold, a kind of diaphragm whose 'focal length' can be precisely controlled.

Intimately linked to the theatre's depth is a powerful accent in the vertical dimension. The stage surface is a constant refer-ence, a shared ground. Fourteen cast-iron columns arranged in an ellipse depart from this level. The ellipse is 16.5 metres long by 14 metres wide, and is divided into sixteen equal struc-tural bays of 3 metres, of which three are spanned by the proscenium arch, the rhythm of the absent columns being taken up in the arcade above. The side walls were formed by filling the space of the two structural bays bracketing the proscenium with plastered-over brick. They have extremely tall proportions: 3 metres wide by nearly 13 metres high. This proportion, combined with their material and colour, gives them a special role as 'offcuts' of the huge back wall scaled to work with the intimate acting area – a kind of near back-ground.

The theatre's three balconies begin (like the ground-level seating) at the edge of the side walls. The first balcony leans further into the void than the second, and the third (which is

Bruce Myers met Peter Brook at the Royal Shakespeare Company in Stratford in the late 1960s. A constant pres-ence in the Centre's theatrical work, he played Krishna in the English version of *The Mahabharata*, the pio-neer neurologist Luria in *Je suis un phénomène*, and Polonius in *The Tragedy of Hamlet*.

Mireille Maalouf and Ryszard Cieslak in *The Mahabharata* at the Bouffes du Nord

not used today for spectators) threads between the columns, exposing their height as they climb towards the dome. The dome expresses the ellipsoidal disposition of the columns in a series of decorative metal grilles with a design based on a lyre (recalling the theatre's musical beginnings); it gathers the columns into a unified design, resolving the geometrical variety generated by the balconies, the proscenium and the side walls. Finally, in the two foci of the ellipse there are circular holes for suspending two chandeliers.

The proportions of the Bouffes du Nord are unusually satisfying. The principal accent is provided by the contrast between the shadowy horizontals of the balconies and the ultra-thin columns, whose close spacing emphasizes their height. There is a taste of the Victorian engineer's daring in the stark expression of the uprights from the level of the second balcony to the dome. The side walls are also particularly important for this effect of height, as they extend all the way from the stage floor to the top without interruption. There is a rhyming of certain key dimensions of the theatre which generates a sense of unity in the space. Cut along the axis of the stage, the volume described by the columns is as broad as it is high; in other words, the theatre is inscribed in a square, or wrapped around a circle of 14 metres in diameter. The horizontal centre line of this circle – the halfway point in the height – lies on the second balcony, which divides the theatre at a key line of force between

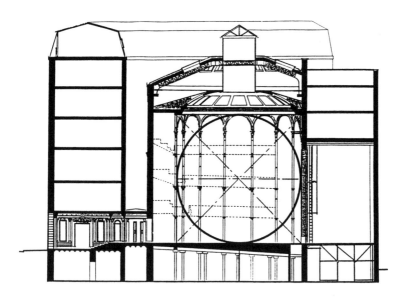

Geometrical diagram of the Bouffes du Nord's long section

the inhabited bottom half and the upward and outward acceleration towards the dome. Cut parallel to the proscenium the overall volume of the theatre to the auditorium walls corresponds approximately to a golden rectangle (having proportions of 1:1.618). The back walls and the two others closing the former stage box– never designed to be seen, and haphazardly limited by the floor slab put in by the owner to make some rentable space in the flytower – are all rectangles with the proportion of 1:$\sqrt{2}$ – another of the 'sacred' proportions discovered by the ancient Greeks.

These objective facts of the theatre were, for the most part, composed by its architect (although he did not intend it to be used for performance in its current configuration). The quality of the space is inseparable from the decisions he made; but today its unique atmosphere depends upon a subtle balance between these forms and factors which were out of his control, such as the forces of entropy which have given the walls their traces of the passage of time, and the changing spirit that Brook's company has brought to the theatre.

PETER BROOK: *When we found the Bouffes du Nord, I saw at once that it was a 'good' space. What is a 'good' space? First of all, it mustn't be cold. The Bouffes is warm, because of its walls, which bear the scars and wrinkles of all it has been through in over a century of ups and downs. A good space can't be neutral, for an impersonal sterility gives no food to the imagination. The Bouffes has the magic and the poetry of a ruin, and anyone who has allowed themselves to be invaded by the atmosphere of a ruin knows strongly how the imagination is let loose.*

A good space is intimate: it is a room in which the audience sit with the actors and see them in close-up, showing what is true in the acting and revealing mercilessly what is false. Yet a good space is more than that – it is challenging, calling on the actors to go beyond themselves, beyond a cinematic naturalism. The Bouffes is at one and the same time intimate and epic. Its relationship with the ring of spectators enveloping the actors is close and easy-going. But its soaring arches, its mosque-like proportions, make it very demanding. Uniquely, it is a shadowy interior and a sunlit courtyard at one and the same time.

The Bouffes is a chameleon. If we want it to be a temple in which at different times Tibetans have performed ceremonies and Sufis have practised rituals, the space will comply. This is because of more than just its romantic atmosphere. Rituals take

their place here because of the rigorously mathematic rightness of the proportions. Proportion is harmony.

The Bouffes has something very special and unique, which is that in the natural structure of the space the depth is articulated. There is something which delineates the big space into two linked areas because of our playing way in front of what was the proscenium; and there are still the remnants behind of what the French call the cage, in English the flytower. We have a circle coming round and framing something which for us is no longer a picture frame but a flexible division, because as you go through

it another space opens out. *Through this, something very interesting is happening architecturally speaking, and I don't think
anyone could have invented it from a theoretical standpoint.
There is a new principle that could be used, which is that of a
double-depth theatre space. The first area has its front and back,
surrounded by the semicircle of the audience; when an actor
passes in front of the plane of the proscenium by a matter of only
2 metres there is an enormous gain in intimacy which the actors
use very consciously, like going into close-up. There are scenes
which, in rehearsal, have to be brought only less than a metre
downstage to suddenly be brought into focus, just as one would
with a camera. There is a great psychological difference between
someone at the back, the middle and the furthest forward point
in that particular area. Then the second zone has the very back,
the middle and front; but, because this is always framed, the
impression of distance is greatly increased wherever one goes.
There is a curious perspective which means that, if you walk
backwards in the first space, one goes in filmic terms from close-
up into full figure; then, as you go back beyond the proscenium,
you suddenly go into a long shot – a device that we used very
much in* The Mahabharata, *putting things right at the back
during the battle scenes, exploding the view into a distant
panorama.*

MARIE-HÉLÈNE ESTIENNE: *First of all there's the preservation,
the openness of the space. There's a strong silence – which is not
necessarily just a physical silence – a kind of gentleness, an openness to different possibilities, a listening quality. It's not a church,
but one feels that it could be, it has that certain tranquillity. It's a
place where one can open oneself, reflect in peace, take risks without being too hurried. It still imposes a certain rigour, but not too
strongly.*

Marie-Hélène Estienne
has been Peter Brook's
artistic collaborator
since the mid-1970s.
She co-wrote with him
the texts of *The Man
Who, Le Costume, Qui
est là?* and *Je suis un
phénomène.* She trans-
lated, with Jean-Claude
Carrière, Brook's adap-
tation of *Hamlet* for the
French version of *The
Tragedy of Hamlet.*

*I remember there being terrible acoustic problems before the
void of the former stage was covered. It's not necessarily an easy
theatre: you have to make it work for you; it demands more
vigour than you might think for such an intimate theatre. It's
actually well made for music, but an actor who can't play strongly and subtly at the same time will have problems. It feels intimate, but it's actually very big, very high. Even the colour seems
to change the size, the echo of the space. It's always evolving, it's a
combination of the space and the spirit Peter brings with his
work.*

I have the impression we've been at the Bouffes for ever; it's our territory, our core, our centre. We like to work on Sundays, because the streets outside are quiet, there is no one there except us, and we can have an unbelievable quality of peace. But during the time we're closeted away secretly we always keep a vision of the audience who will eventually come – they're somehow there all the time. We also keep in mind that eventually the work will leave the Bouffes on tour. We try to appreciate all of these things – they each have their value.

YOSHI OIDA: *The Bouffes du Nord is not symmetrical: there's a subtle difference in the colour of the right and left walls, so there isn't a stable balance. There are other small differences, such as there being no doors under the left balcony. My background in Noh has made me sensitive to this, there being a qualitative difference between left (aggressive and strong) and right (weak and peaceful). We have responded to this in our work here, always placing important things (the pool in* The Mahabharata, *the rock in* The Tempest*) on the right.*

The side walls in the Bouffes have always felt completely natural to me, because the same kind of surface exists in the Kabuki theatre, with the musicians on one side and the storyteller on the other. It extends the kind of proscenium arch on to the stage, making a link with the decor (say a house or garden) which begins just behind.

A lot of theatres put black curtains up, as if this makes anything possible; but this is wrong, as black is a very strong colour, very dominant. The red in the Bouffes is domineering but warm – like the red you find in some very welcoming Italian piazzas. It gives you a good feeling. You never feel happy in a black space: you want to leave straight after the performance. Here people want to linger afterwards.

The space asks the actor, 'Who are you?' It asks this directly to the being, the personality of the actor. You have to take responsibility for answering this yourself, or whatever you're doing won't work. In a proscenium theatre you don't feel the same demands: it's enough just to play the character well. But there's an overlap between acting and being in the Bouffes. You can't succeed through the skill of your acting: you have to charm with your being in order to charm with the play.

MAURICE BÉNICHOU: *This space itself creates an exceptional concentration: everything is visible from almost everywhere. This demands from the actors a precision, a presence, a warmth which*

Maurice Bénichou joined the International Centre shortly after it moved into the Bouffes du Nord. He has played roles such as Krishna in the French version of *The Mahabharata* and Solomon Shereshevsky in *Je suis un phénomène,* and was Brook's assistant director for *La Tragédie de Carmen.*

one could avoid or neglect elsewhere, but not here. It's not being pretentious to call it a house of the spirit. I have the impression that I don't have to make a considerable effort to play, to show, because I don't feel any need to prove myself here. I'm in a trusting relationship with the material, with the space, with the audience, with Peter. I don't like to act: I prefer that the actor's presence and what emanates from him is correct, but doesn't provide anything superfluous. On the occasions when I have over- acted in the Bouffes I sensed immediately that I was disturbing the balance of the space, its concentration.

JEAN-GUY LECAT: *Apart from in the recent production of* Oh les beaux jours, *we've never been attracted by the old form of the theatre. It's as if we've found the natural form of the theatre, reverting to the Elizabethan circle, and the former stage has become a kind of background. This move has been helped by the fact that we've never developed a need for stage machinery, for hanging things from the ceiling, which would be impossible in the Bouffes. Instead, everything is built up from the floor.*

The proportions of the Bouffes are unique: as soon as an actor walks onstage it has a scale. When all thirty performers were

The theatre trans- formed for Beckett's *Oh les beaux jours*

onstage during The Mahabharata *the theatre seemed vast, whereas just before it had seemed very intimate. I think this has to do with the height: paradoxically, the higher the ceiling in a theatre, the more intimate it feels, whereas a low ceiling makes a space feel big. Something one doesn't find in other theatres is the vertical accent of the columns: the eye is always stopped at the balconies and never seeks further, so we see half the volume.*

The theatre has an extraordinary quality. The slightest sound takes on a great importance. We can speak at a normal level and be perfectly understood. But it's also a question of being able to hear oneself well: the actors can't perform with subtlety unless they hear themselves with full sensitivity. There's a space right under the centre of the dome where there is a direct vertical echo; an actor standing there can fool himself into speaking very softly, when the audience doesn't necessarily hear that well. Fortunately it's a microscopic spot, so the problem is not very serious. Because of the great quality of the acoustic, when there is silence it is not just an absence of noise, a register of zero decibels: it's an active thing, something which penetrates the audience, something which comes upon us. It's linked to the physical presence of the theatre.

It is interesting how some feel that our theatre has a religious quality. On entering, your gaze is at once drawn upward. This attraction comes from the narrow vaulting, elegant and rhythmically divided by slender columns, crowned by a dark, restrained cupola. It is a place oriented towards sky and light, and in our cultures verticality, sky, light and religion go together.

Natasha Parry has worked with the Centre since the earliest experiments in the Round House, Africa and Persepolis. She has also performed in *The Conference of the Birds, The Ik, The Cherry Orchard* and *Oh les beaux jours,* and played Gertrude in *The Tragedy of Hamlet.*

NATASHA PARRY: *I've never seen a theatre with such a living presence. It has its likes and dislikes. I've seen it with certain outside productions when it sort of shrinks back into itself and becomes dismal and grey: it's tempting to say the theatre isn't happy. Then when you feel that something is right it comes greatly to life. It can change feeling and period and decor with nothing in it: when I saw a group of whirling dervishes it had the feeling of a mosque; the next week, with a performance of French songs, it was absolutely part of Parisian life; and it felt perfectly Russian during* The Cherry Orchard.

ANDREW TODD: *On the hundreds of evenings I have spent at the Bouffes it has been interesting to eavesdrop on other people's reactions – particularly those of people who are not part of the cognoscenti who have pre-established views about Brook and the theatre. At Saturday matinees I've heard older people compare the building to a circus; many people have commented on a certain religious quality.*

The very ordinary, very pleasant and somewhat overcrowded café is also an essential part of the experience: the performers and Brook are usually to be found there before and after the show, mingling with the public, not self-conscious – this is an extension of the barrier-free, compacted, intense quality of the theatre itself. There are other quirks thrown up by this aspect of the space, such as a door secretly connecting the café to the corridor around the auditorium. The door is supposed to be used only by those working at the theatre, and has the unusual distinction of being marked 'Private' on both sides, even though one discovers, going through it, that it in fact separates two public *spaces.*

Declan Donnellan is the founder of the theatre company Cheek By Jowl. His productions of *As You Like It* and *Le Cid* have played at the Bouffes du Nord.

DECLAN DONNELLAN: *I think that a work of art cannot exist without a frame, and the frame is every bit as important as the work. A piece of theatre changes completely according to the space it's in – a fact to which I have become increasingly sensitive, having spent most of the last twenty years on tour. This has often been a dispiriting experience: the increasingly prevalent cultural* 'administrators' have tended to impose on us their latest 1,500-seat concrete bunkers, built to survive nuclear holocaust, replete with sleep-inducing armchairs. A suggestion that a 400-seater might be better is usually met with blank looks. In England at the National we have one vast space – the Olivier – which demands the energy of plutonium just to get things across to the front row, and is extremely constraining in spite of its size, and the Lyttelton with its audience cut in half on two shelves.

For these reasons it's always a refreshing and renewing experience to return to the Bouffes, which has come to feel like a home to me. It has, first and foremost, a humanity of proportion, creating an intimacy among the audience and between audience and performers. This is contrasted by the epic gesture of the proscenium – a soaring height which would be unfashionable in a new theatre. The theatre and the equally welcoming café make up a proper place with a proper function: the Bouffes serves real theatre in the context of the culture of the city it's in; it doesn't scream 'art' at you – it's very much a part of the city.

The Bouffes demands a heightened level of energy from the actors, in spite of its intimacy, and this is perfectly correct, because theatre is a concentration of life. The audience has to offer a heightened level of energy too, and the performance is something that results from this meeting. It's a theatre that's made to be changed, that gives energy from the past life on the walls. As a pole it's as special as Peter, who is himself such a reference point, and has infused the space with his spirit. There's something very moving about the Bouffes – it shows how things can *be*.

2 : Preparation: 1968–1974

PETER BROOK: *The name 'show business' is very revealing. It's not for nothing that we talk of putting on a 'show'. We make theatre in order to excite the eye of the beholder, and the first thing that the theatre has to do is to make us wish to go on watching. A good storyteller knows that, if he pauses, someone will say, 'Go on.' The visual aspects and the physical aspects of the theatre are there to make everyone in the audience wish to say, 'Show us more.'*

On the other hand, all forms of bad theatre come from 'show' being all that matters. We find all too often that a performance is indeed a show – and this means that completely separate worlds confront each other: performers with their own ideas, their own convictions, and an audience which is a mixture of people who have got together as though by chance. This has led to an architectural division between audience and performer which one can call 'the two-room theatre'. The division into two rooms is, like all architectural facts, an outer expression of something much more fundamental. The two-room structure is inevitable when there is no deep wish for the experience to be fully shared. Any audience is a chaotic mixture. This is not a bad thing: the bigger the mixture, the more vital the audience. But we cannot expect all these people with so little in common suddenly to enter into a shared event. A process is necessary. The aim of this process is to make the 'inner' and the 'outer' merge, to convert a 'show' into an 'experience'.

Ceremonies in great cultures – whether in Bali or in public events and carnivals over many days in India, in Africa or in other traditional societies – are always quoted as an example of a performing art which is not a spectacle that people watch, but something in which an entire group is participant. In those communities there is an equally profound preparation of the spectator as of the performer. One participates from birth in the same religious and social structure; so whether in the Greek theatre with the appearance of a god, or in an Indian street with people following the procession of Kali, the ritual as such takes place within a pre-existing body of belief. One is no longer an observer: one is part of the experience.

More than forty years ago it was clear to me that space is of vital importance in any theatrical gathering, in that it can kill or nurture a vital rising to another level of perception. The search for all the possible ideal, ephemeral, lasting, clear, obvious and unexpected forms that a theatre could take became an obsessive quest – something no less important in our research than the work of the actor or the work on the text. Following an initial suspicion in the sixties that things were badly wrong – that something was clogged up and preventing a healthy exchange with the audience – a vast field of surprises and discoveries opened itself up as soon as we sincerely faced the question 'What should a theatre be?'

The Bouffes du Nord has been the pole of the International Centre's work since 1974. As of 2003, it has been the seedbed for eighteen of Brook's productions – of enormously varying character – and it has anchored their identity each time the group has left to tour in a wide variety of other spaces, which have themselves been spawned partly in the image of the home base. Each of these journeys has in turn brought new insights, materials and forms to bear on the Bouffes, which continues to evolve in dialogue with the experience gleaned from the foreign spaces.

However, the process of spatial exploration did not *begin* with the discovery of the Paris space in 1974: the transformation of the Bouffes was, rather, a vital development in an ongoing search which the International Centre had initiated in the late 1960s. In fact one could look back even further for the first signs of this process. The first twenty-three years of Brook's productions were performed exclusively in conventional proscenium (or 'two-room') theatres. However, the separation of audience and actor in this form was challenged as early as 1962 at Stratford: in *King Lear* the house lights were abruptly brought up after the blinding of Gloucester, leaving him to wander helplessly around in the same light as the audience. A similar moral searchlight was shone across the proscenium divide in *The Marat/Sade* in 1964 and in *US* in 1966: in the former case there was a complicated blurring of the differences between the spectators and the 'characters' (actors playing lunatics playing figures from the French Revolution debating political topics which were being confronted in the sixties); the performers faced the auditorium and ironically applauded the public at the end. The central question in *US* – does the Vietnam War mean anything to people in London? – was real and alive for spectators and performers alike, and it literally invaded the auditorium before the interval, when actors descended from the stage with bags over their heads, forcing the audience to confront the question of whether or not to intervene and help them to the exits, or leave them floundering in the alleys. In Seneca's *Oedipus* two years later the invasion became an occupation, with the chorus positioned throughout the Old Vic auditorium, chained to the proscenium and standing on pillars in the stalls, exploiting their distribution to create three-dimensional soundscapes.

The Mobilier National and the Round House

It was at this stage – roughly the same time as the writing of his book *The Empty Space* – that Brook's urge to leave the conventional theatre altogether had increased to the point that action had to follow. He had been invited by Jean-Louis Barrault, then director of the Odéon and the Théâtre-des-Nations Festival, to participate in an international workshop in Paris. This was to be an open-ended two-month collaboration between practitioners drawn from various nationalities and traditions; Barrault arranged for the use of a space in the Mobilier National for the duration of this 'work in progress'. The Mobilier is a 1930s building, designed by Auguste Perret, in which the French state's furniture collection is conserved. Within it there is a vast space some 46 metres long, 14 metres wide and 9 metres high for the storage of tapestries. It corresponds well to the metaphorical blank slate invoked in *The Empty Space*: writer Anthony Smith described it as a place 'as austere as a monk's cell, [or] a research laboratory . . . a marvellous place for concentration'.* Scaffolding structures which divided the space up into bays were stripped of their cladding and put to use in improvisations for actors to play at different levels.

*Anthony Smith, *Orghast at Persepolis*, p. 130.

No sooner had the group started their work in the Mobilier than it was truncated by the revolutionary *événements* of May 1968; they were ejected from the space when all official build-

The Round House
during a performance
of *The Tempest*

ings were closed down in response to the violent protests taking place in the streets of Paris. The French members of the
group tried to keep involved in the work while at the same
time participating in the events outside, but eventually the
external conditions made work impossible even for the for-
eigners, who had felt a strong need to keep the work going in
parallel to the *événements*. The company fragmented, and the
non-French had to leave the all but war-torn country.

After a pause, funds were hurriedly sought and some of the
group reassembled in London and continued the work in the
Round House in Chalk Farm, north London. This vast brick-
and-iron train-turntable shed was well known as a meeting
place for radical political groups in the late sixties (it made an
appearance in this role in *Tell Me Lies*, the film version of *US*);
it was also a venue for 'happenings', art exhibitions and concerts.

Work had been started in Paris on the basis of the themes of
The Tempest, and this was developed into a one-off performance of a 'work in progress' combining song, mime, 'ritual',
acrobatics and fragments of the Shakespeare text. The audience were treated as temporary visitors, and were able to move

at will to follow the action. The space was structured by six movable scaffolds 4 metres high. The scaffolds – inspired by those found in the Mobilier – supported platforms where the public could sit or action could take place.

The CIRT

The guiding idea of the CIRT is that there is no theatrical representation without 'something other'. This idea assumes that it is not enough to put on a play. One must offer a whole, a complete cultural environment, a contact without barriers. Then one can say that the theatre, offering a mutual enrichment, rediscovers its first function, which has sometimes been forgotten or distorted . . . A group of actors must be a community: it needs to be conceived not as a 'company' for certain hours during the day, but as a social experiment, in which the actor seeks to assume a mature adult responsibility. Only in this way can an actor truly know what he is doing when he makes contact with an audience without the protection of conventional ways – in conditions that are new and free. Free conditions mean moving out of theatre buildings. Theatre buildings that exist today are often beautiful and can be very satisfying for certain particular requirements. But the act of entering a theatre building carries with it a whole structure of associations and practices which largely shape the experience that eventually takes place. These associations deter a large number of young people from ever setting foot in a theatre building. A fresh experiment must occur in a neutral place which only becomes a theatre as the living event unfolds. In this way, the same group can present many different kinds of work – intimate, popular, serious – in a free space that continually redefines itself. In a free space, all conventions like the placing of the public, the complex question of audience participation, the length of the performance, the time of day, can be re-examined.

Excerpt from the annual report of International Centre of Theatre Research, October 1969

The aims of this work found an institutional form in 1969, when Brook and the celebrated French producer and agent Micheline Rozan created the Centre International de Recherche Théâtrale (International Centre of Theatre Research). Brook had previously been sponsored for limited periods by Barrault or the RSC (at the Round House); he and

Rozan now sought enough funding to sustain the work for three years, with a core company and several visiting collaborators. A budget of $1 million was established: $100,000 to set up the organization, and $300,000 each for 1971, 1972 and 1973. Money was raised from the Ford, Gulbenkian and Anderson Foundations and from the government of Iran (in the form of a commission for a work at the Shiraz Festival in 1971). Work was begun even though the full three-year budget was not secured at the outset.

In 1970 Brook was to return to the RSC in Stratford for *A Midsummer Night's Dream*. This production, while intended for the conventional theatre (and, as it turned out, enjoying a triumphant international tour in such spaces), was shown to an audience during the rehearsal process in unconventional locations (a method still used today). It was also performed, without costumes or settings, at the Round House.

Afterwards, in Paris, several months were spent auditioning actors for the Centre and seeking out a space. Houses, garages, warehouses, even a disused railway station were considered. It was actually at this stage that the Bouffes du Nord was first considered as a possible home:

> MICHELINE ROZAN: *A friend of mine told me about an abandoned theatre behind the Gare du Nord. Someone she knew had rehearsed there the year before, though it was in a very crippled state. The minute I told Peter it was in a rather weird area and totally dilapidated, he was charmed. We asked Georges Wakhevitch, an important movie and theatre designer and close friend of Peter's, to do a scheme and an estimate of how much renovation would cost. He made a marvellous model, putting the theatre back to its original state. The cost came out to be exactly two years' subsidy for the Centre, so we dropped the idea and concentrated all our efforts on recovering the Mobilier National.*

The company gathered at the Mobilier on 2 November 1970 for their first meeting. Work concentrated on three areas: physical development and control, in which the techniques of the varying traditions embodied in the group were shared and compared; vocal exercises, drawing on the various languages represented – a research which would lead towards the ur-verbal expression of *Orghast* – and techniques of improvisation. This work was put to the test after six weeks in a performance for ninety children. The space of the Mobilier was used in two

Micheline Rozan was co-director of the CICT from 1974 to 1996 (from *Timon of Athens* to *The Man Who*). An agent and producer, she collaborated with, among others, Albert Camus, Jean-Paul Sartre, Arthur Miller and Orson Welles.

The Centre's team in 1974 with, at right, Nina Soufy, Micheline Rozan and Peter Brook

ways: in a concentrated way for intimate work in an arena formed by the bodies of the audience, and in its entirety for a 'promenade' led by the actors through spatially diverse settings. These two forms basically described the twin poles of the Centre's work, which was declared at the time as an attempt 'to link two traditions, the hieratic and the popular',* 'to bridge the false and sterile separation between popular entertainment and the avant-garde'.* These uses of space presented a challenge for the Centre's actors, who themselves were conditioned by the architectural forms developed for their respective traditions:

*CIRT Report, 31 November 1970.

*Ibid., October 1969.

BRUCE MYERS: *In my training in the 1960s absolutely no attempt was made to make you sensitive to space: you were trained to obey the director, and there was always a lot of conflict about whether one should look at the other actors. When I toured with the Royal Shakespeare Company all you really wanted to know was that you were being heard: for foreign audiences, people thought it was better to play slower. One knows now, from a very strong following in Germany, that communication takes place through the details of the acting. I remember thinking that no one could even see me: one felt alone with the other actors – which I'm sure some people prefer. The attitude was that the audience were of no particular interest: one never tried to adapt to each crowd, to listen to them. If you had a comic role and nobody laughed, you might speak a bit louder or get it over with quickly. Having said this, with experience you can detect certain qualities of silence in those great theatres. There's an artificial privacy and charisma which are presented by that platform in those illustrious spaces – a kind of false respect generated by the architecture. This could occasionally lead to remarkable work, but it just doesn't compare to the work we do now, to the endless possibility of a more human relationship.*

Working with Peter was terribly hard at first. I really didn't enjoy seeing the audience; I was very anxious. There was a comfort given by the footlights: you never knew who was out there. Now I find that uncomfortable. I enjoy seeing people, being with them. I can barely remember the sensation of being cut off like that.

YOSHI OIDA: *With Kabuki I was used to seeing highly stylized representation, like a Japanese woodcut, and highly stylized performance techniques and costumes. Then, when I was around fourteen years old, I saw a Western-style performance with realistic scenery. There was a mountain which became dark as night fell until you could see only its outline; there was real water, unlike the silver paper used for this effect in Kabuki. The actors were wearing authentic costumes, and you could see their faces. I thought it was a fantastic artifice, and this is what first aroused my interest in European theatre, this realism.*

But of course that's not what I discovered when I arrived in Europe and started working with Peter. For the Round House experiments we were in the space even before the audience came in, taking up positions in the seating area. Someone would stand and perform a scene: in so doing he became an actor, and the others became spectators; then he would sit down and be absorbed again into the audience. As an actor, I had been used to hiding from the public before; but here suddenly I was in the middle of them. How do you make theatrical magic in these conditions? In Noh theatre you can control and direct your performance in a very formal, specific way, but here you had to give up that kind of trick, form or technique, because the people were all around. You have to build up from your own interior in order to convince the audience. The actor isn't a special person any more, framed by an arch, raised up on a platform. He's just ordinary and naked, and that's very hard to accept as a performer – to be observed and controlled by the public.

Orghast at Persepolis

The international character of the Centre had two primary ramifications: actors, designers, directors and musicians would be brought together to share their different backgrounds, and the work so produced would be exposed to audiences in different countries, then re-evaluated at the home base. There would be an oscillation between home and away, between near and far, the one affecting the other in a continual reciprocal process.

The first important journey undertaken by the Centre was a three-month experiment in Iran, beginning in June 1971. At the invitation of the Shiraz Festival, the company installed themselves in the great hall of Baghe Ferdous, a decaying mansion near Tehran which was to be their working base for the first two months. They were living in the less than ideal conditions of a government-owned motel, still under construction, with a very noisy house band and – probably – the Shah's undercover police to monitor the group.

Brook had been on an advance visit to recruit Iranian actors, ten of whom would eventually perform with the total group of twenty-eight. The first month was occupied with the integration of the Paris and Iranian groups through improvisation, physical and vocal work. The British poet Ted Hughes was present, and had started work on a text in Orghast, a language he was developing with the actors. The aim was to create a performance based on the Prometheus myth, using ancient Greek, Latin, Avesta (the language of Zoroaster) and Orghast. 'Bashtahondo', a collection of sounds developed by the group in Paris, was also used in rehearsal. Hughes and Brook wanted to test the power of these dead or occult languages to communicate merely through their sounds, their 'deep structure.'

The designer Jean Monod had created a maquette for the staging of the project at Persepolis among the Zoroastrian royal tombs. It was a development of a spinning, unfolding metallic cube which had occupied the Old Vic stage in *Oedipus*; here it was big enough to contain an audience of 1,500, some of them on scaffolding on the sides. Actors would be flown in on cranes, and the whole thing was supposed to move on rails throughout the ancient site. It turned out that it would be exceptionally expensive to build (a French construction company had a monopoly on scaffolding in Iran).

With a more modest version under examination, Brook, Hughes, Monod, two actors and various assistants set off for Persepolis to see how it might fit in with the site. They climbed from the planned position of the cube to the rock-cut tombs of Artaxerxes II and III. Nozar Azadi and the British actress Irene Worth recited passages of Orghast to test the acoustics, and the team was immediately struck by the possibility of hav-

ing the audience climb from the cube to one of the tombs for the end of the performance. The site for the cube was found to have weak acoustics. However, the tombs both had a terrace in front of the façade, bracketed by triangular side walls hewn from the rock (they were cut from a sloping rock face), and this space had excellent sound qualities, as well as a view over the ruins of Persepolis.

Brook and his colleagues then visited another site, ten minutes' drive away: the cliff of Naqsh-e-Rustam. Two hundred metres long and sixty high, the rock is punctured by the tombs

The tombs of Artaxerxes I and III

of Darius I and II, Xerxes I, and Artaxerxes I – all high off the ground. Parallel to the cliff is a low mound, halfway along which is the Cube of Zoroaster, a 13-metre-high monolith, probably a fire temple. To everyone's astonishment, the voice of an actor on the cliff could be heard perfectly on the ground at 100 metres' distance. But talk of performing here foundered on technical difficulties of lighting and electricity. Anthony Smith (who documented the trip in the book *Orghast at Persepolis*) describes what happened next:

> The party turned to go. 'Wait,' Brook said. 'Suppose we did it in two parts here. The first half starts at sunset and goes into the night; we stop at some tragic break; and do the second half when dawn comes up. Then we wouldn't need lighting or electricity at all.' Where would the audience go during the night? 'All right, we let them go home to bed, and do the second part at dawn the following night.' Would they be willing to come out from Shiraz, where they would be staying, so early? 'Only those who were really interested.'[*]

*Anthony Smith, *Orghast at Persepolis*, p. 103.

After a return visit at sunset to the first tombs, it was decided to play the first part there – 'a place of mystery, extraordinary for intimate work' – and the second part at Naqsh-e-Rustam – 'epic, like Epidauros, a place for big voices'.[*] The space had therefore dictated the final abandoning of Monod's cube, and had determined the structure and tone of the text. Brook said, 'the best we can do in designing and lighting a set turns out to be: nothing at all'.[*] He attributed this process of discovery to the 'rule of luck': 'It's not a process of building, but of destroying obstacles that stand in the way of the latent form'.[*]

*Ibid., p. 108.

*Ibid., p.109.

*Ibid., p.107.

All well and good in theory. But in practice, in tandem with the rapid development of Hughes's text with the actors, vast amounts of energy were expended from hereon in the practical wrangles of putting on a show at the most politically sensitive archaeological site in Iran. (Preparations were under way for the Shah to celebrate the twenty-fifth centenary of the Persian monarchy, and the Persepolis remains – embodying the origins of Iranian history as it was officially told – were carefully guarded, to the extent that actors strolling through the ruins at night would regularly stumble on hidden and well-armed policemen.) Permissions to play there had to be sought from several different government agencies, and were granted very late in the day and after much complaint. *Orghast* became a pawn in power struggles extending far beyond the Festival –

another source of delay and frustration. And there were worries that reciting speeches from Aeschylus' *The Persians* before the tomb of Xerxes, the fallen king in the play, would arouse nationalistic ire. Other participants in the Festival – notably the composer Iannis Xenakis, who was performing just below the tombs – held up the work and created artistic and practical conflicts. And there were the simple physical problems of rehearsing in hot and unpredictable conditions, with unwelcome interruptions from snakes and other wildlife.

Part I of *Orghast* was performed four times over two evenings in front of the tomb of Artaxerxes II. The setting was fully integrated into the drama: 'Prometheus' was bound to the tomb face on a ledge near the top, and a fireball descended slowly past him on a crane as actors chanted below. A figure representing 'Light' stood on the side wall, silhouetted against the evening sky; 'Man' crawled on to the terrace from a platform hidden below on the cliff face. The space was lit with flaming torches carried by the actors. As in *Oedipus* at the Old Vic, the whole volume was used to create a fluid soundscape. But practical headaches remained: the Iranian army carried out manoeuvres at their base below the tombs, in contravention of an order from the Festival director, and on the second night a strong wind changed the acoustic and blew fire from a torch into the face of one of the actors.

But these were minor incidents compared to the near-catastrophe provoked by the performance of Part II. The Queen watched Part I, and remained at the site for a late-evening dress rehearsal of Part II especially for her and her retinue. (Because the action took place around a slow procession of the audience along the base of the cliffs, it would have been impossible to guarantee her security in a normal performance.) Arriving to set up after the first show, Geoffrey Reeves, Brook's assistant director, found that the entire site had been closed off by the security forces, who would not admit anyone until they had the official list of participants from the Festival director, who was away entertaining the Queen. When Brook tried to walk into the site he was physically repulsed by a guard. The company withdrew in protest, walking along a desert road towards a restaurant where they planned to wait until the situation was resolved. On the way they found the director and a general, to whom Brook returned the shove he had received from the soldier. Finally they were able to set up (the Queen had to wait for an hour

and twenty minutes in her bus), and a conflict which would have reverberated internationally was narrowly avoided.

Part II used the whole length of Naqsh-e-Rustam. Actors called out from the clifftop, where bonfires had been lit before the performance and walked along the cliff bottom, lighting it with the torches they carried; voices called out from clefts in the rock; actors rushed through the slowly walking audience. The procession paused before the tomb of Darius, cut high into the cliff, and an actor representing the dead King emerged from the tomb speaking in Avesta. Further along, the Cube of Zoroaster was ringed with fire and became the scene of another vignette. The performance ended with the actors climbing the cliff as a solitary man led a cow through the audience, chanting in Avesta. The scale was the obverse of that of Part I, and, unintentionally, Part II also represented the 'popular' obverse of the 'hieratic' tomb performance: the crowd had failed to remain in awe-struck silence, but instead chattered throughout; the dramatic distance of the mythical subject-matter sometimes collapsed into the participatory frenzy of one of the children's shows at the Mobilier. Brook said it was like going to a pop festival.

Peter Wilson wrote of *Orghast* in the Shiraz Festival bulletin, 'Perhaps the best thing about the concept as a whole is the use of "place". *Orghast* does not set out to "wake up" the past; the temple-tomb is treated as exactly that. It is neither worshipped nor desecrated, but its proportions and acoustics make up the central fact of the drama.'*

*Quoted in Anthony Smith, *Orghast at Persepolis*, p. 241.

Spatial discoveries made during *Orghast* would resound through the company's later work in quarries (especially on *The Mahabharata*): the use of multiple levels, a rock face as a background to the action, the use of twilight and dawn in the drama. What was unique about *Orghast*, and what puts it into a slightly different category to the performances in later spaces, was that the spaces were used almost *as found* (lights, loudspeakers and some scaffolding were the only additions): they retained their specific identity and historical associations, which were intimately bound up with the subject of the play. A visit from the International Centre did not change the way people thought of the spaces: the next day they reverted to beautiful archaeological sites as if nothing had happened.

Another important innovation was made during the Iranian experience: for the first time the company played in non-Western villages to people who had no preconceptions of European avant-garde theatre. The first show, very much towards the 'popular' pole, was at Uzbakhi, 50 miles west of Tehran – a place 'too primitive and hot for holidaymakers'.*

*Ibid., p. 159.

The company prepared Hughes's script *Difficulties of a Bridegroom* to play for the villagers. It was a considerable success, and, according to Geoffrey Reeves, the most valuable experience of the entire trip. Having encountered bureaucratic difficulties upon their arrival (proportioned this time to a sleepy backwater rather than to a nervy state), they obtained the headman's consent to a performance in the prime spot, the central yard of the village. There was some concern about representing sexual topics in a conservative culture, but this turned out to be no problem, and a source of instant communication. (The locals didn't find the policemen in the drama funny, however.) After the Persepolis shows, Part I of *Orghast* was put on at Jar-Baravoon, a village near Isfahan. A ruined arch, all that remained of a mosque just outside the walls of the settlement, was chosen as the focus because of the possibilities of playing at various levels and *around* the audience (rather than in the natural arena they had formed at Uzbakhi). The results here were superficially disappointing: the acoustics were not as good as in the semi-enclosed space of the tomb terrace, and the performance dissolved in chattering among the locals. But for Reeves it was worthwhile merely because *some* parts of *Orghast* managed to traverse the void of cultural non-preparation, which was 'much more useful to us than any hermetically sealed "success" could have been'.*

*Ibid., p. 233.

Back in Paris the group performed with the American National Theater of the Deaf and put on a version of Peter Handke's *Kaspar* in various everyday locations, along with a few performances at the Récamier theatre. Work was started in preparation for the next expedition – an enormously ambitious continuation of the village work in Iran.

Africa

When the group reached Algiers (after travelling from Paris via Marseille) in December 1972, they were prepared as if for a military or archaeological expedition: a fleet of six Land-Rovers was loaded with food, camping equipment and spare parts, and guides were engaged who knew the treachery of the desert and some of the customs of its inhabitants. Except for a brief advance visit Brook had made to Nigeria, the group were entering unknown territory – which was the object of the exercise. Rather than a Western avant-garde troupe visiting 'authentic' settings in their spare time in Iran as an appendix to their 'serious' performances, here the aim was constant contact with people who in most cases had never seen Western theatre before. The practical difficulties which had been a source of frustration in Iran were expected and even welcomed here as an unavoidable part of the experience, a harsh test of the group's ability to remain focused on their common aims of learning and discovery, uncovering aspects of the fundamental nature of theatre by immersion in a context where, in Western terms, theatre did not exist.

The spaces where the company would perform were an essential part of this openness to chance. There were no preconceptions, no recipes for success: it was as if Africa itself was a vast potential theatre, brimming with energies and forms which the company would negotiate in the here and now. Work – based on a daily discipline of coordination exercises with bamboo poles, improvisation and physical exercises such as t'ai chi – would consist of a series of improvised

shows using minimal language, revolving around everyday objects and situations (boxes, shoes, walking), and also excerpts from the twelfth-century Sufi poem *The Conference of the Birds*.

Helen Mirren contemplates Andreas Katsulas' magically-powered army boots; Lou Zeldis at right

There were to be some performances in spaces prepared – however crudely – for theatre: a simple open-air auditorium in Oshogbo (in Nigeria) and the courtyard of the Emir's mud palace in Agadez (in Niger), where rudimentary lights and a curtain were strung up above a concrete stage. In most cases, however, the actors simply spread out their blue carpet in what appeared to be the best place to be found, and waited for an audience to gather. There were shows in medium-sized towns such as In Salah and Tamanrasset in Algeria (some advance permissions had been sought here). In the former, where the first performance in Africa took place, the show was a spectacular success among the crowds who had been going about their daily business in the marketplace. They were enthralled by Andreas Katsulas's spontaneous improvisation concerning the magical powers of his army boots. But the show in Tamanrasset, the next stop, was marred by, among other things, a lorry needing to get through the performance space – the first

of many such interruptions, some of which would border on violence.

The encounters with local people tended to be at their most intense in small hamlets, which were selected on sight. John Heilpern, who documented the trip in the book *Conference of the Birds*, explains:

[Brook] chose the villages haphazardly, though there were now several rules about size and playing areas and the number of people who might attend. Often a child would translate for us or guide Brook to better locations. One village was too large and noisy, too worldly. 'It's the Chalfont St Giles of Nigeria,' said Brook, ploughing on through lush pastures in search of another village.*

The actors would then explore the village, meet the locals, and sense where and when it might be best to perform.

> **PETER BROOK**: *With a simple pragmatism (which is the basis of everything), we would look around and see that in one place there are some nice trees, or a tree where the villagers normally gather; or there'd be another place that's exposed, with a breeze.*

The group's resident composer, Elizabeth Swados, beside her gong-player, Peter Brook

*John Heilpern, *Conference of the Birds*, p.199.

49

In one place the soil is bumpy; in another it's flat. In one place there's a little clearing with earth that rises to the sides in a natural amphitheatre, so more people can see. We played in a number of school courtyards where, because there were walls of different heights all around, the kids could scramble and sit on the walls, as well as in the front row. Spatially speaking, one is here touching on things that I would say every architect should experience for himself, which is finding what is conducive; this conducts and that doesn't.

The encounters often revolved around a delicate, shifting balance between the parties. Gone was the duality of the Western theatre, in which a 'prepared' troupe expose their work before an 'unprepared' public in separate spaces. Here, in most cases both groups were equally *unprepared* for what would happen, and the 'audience' and the 'performers' could find themselves exchanging roles. In a Tuareg village near Agadez the carpet was set up as usual, but to the complete indifference of the villagers, who, it quickly became clear, intended to perform for the visitors their extraordinary leaping dance. The tables were turned by Yoshi Oida leaping up and down on his knees with a tiny stick (in self-effacing emulation of the Tuaregs' pile-driving walking sticks), then gradually leading the whole dancing Tuareg troupe over to the carpet, where the company immediately launched into their routine, inspired by the beginning into an event which John Heilpern found to be a 'real exchange, real and precious sharing'.

In other cases one would be hard put to describe the events as 'theatre' at all: they simply involved exchange and meeting. On one occasion the group were visited at night in their camp by some children, who led them back to their village. A villager had died; the visitors sat and watched the singing and dancing of the funeral ceremony. Eventually they were asked to sing a song of their own. Moved by the occasion and by the depth of the bond suddenly created, this simple gesture by the actors became for Brook 'one of the best works of the whole journey'.*

As the journey progressed, the separate strands of the work – the first contacts, the selection of spaces, the deepening of contact during improvisation and performance, the rehearsal work and physical exercises, and also the arduous regime of establishing and running the camp – began to fuse into an organic overall project. The spaces for performance consisted of not much more than the carpet and the ways people gath-

*Peter Brook, *The Shifting Point*, p.124.

ered spontaneously around it: they had only a provisional form, whose success was determined to a great extent by chance factors and flows of energy between the group and the public. Nevertheless, the 'simple pragmatism' with which Brook says the spaces were selected was being conditioned by accumulated experience – a far from simple *intuition* of what syntheses of forms, materials, social conditions, climate and time could open the pathways of communication.

PETER BROOK: *People have said repeatedly that my recent work is 'simple', and this has become a very friendly cliché. The warning I would always attach to such statements is that the road to simplicity is extremely long, and I discourage anybody else from trying to start with the notion of simplicity, because it is something that arises as a result of diverse, sometimes convoluted, processes.*

An ethical idea of simplicity as a point of departure can be revealing if it involves discarding everything moot, whether it is a protection or a defensive reflex, and seeing what happens. This is what our first projects in the early 1970s were all about. The first surprising discovery of this work was just how much is there waiting there beyond one's preconceptions if one can come to know and trust it. When there is simply an intimate contact between performers and spectators, one discovers an enormous amount already given which one had ignored before; one doesn't have to fight and struggle to get something across to the audience. There used to be an expression 'getting it across the footlights'. The easiest way to get across the footlights is to take them away. Being in the open air in one light with nothing else to draw on but the living contact with the audience is something that one couldn't have known without experiencing it.

The other revelation of this work is just how little is needed to capture and develop the imagination. I was brought up with a set of theatre conventions which held that it was axiomatic that you have to have scenery, costumes and props, otherwise the magic of the theatre won't work. One accepts this as one grows up. When one begins to question this, it is not enough to question it intellectually: one must be able to see in practice what actually happens if the conditions are changed. The new conditions we encountered in Africa suddenly revealed that almost all one needs is already there and you need only very few extra, imported, elements for the audience to go with you into a completely new world and a new set of imagery.

This early work revealed a distinction which has continued to be relevant ever since: between work which demands a solid ground, a real setting, and a performance which can begin by being detached from a real space. One could say that the African work tended towards the latter, and Orghast *towards the former. Without the experience of* Orghast *we would not have started working with our first quarry in Australia for* The Conference of the Birds, *and without that experience we would not have gone into all the quarries which were vital for* The Mahabharata. *That came from the direct relationship with solid, real, outdoor elements, whether these were pillars or rocks or stone or earth or fire.*

In Orghast *the surroundings were part of the story. In Africa the surroundings were the basis of the relationship between actor and audience, and the story came from what was being done. Everything had that other aspect, the direct involving and integrating of the actors and the audience's imagination, so that together one entered another world – that 'other world' which conventional theatre 'magic' evokes by denying rather than underscoring the common, shared world of the event.*

Sitting around the carpet on the same ground as the actors in the same light and time is a form of reality, but the imaginative world jointly created on this basis has a different – virtual – quality, and both the real and the virtual qualities coexist. This harks back to Meyerhold, who emphasized that theatre is theatre: *it is not pretending that the image we are looking at really exists. At every moment we keep this double vision: we are in this place where people are playing a game, and we are watching them performing (Meyerhold always referred to playgrounds and games as fundamental metaphors for the theatre); it is a game. And, as when watching a football match, you don't need this thing called 'illusion' to be completely caught up in it. Nobody can be more caught up in an event than 20,000 football fans, yet never for a moment do they lose sight of the fact that they are sitting in a stadium, they have people next to them. They don't switch off and think that they are transported into a never-never land. The peculiarity, over several centuries, of what we call the* théâtre à l'italienne *is that the audience is invited – although this never works completely – to enter into a different game, which is pretending that they themselves and their world have completely disappeared and this other world on the stage is absolutely real. Stanislavsky says we are taking away the fourth wall, looking through the keyhole. But the theatre is not another world: the game is the game.*

The experience in Africa completely affirmed this. We were Western performers: they were an African audience. We were together under the same light, and never lost sight of this. But together we were playing a game which took us somewhere else.

America

The following year the group repeated the format of their African voyage in a fifteen-week tour of America. Less was left to chance: working sessions with the Teatro Campesino in California and with Native American groups in Minnesota and Colorado had been organized in advance. With Luis Valdez, director of El Teatro Campesino company, the CIRT group played in the electric atmosphere of the strikes led by Cesar Chávez – a situation which briefly transformed them into a kind of agit-prop outfit. They played at demonstrations, in the vineyards, and in conventional theatres in Santa Cruz and San Francisco. They adapted passages from *The Conference of the Birds* into Spanish for this work. There were structured exchanges of technique and method with various established groups, a repeat collaboration with the National Theater of the Deaf, and a week-long living/workshop encounter with the Native American Theatre Ensemble in Minneapolis.

The trip, and this phase of the Centre's work, concluded in New York. The group were guests of the Brooklyn Academy of Music, which made a new venue, a converted ballroom (later named the Leperq Space), available for their work. The room was long and high, with windows on one long side. Steep rakes of seating were built on one short side and along two of the long sides, putting much of the audience into a face-to-face relationship. 'Theatre Days' and open-ended collaborations and workshops with local groups and visitors such as Jerzy Grotowski were combined with 'animations' – spontaneous interventions with local inhabitants (primarily poor African-Americans) in their neighbourhoods. The evenings were used for focused performances of excerpts from *The Conference of the Birds*. The final night ended at dawn, after evening and midnight shows. The group disbanded – its funding exhausted, its initial aims, particularly with regard to spatial exploration, fully satisfied, and poised for further definition.

3 : The Rough Arena: *Timon of Athens, The Ik, Ubu aux Bouffes*

Deciding to settle in the Bouffes du Nord at the time of the 1974 Festival d'Automne was an entirely logical development of the peripatetic work the Centre had undertaken since 1968. (Yoshi Oida described it as 'like doing a big carpet show'.) In its ruined state the Bouffes was a kind of anti-theatre, a negation of the meaningless bourgeois certainties of plush upholstery, gold leaf and sparkling chandeliers. It had something in common with the village squares of Nigeria and Iran, the tough street corners of the Bronx, and the impromptu performance spaces made around Paris in barns, railway stations, schools and hospitals. However, this was not a 'disposable' space, and, as we have seen, its underlying design was careful, inventive and inspiring. Over the first few years of use it started to mould the Centre's work in a certain way: its proportions and materiality presented unique scenographic possibilities.

Three early productions – *Timon of Athens, The Ik* and *Ubu aux Bouffes* – were prepared and performed in tandem during the period 1974–9, with very similar styles of staging. *Timon* was staged with the minimum of modifications to the building's fabric. The space was 'stabilized' as quickly as possible in order to permit an audience to gather around the central area, with the battered grey-black walls performing the same supporting-ground function as the mud walls of the Emir's palace in Agadez or the rock-cut walls of the tomb of Artaxerxes. Crude benches were built at the stage level from planks nailed on to lumber uprights, with long straw cushions on each board. There were no backrests, seats were not numbered, and the audience packed in much more closely than they do today (100 additional spectators were accommodated, some on the precipitous third balcony).

The actors simply played on the raw concrete of the new stage floor, with a pile of cushions as seating. The pit where the

François Marthouret and Michele Collison in *Timon of Athens*

stage had been was used for entrances and exits by means of a wide staircase (particularly for Timon's first appearance in glory, and his final exit in shame). Metal rungs (of the type used everywhere in Paris to permit access to chimneys and roofs) were anchored in the back wall and used as supports for climbing. (They would remain and be used in certain productions until after *The Mahabharata*.) A scaffolding walkway about a third of the way up the wall was simplified in order to fit in with the space. The general level of lighting was kept high in the auditorium; in fact there was no 'theatrical' lighting per se, with the possible exception of a floodlight washing the back wall from deep inside the pit.

The fabric of the building was modified for incorporation into the play: a hole was roughly broken through the left-hand side wall at the level of the first balcony; another was made higher up on the right side. The roughness of the hole was in keeping with the roughness of the theatre: it was as if the process of destruction had been unconsciously continued for a specific theatrical purpose. The partial ruination of the Bouffes had given the space a wonderful flexibility: one could patch it up or destroy it a little further. As the auditorium's previous 'cultural' skin had been cauterized away, the hole was authentic and rather innocent: it was simply a hole in a wall. (Try – if it were bureaucratically possible – to make a similar hole through the gilt mouldings of the Odéon or the concrete of the Lyttelton and you would end up with something much more self-consciously 'theatrical' or decorative.)

This treatment of the space as 'empty', as just a ground for the acting, was repeated in *Ubu aux Bouffes* (based on Jarry's *Ubu Roi*). The actors transformed the space with objects which they brought on to the stage themselves: a few bricks were piled up to create a village, which was demolished by Ubu riding on a make-believe tank represented by an industrial cable drum. The bricks became mountains for actors to perch on, or stepping stones through a flooded basement. Turned on its side and with two others on top, the cable drum became the tower of the king's palace, around which the characters chased each other as if mounting an endless spiral staircase. On a conventional stage such antics would have been coloured by a fatally strong dose of self-consciousness. The fact that they were performed on the floor that the audience sat on, in the same space, removed from the architectural quotation marks of a proscenium, invited the participation of the public's imagination.

Because the actors had nothing to hide and nothing to lose, we could join in with them and *see* a brick as a mountain.

Michele Collison and
Andreas Katsulas in
Ubu aux Bouffes

PETER BROOK: *For* Ubu *we rehearsed the play in the whole theatre, and for several weeks we used the entire extent of the acting area. After we had rehearsed for some time with the same actors, using just minimal props such as bags, I began to feel that something was missing, something was not concentrated enough, and I had no idea what to do about it. We were using this marvellous exciting space in the Bouffes, with its holes and doors and windows and backstage, we were using everything we could, and this gave great vitality, but somehow there was a lack of concentration. One night, coming to the theatre, I saw one of those great spools for cables outside. Everything clicked: I said we should go outside and pinch it. We brought it in and rolled it on to the stage, and the entire production fell into place in two hours around the presence of this single object. Most of the show was grouped around this one object: it became a table which people sat at, a castle, a tank rolling across the stage destroying a village of bricks. This was also the first time we had a very concentrated area within the bigger acting area.*

MAURICE BÉNICHOU: *Starting in the Bouffes was a great shock. I felt unarmed: I didn't have the familiar references of the stage, costume, lights, proscenium etc. that I had worked with exclusively before. I didn't know how to position myself in the space, which bothered me a lot. We did a lot of improvisation – another thing I'd never done before. This space seemed huge to me at the beginning. I spoke either too loud or not loud enough; I didn't know where to stand, how to move.*

Peter left the actors fairly free to find their own way, their own relationship to the space and the audience. I quickly got to love this openness – also the freedom we had improvising in the street, in the suburbs. There was a kind of unrestricted discipline to the work. I could allow myself to approach it in a somewhat chaotic way, and this was very pleasurable. The actor has the liberty to move anywhere in the space in such a way that the spectator thinks that he is creating that action now, for the first time; it doesn't appear to be a careful, elaborated artistic choice.

In *The Ik* the performance began and ended with the blank stage, but a new kind of transformation occurred during the performance. This production had been devised by the actors

The Ik at the Bouffes

along with Brook and the writers Colin Higgins, Denis Can-
nan and Jean-Claude Carrière. It was based on a book by the
anthropologist Colin Turnbull – an old friend of Brook's –
who had lived with the Ik tribe of Uganda for two years and
had documented the degradation of their society due to
famine and government interference. (A nomadic tribe, they
had been forced to settle in a place disconnected from their
sacred landscapes. Used to moving to wherever there was
food, they were incapable of farming, and gradually began to
starve and to destroy themselves.)

After the introduction of the Colin Turnbull character
(played by Andreas Katsulas), the villagers created their space
by spreading dried moss on to a circular zone on the stage, and
by building a wooden hut with sticks poked into prepared
holes in the stage floor. Other objects such as wooden seats
were brought on, and some rocks were placed around the acting area. The mossy circle changed the space in two important
ways: it delimited an acting area which could mean something
quite different when one was inside it as opposed to outside,
and it also brought a specific material representation, a sense
of the parched vegetation of Uganda, into the space of the

Bouffes. Its shape and size with respect to the architecture played on a delicate set of balances: in the ellipsoidal arena of the Bouffes a circle is a neutral form, not setting up a specific counterpoint with the shape of the building. At around 8 metres in diameter, the circle filled the width of the proscenium opening, and left a blank zone before the first row of cushion seats. The audience therefore understood it as an 'acting area' apart from their own space, but also as representing a specific place, the Iks' settlement, with a 'real' material – as 'real' as the scarred walls of the theatre up to which it crept. Its circular form also served to avoid a literal description of the Iks' space: it was understood as a general, self-contained sign of 'village', left up to the actors to interpret. Its role was not rigidly consistent, however: a ladder leading up to the chief's space (the other side of one of the holes made for *Timon*) was outside the circle itself, but could still be interpreted as belonging to the village.

A fire was lit on stage during *The Ik* (a campfire used to cook a rabbit), and this was something that would reappear in *La Tragédie de Carmen* and *The Mahabharata* with considerable force. Once again, the space dictated that this went beyond mere theatrical effect. The fire was *grounded*, given context, by our awareness that this element, out of control, had touched the actual walls of the building.

When the few surviving Ik were forcibly dispatched to different territories at the end of the play, the actors cleared the stage, stuffing the moss back into canvas sacks and taking it off with them. The space reverted to the Bouffes du Nord; we became implicated in the disappearance of the Ik.

PETER BROOK: *When one decides to stage an Elizabethan play, artistic criteria alone no longer suffice. One finds oneself swept away by opposing currents, as when one jumps in the sea, and all one can do is to try to swim with the flow, try to use the multiple scenes and actions to make a multidimensional picture of life emerge. It's like going into the street or into any vibrant public place, diving into the crowd, allowing oneself to be open to all of the conflicting, criss-crossing energies present. Above all the Elizabethan theatre is dynamic. It is the expression of a society in conflict with extremely powerful forces, as yet unclear, with its values being redefined. Today the world is in a similar situation, so there is a chance to recognize ourselves in this marvellous, strange morass.*

Because of its simplicity – performances being given in the open air on simple wooden boards, with few special effects – the Elizabethan theatre was long considered primitive by the rest of Europe, in the sense that the théâtre à l'italienne, with its cunningly contrived perspective scenes and machinery, was taken to represent progress. This was mistaken. The Elizabethan theatre is the ideal form for a perfectly free theatre, which ignores the unities of action, time and place that were so precious for the Greeks and then for the French. There are certain actions of which it is impossible to say where they take place: they begin in one place and appear to end in another. A play can last two hours and yet cover two months. This freedom to move at will in space and time, to evoke vast armies and intimate introspection, is made possible by the simple open platform on which the action takes place: a forestage for exterior scenes; an elevated, covered space for interiors. There was also a gallery, and therefore the possibility to show vertical schisms between places and qualities: between desire and its object in Romeo and Juliet, *between the powerful King above and the dispossessed populace below; between the spirit world and the world of men. Most importantly, there were no barriers, no partitions: these worlds were all open to one another.*

We found the same free qualities in the Bouffes du Nord. The space is simple, intimate and without boundaries; it possesses an Elizabethan sense of verticality, sadly missing in so many modern theatres. We created a great crevice in the stage space, breaking holes in the side walls for Timon of Athens. *Today, with* The Tragedy of Hamlet, *we stay on one square in the middle of the arena, and the text with its constant reference to the above, the below and the human level, the sense of the ground – a shared, open ground – and the heavens, in the great cupola and the dramatic height of the columns, are present for all. In* Timon *a high gallery ran across the back wall; in* The Ik *this was replaced by iron rungs, so that the actors could climb from one mountain to another, while in* The Mahabharata *other rungs made an upward movement as possible as all the horizontal ones.*

Timon in France; *The Ik* in Europe and America

Almost immediately the question of how the Bouffes du Nord would influence the selection of touring spaces had to be confronted. *Timon of Athens* went on a short tour of France, mostly in established theatres. It also made a brief sortie into

Switzerland, where it opened a new venue in Zurich, the Gess-nerallee Theater, which was used as found. (This theatre was later transformed for *The Tempest*: see p. 200.) Often there would be street exercises and 'animations' in the town during the day, of the type developed in Africa and Brooklyn. These served to sensitize the actors to the citizens who would join them in the evening, and also to generate interest in the production. A few 'found' spaces were used for performances, in the spirit of the earlier work, with makeshift seating built for the occasion. (There was a near-disaster in Cergy-Pontoise when the wooden structure started to move under the weight of the audience, who fortunately vacated it immediately.)

The Ik was the first production to undertake a serious international tour, travelling to London (the Round House), Berlin, Vienna, Venice, Belgrade and the United States. Jean-Guy joined the Centre at the beginning of this tour:

> JEAN-GUY LECAT: *In 1975 I was working as an actor and stage manager for Ellen Stewart's La MaMa company in New York. During a long tour we played* The Trojan Women *at the Bouffes du Nord and* Electra *and* Medea *in both spaces of the Sainte-Chapelle as part of the Festival d'Automne. Peter was looking for someone to organize a tour of* The Ik *in the United States and find the performance spaces: the company was being sent as a gift from the French government for the American bicentennial. I went to see him and Micheline Rozan and explained my past experience as a stage designer and as technical director for Jean-Louis Barrault (who was responsible in the first instance for bringing Peter to Paris). At that time, not being overly familiar with his work, I asked Peter for some advice, some rules which could guide me in my research. He simply said to me, 'I cannot say anything to you that would help you. You see on your own; you will recognize the spaces. What is most important is that these spaces should be full of life.'*
>
> *I started my career at the Vieux-Colombier theatre in Paris. It is a place with a strong history: a small room for 300 people, a single-space theatre originally opened by Jacques Copeau. As I was the only technician there, I got to know every aspect of the space, the quality of the relationships it set up, and how all of the theatrical disciplines – light, sound, design, direction – interacted to form a whole. Then I worked at the Avignon Festival with the Living Theatre in 1968 (my second year at the Avignon Festival), and through relationships made there I collaborated on*

the creation of the Cartoucherie in the Bois de Vincennes with Jean-Marie Serreau. (Ariane Mnouchkine was opening another space, and Jean-Louis Barrault a third space for storing his sets.) I worked for Claude Perset, a theatre architect, in my spare time, and helped Serreau with the design and construction of his space, as well as carrying out the technical direction of his productions. Serreau and I also developed a prefabricated seating structure which could be used in Avignon at the Cloître des Carmes and then, during the rest of the year, in the Cartoucherie in different configurations.

Later I worked for Jean-Louis Barrault at the Récamier theatre. He put on a play by Paul Claudel in the Gare d'Orsay, inside a tent (the train station was still functioning underneath); all the public entrances were integrated into the decor of the play to make a 'total' environment with good acoustic isolation. This gave him the idea the following year to build a more permanent theatre in the same space rented from SNCF, the French railway company. I participated in the five-month-long design and construction of this wooden theatre, which was eventually moved into an empty ice rink on the Champs-Élysées – a space with completely different proportions, which killed the spirit of the original building. (Barrault had started his career in the Théâtre de Marigny just opposite. He used to say it took him his whole life just to cross the Champs-Élysées.) At the Gare d'Orsay we had to confront some of the absurd problems which continually crop up working in 'found' spaces: we had to persuade the SNCF to change the platforms of certain trains, so that there was never any noise when Madeleine Renaud was speaking. We had to read out the play on the platforms with a stopwatch to determine when we needed to move a train. This gave me the idea later, with Peter Brook, that we could convince people to change their activities in order to bring a play to life in a given space – whether it involved stopping cars, planes or trains or whatever was needed.

The Ik was due to travel to Berlin, Vienna, Venice and Belgrade before the States. I went to Berlin and Venice with Miriam Goldschmidt, one of the actresses in the play, who helped me understand the proportions and technical requirements of the production. I discovered quickly by instinct what worked and didn't work as a space with the very particular world of this play. It was only through what I could see was unnecessary that what was necessary became clear. It wasn't a question of making a space: it was rather a matter of recognizing the right one which, with the necessary transformations, would feel correct for the *play – and that still remains true today. When people asked what kind of space we were looking for it was very difficult to say: one can't describe a space, but one can describe a relationship which should exist there. I could see immediately that if the space told a story which was in conflict with the play – if it was too decorated, too beautiful, too violent, too aggressive, too well-prepared – then it would never work. We needed a strong, raw, neutral space.*

University cinema,
Belgrade

In Belgrade the Centre used a cinema which was still under construction for the university's dramatic arts faculty. The audience sat on benches placed on the unfinished steps of the auditorium. Because the concrete had just been poured it was rough to the touch: there was a toughness to this surface which went well with the world of the play, the harshness of the tribe's life in Uganda.

In Venice the company played in the open air, in the cloister of San Pietro di Castello and in the campo Angelo Raffaele. This posed problems for the intimate acoustics needed in *The Ik*. Every single resident around the campo had to be visited and convinced not to watch television, listen to the radio or talk loudly during the hours of the performance for a whole week – a fearsome task given the natural volubility and conviviality of the Italians. They stayed at home at first, but little by little they came to see the performances – always bringing their own chairs, rather than sitting on the newly constructed benches.

Cloister of San Pietro
di Castello

PETER BROOK: *In Venice we learned an important lesson about the value of chance factors when playing in an uncontrolled envi-*

ronment. The Ik are dying of thirst and hunger under Africa's punishing sun; but in Italy in August the play was performed in driving rain. At first we were worried that this might destroy the atmosphere of the piece, but in the event it didn't matter a bit: the audience immediately related the actors' suffering in the rain to the heat and dryness in Africa. This showed us the power and flexibility of theatrical metaphor: people are capable of using their imagination to join things together. Not only is it unnecessary to provide a 'complete' image, it is also dangerous, because this so-called completeness is brittle and can be shattered.

The American tour was to be hosted by the theatre departments of seven major universities, most of whom had their own purpose-built performance spaces. Advance visits revealed these to be of widely varying quality and character: there were modern theatres at the University of Pennsylvania (the Zellerbach), the University of Houston, George Washington University and Berkeley. Of these, the latter two had the recently-become-fashionable Elizabethan or arena form, which lent itself well to the style of the Centre's work. (The Playhouse Theatre at Berkeley was particularly successful.)

Above: Improvisations at the Mestre bus terminal

Above left: Peter Brook and Jean-Claude Carrière sheltering from the rain in Venice during rehearsals of *The Ik*

The Zellerbach auditorium was too big and lacked the essential 'living' atmosphere. However, the backstage walls, which had been neglected because they were always hidden behind a stage set, carried a random scrawl of accidental markings, dirt, graffiti and stains. With the safety curtain down, the area of the stage itself was just the right size to gather the audience on some simple benches with these accidentally 'live' walls as the backdrop to the drama. In Houston the theatre seating had too shallow a gradient; the university undertook to build a steeper slope above the normal seats – an ambitious and generous gesture given the very short run the Centre performed there.

In Chicago the 'theatre' on offer (a hammerbeamed pastiche of a Gothic hall) was completely at odds with the world of *The Ik*. A trawl through all the possible interior and exterior spaces in the university turned up few suitable alternatives, and for a while the space housing the world's first atomic reactor was considered, but its associations were rather too strong for the play to be able to find its own level. In the end an old gymnasium was screened down to the correct size for performance. An abandoned theatre in Minneapolis – the Guthrie II, which resembled the Bouffes, but was a fraction of the size – was used

Marva Katsulas, Toshi Tsuchitori, Joseph Towles, Bob Applegarth and Colin Turnbull unloading the set for a performance at a prison in Philadelphia; *below*, Yoshi Oida waiting outside for his entrance in the tiny cinema studio at UCLA in Los Angeles

THE ROUGH ARENA

exactly as it was; and at UCLA the group performed in a small cinema studio which had dirt and graffiti on the walls.

Ubu, Certificat and *L'Os* undertook a frantic tour of France – a town every one or two nights for two months. Lecat travelled a day ahead of the actors, finding and transforming spaces that would be inhabited by the actors (with the help of technical director Philippe Mulon and assistant director Marie-Hélène Estienne). Afternoons were used for rehearsal in the space, with the performance in the evening:

Ubu in Bordeaux

JEAN-GUY LECAT: *This tour was a crucial lesson in how to improvise spaces. Because of the timing, we simply couldn't afford mistakes: if something didn't work, another solution had to be found in a few hours. In Carcassonne I found a beautiful covered market which the traders let us use; we washed it down with the actors after the day's market, and performed in the evening. (We also had to rearrange it rapidly afterwards.) In Istres our contacts had proposed a train shed, which I rejected because it was close to the tracks and wouldn't be silent enough. They assured me this wouldn't be a problem, because the tracks*

Ubu in Munich

were never used. Right then a huge train passed by, taking about half an hour. We were mortified: the contracts with the city to play Ubu *were signed and we had to find somewhere fast. Next door there was a refrigerated vegetable store, which was well protected from the outside noise because of its thermal insulation, but unfortunately very white and pure, with a terrible acoustic. Outside we found hundreds of crates of apples. We shifted them inside – which took all day – and built a solid wall. This created a backstage area: the actors could peer through the apples towards the audience. The heavy crates changed the acoustic and atmosphere of the space –and also gave off a lovely smell.*

I don't think we could have done a tour like this with The Ik. *This and* Ubu *were performed in a similar style with just a minimal 'decor' built by the actors themselves, but* Ubu *offered the great advantage that the actors could manipulate the audience, improvising their positions during the show if something wasn't right. The* Ik *was much less physical, and required a stable balance which the space had to establish on its own.*

Ubu in Caracas

An experiment which opened the way for many of the later strategies of spatial transformation was the week-long conversion of a former cinema in Caracas for the 1979 touring productions of *Ubu*. When the space was discovered it was being used as a garage. The walls on either side of the proscenium had been broken through to allow cars to circulate; there were stains on the walls from exhaust pipes, and a makeshift apartment on the balcony. Some quirky Moorish decoration was still intact. On the customary mad dash to the airport it was decided to use the space almost exactly as it was. The Minister of Culture bought the building, moved out the cars, and rebuilt the entrance wall. Rough breeze-block walls closed the holes smashed open for the cars, with openings left for one exit during *Ubu*.

The former Alcazar cinema in Caracas

The production drew an enthusiastic public from the immediate working-class neighbourhood and beyond. Often there were more people crowded outside the door than the simple seating was designed to accommodate: the extra spectators were allowed to arrange themselves in up to five rows seated on the floor of the stage.

PETER BROOK: *We had a terrible problem one night when the audience burst into the space an hour before the show and simply took over the theatre, overflowing on to the stage. We managed to close the exterior iron gates, but there were even more people there – who could see in – clamouring to get in and join their friends. This electric, popular atmosphere was certainly encouraged by the roughness, the improvised quality of the space. Suddenly the audience went silent: the Venezuelan Minister of Culture and Chief of Police had walked in. The silence was not respectful: slowly, a chant of 'Fuera!' ('Get out!') started up; nobody wanted to relinquish their seat for these unwelcome spectators, and they had to stand there in the middle of the crowd. We were all hiding behind the breeze-block walls we had built at the sides of the stage, wondering if we would witness a riot or a lynching, and with some time to go before we were due to start. Not having any idea what to do to defuse the situation, I turned to Bruce Myers and said, 'You're on! Go and improvise.'*

Andreas Katsulas, François Marthouret and Malick Bowens

BRUCE MYERS: *I walked into the middle of the stage, climbed on to the cable drum that was positioned there, slowly raised my arms for silence, and said, 'I have something very important to*

tell you.' Of course I had no idea what I was going to say – my mind was blank with terror. At that instant someone grabbed a piece of cardboard that was lying around, wrote 'UBU' in big letters on it, and walked over to the Chief of Police. They held the sign over his head. I said, as naturally as I could, 'We have met your Ubu. Now we would like you to meet ours.' Andreas Katsulas recognized his cue, bounded on to the stage, and shouted his first line, 'Merdre!' The audience immediately turned their attention away from the objects of their hatred and the play began.

This space – tough, vibrant (thanks, in part, to the acoustic properties of the concrete surfaces), and open to interpretation and adaptation – was one of very few that would have been suitable for any of the Centre's subsequent productions. It *did* retain a theatrical vocation for a few years, but it was later demolished during building work on the Caracas Underground system.

During these three tours the Centre encountered all the types of space (old and new theatres; indoor and outdoor 'found' spaces) it would use throughout the following years. In keeping with its origins in the Bouffes du Nord, the appropriations and transformations were rough, improvised and public-spirited: they stimulated and gave a dose of fresh energy, a new perspective, to the places that the Centre visited, in much the same way that Parisian theatre-goers were (and still are) gently surprised out of their expectations by the Centre's 'found' space at home. A line back to Iran and Africa was also very clear.

This work – spinning in all directions, grabbing and gathering insights and material – was laying the ground for the next phase, which would involve a concentration of this energy into much more precise and refined forms.

4 : *The Conference of the Birds* and *The Cherry Orchard*

Having been in the Centre's repertoire for seven years as a series of loosely structured improvisations, *The Conference of the Birds* was given final form in a text by Jean-Claude Carrière in 1979, and a full-scale production was prepared. Instead of starting in Paris, the show was prepared for the 1979 Avignon Festival. The space selected was the Cloître des Carmes (which was an existing venue for the Festival). *The Conference* was unlike the previous work in that it used music, masks and movement in an almost abstract way. The spiritual character of the birds' journey across vast distances to find an elusive god required the kind of pure, sober atmosphere which a monastery cloister provided, and there were other beneficial characteristics to such a space: a strong geometry and a particular architectural 'style', together with the presence of the earth of the former garden and the open sky above.

The Cloître des Carmes in Avignon

The designer Sally Jacobs (who had worked on Brook's production of *A Midsummer Night's Dream* at Stratford) conceived with Jean-Guy an environment which anchored itself in the character of the garden: a mound of earth topped with a tree would be built in one corner of the square, with the audience gathered around on three sides; the actors would emerge from the cloister arcade, which formed a backdrop to the scene. The tree presented certain technical difficulties: it had to be lifted into the cloister with a crane lent by the army. It was bedded in sand from Roussillon, which had been specially chosen for its delicately varied colours. In the heat of a Provençal July its leaves promptly tuned brown and fell off. They had to be glued back on one by one and restored to their original green colour by careful painting. The audience were accommodated on a scaffolding structure in three blocks which brought them into an embrace around the acting area.

Maurice Bénichou.
Alain Maratrat, Mireille
Maalouf, Malick
Bowens and Yoshi Oida
performing *The Confer-
ence of the Birds* in
Avignon

MAURICE BÉNICHOU: *After Avignon we played in Rome out of
doors. The space was charming, but conditions were not ideal.
There was a little background noise on the first night. Then on the
second night it rained, and we had to go into a conventional theatre and perform on the stage. For me it was a huge disappoint-
ment: all the interiority and the intimacy of the piece were lost
because of the huge threshold imposed by the proscenium.*

PETER BROOK: *The crisis in Rome, which for the first time forced
us indoors, proved unexpectedly to be a source of discovery. Circumstances obliged us to find a completely new way of staging the
play. We called on the first simple solution at hand, which was to
play on a large, beautiful Persian carpet. We tried to rebuild the
scenery used in Avignon, but the tree looked horribly lost in this
neutral setting: it appeared arbitrary and theatrical, whereas in
the cloister it seemed natural and right. I became concerned that
we would have the same problem when we returned to the Bouffes
du Nord for an extended run, so I asked Jean-Guy to investigate
how we could capture the spirit of the play in that very particular
space.*

JEAN-GUY LECAT: *I did a number of drawings, and we realized that we couldn't put this somewhat realistic decor into any interior space. We tried in Berlin inside a temporary theatre but it was not successful. Although the cloister was enclosed, its success depended upon the openness to the sky, making a kind of real garden. In the Bouffes we can very well imagine we are in a garden, but not of this type – the walls dictate a different approach. This made me realize that the strength of the theatre exists everywhere except in the floor. The walls and the dome all have great force, and one can't change them much. Peter then recalled the*

Berlin

experience in Rome, and suggested we try using Persian carpets in the Bouffes. They were perfect, because they chimed with the walls but without touching them; one could take off with the story of the birds because the world of the play was supported by the carpet but detached from the walls.

We needed a great depth of the stage for the very long first entry, when the actors came on murmuring softly, with just a little music, so we built over the hole left where the theatre's former stage had been. The resulting slowness helped build up the pressure, preparing the audience for the Hoopoe's introduction when the actors were all gathered in the central zone.

There were three carpets: one in the central acting zone, another covering the new stage surface (which also dampened the booming acoustic of the huge volume behind the proscenium), and a third suspended against the back wall. The downstage carpet, which was the most heavily used, had a similar status to the mossy circle of *The Ik* as a zone denoting the limits of a specific theatrical world. It held this identity more intensely than the moss, because in *The Conference* the world of the play changed rapidly and without rules. The zone was more highly charged as a theatrical tool in proportion to the heightened theatricality of the piece, in which actors played birds with masks and puppets, and oscillated between appearing as birds, human characters and themselves. The carpet became a territory of make-believe, a world apart from its immediate margins (where the actors could loll around as themselves) and the space in front (which belonged to the audience).

In the context of the Bouffes, a Persian carpet takes on certain meanings quite naturally. Its geometry is different from the neutral circle of *The Ik*: it has direction, structure, and a form which sets it into contrast with the curves of the theatre. It is a hand-made object, crafted in detail and richly decorated (like the building). Its design and fabrication mean that it has integrity as an object: it is not cut off a roll, and has specific boundaries which cannot be altered without disrupting its unity. All this reinforces its role as a specific artificial zone for theatrical creation. In this case, as is quite common with Persian carpets, it was antique and somewhat worn – characteristics which chimed perfectly with the walls and balconies of the theatre. It imported a history which was unique to itself, but, because this history was inscrutable, it remained open to

imaginative interpretation by each of us. And, unavoidably, it resonated with the world of this Persian poem. This exotic character was, however, tempered by the familiarity of Persian carpets in many homes in the West. It was therefore an ordinary-extraordinary artefact par excellence – a launchpad for the imagination which has its foundations in our world.

This production saw other innovations for the Bouffes: conventional theatrical lighting was installed and used to create a focused atmosphere and particular effects of mood and space, and non-everyday costumes (vaguely Eastern flowing robes, which had been designed by Sally Jacobs for the Avignon run) were used for the first time, in combination with Balinese masks and bird-puppets.

The Conference of the Birds at the Bouffes du Nord

Lisbon: Convento do Beato António

Away from the Bouffes again, the Centre had the curious fortune to find itself using another monastery cloister, which, like the Caracas cinema, also served as an improbable garage. The venue was the marshalling yard of a biscuit factory belonging to the Companhia Industrial de Portugal e Colónias. Their premises had grown over time to engulf the fifteenth-century monastery of the Beato António, and their lorries manoeuvred and loaded up in what used to be the cloister. A square space of 26-metre sides, this had been roofed over early in the twentieth century, and was covered in grease and stains from exhaust pipes when it was first visited with Carlos Wallenstein. (Wallenstein, producer for this visit, was director of the Gulbenkian Foundation, which had generously funded the first three years of the Centre's research phase.)

Built around 1580, the monastery had been one of the most

The cloister in Lisbon during the first visit

magnificent in Lisbon. It had accumulated a large library and works of religious art, which were lost in the dissolution of the religious orders in the eighteenth century and also in a subsequent fire. From 1834 onwards it served as commercial premises (the church and refectory as warehouse space, and individual bays of the cloister as ateliers), and other facilities were added in a piecemeal fashion until the original institution was all but invisible.

The Companhia Industrial willingly accepted the suggestion to move their lorries out for a few days to make way for Brook's performances, and they also provided labour free of charge to clean the floor of the cloister and wash down the piers. They dismantled one workshop to allow public access from the street, and shifted the furniture in all the first-floor offices away from the windows overlooking the square so that these could be left open during the evenings, returning the building towards the simplicity of its original form.

Following the Avignon adaptation, it was decided to arrange the seats facing towards a corner – the furthest from the entrance. (This was the least dirty, the most convenient for access by the actors, and the most appropriate in terms of the

approach sequence made by the public from the outside towards the stage.) This configuration also gave a larger playing area than would have been possible flat against a wall, and greater spatial richness with the diagonal views through the archways into the cloister arcade. (Actors were able to use these spaces to great effect for multiple entries, and used the full depth for the long first entry of *The Conference*.) Three blocks of seating were made of scaffolding, accommodating 590 people, all within 12 metres of the stage front. The top of the new construction was aligned with the division between the two levels of the façade, giving the rows of benches a fairly steep slope of 21 degrees.

The space was a curious hybrid: an elegant leftover religious structure, but also a modern industrial interior. The floor surface (small beige terracotta tiles) had a lively material quality, with traces of use. It hardly seemed appropriate, in these circumstances, to revive the sand, mound and tree of Avignon; instead, one of the Persian carpets was simply placed on the tiled floor, which was left exposed as a ground flowing between the carpet and the audience. The space was very much like the Bouffes in that one felt surrounded by something real, something natural, even something profound; it also carried the trace identity of having been a place which once served for reflection and thought.

Adelaide

The Ik, *Ubu*, *The Bone* and *The Conference of the Birds* toured together in English-language versions in 1980. The Adelaide-based Macau Light theatre company took the intiative of helping the Centre to find a space that would be easy and inexpensive to inhabit. They knew of a quarry just outside the

The meeting with an Aboriginal group in Adelaide

THE CONFERENCE OF THE BIRDS

city; it had good proportions and – thanks to its high walls and hard, level floor – a good natural acoustic. Its crumbling walls had a blend of nature and artifice, of roughness and magnificence, which could allow the radically different worlds of *Ubu* and *The Conference* to take form in the same space.

Seating and lighting were the only additions made to the quarry. The Macau Light troupe helped with the construction work and remained at the site during the performances to participate in exercises and help out with the running of the theatre. Performances took place both at night and under the punishing afternoon sun. An Aboriginal group came and stayed for several days of exchange with the Centre's performers: they visited a modern city for the first time, taught dances and face decoration, and watched *The Ik* (in a language none of them could understand) with particular sensitivity and recognition.*

*The film *Stages* documents this work.

New York

The same group of productions then travelled to New York. Since the 'Theatre Days' in the Leperq Space in 1973, the possi-

The La MaMa annexe in New York

bility of finding a suitable venue for prolonged visits had become an intriguing challenge. On this occasion the guide was Ellen Stewart, director of La MaMa. Several abandoned theatres were visited, including the Anderson on 4th Street, which was seriously considered until Stewart said she saw a ghost on a visit. (The former director had hung himself over the stage.) Brook remarked that, what with the exploding radiators, lost keys and other practical glitches they had encountered there, it was as if the theatre itself didn't want to be reopened. Eventually it was decided to perform in one of Stewart's own spaces, the La MaMa Annex: a simple, flexible volume situated in what was then the dangerous and unfashionable East Village.

The Cherry Orchard in Paris

The Cherry Orchard, produced (in French) in 1981, marked a development in the focused, precise character achieved for *The Conference of the Birds*. It saw the arrival of designer Chloé Obolensky as a regular collaborator in the Centre's work, and was the first time a unified treatment of costumes and specific scenic elements was applied to the space of the Bouffes.

The play, consisting of four acts in stable, recognizable locations, revolves around the fate of a particular family house and its attendant orchard. The first and last acts are set in the 'children's room', the third in the salon (with a ballroom behind), and the second takes place out of doors, near the orchard. The basic atmosphere of the space was established by a sea of Persian carpets, extending at times up to the feet of the first row of spectators. These carpets touched the side walls of the theatre and went almost all the way to the back. The theatre *became* the house: characters called out from the balconies, the constant stream of comings and goings was channelled through the middle of the ground-floor audience, and the doors in the side walls were put to constant use. The fabric of the theatre belonged very strongly to the world of the play. When Liubov says near the end, 'One more minute . . . I'm going to sit down. It seems to me that I've never seen what the walls of this house are like, nor the ceiling; I look at them now avidly, with such tender love',* there is no mistaking which walls and ceiling she is referring to. (Natasha Parry, who played this role, looked around the space of the theatre at this point.)

Upon this basis the scene was able to shift with ease. A fold-

*CICT edition of *La Cerisaie*, p. 102.

ing screen delimited the space of the children's room, and a single armchair defined how the room was occupied. When the screen was removed (and the lighting changed) we were immediately outside, framed by the vast back wall of the theatre. A rolled-up carpet became a raised path or a fallen tree along which the characters walked; the other carpets became a lawn when characters lounged upon them. The salon of Act 3 was once again demarcated by screens, but this time with the ballroom beyond on the large space of the old stage. This infection of the entire space with the life of the play, the sharing of the play's world with ours, took on a tragic force when the carpets were stripped at the end, leaving the bare stage inhabited only by the servant Firs (who had been forgotten in the rush to move out). As the family left, never to return, the doors of the theatre all around the audience were slammed and audibly 'locked' in turn.

This was the first time the theatre had been used as a whole environment implicated in the universe of the drama. The clearing away of the carpets was a similar device to the sweeping up of the moss in *The Ik*, but here it was carried a stage further in that the carpets had been more than a limited acting zone. We could imagine ourselves guests in the Ranevskaia household simply because the carpets touched the walls and because we too touched them with our feet. The Ik remained remote across the gulf of a margin which said, 'This is theatre, here'; and the players in *The Cherry Orchard* could not slip in and out of character like the actors in *The Conference of the Birds*.

As if further to reinforce the 'total' quality of the theatre as an environment for this play, Brook asked for a study to be carried out to see if the audience could be put on the stage to watch a performance, using the theatre's balconies as the backdrop to the action. Unfortunately only 170 people could be accommodated in this arrangement, which precluded it for financial reasons.

> NATASHA PARRY: *During rehearsals we started using the whole theatre for improvisations – all of the balconies, the windows, the stairs. The whole building became a living thing for us, and I think this familiarity helped to communicate a certain domestic spirit during the performances. We had been working with some elements of scenery, but during a read-through on the day of the first public preview Peter decided to have us all sit on the carpet*

and just get up when we were in a scene. It worked quite well, and he announced that we would put aside all the scenery that night and use only the carpet. Suddenly it seemed like nothing: all we had was one chair. There had been a bench for the second act, but in the end we just had a rolled-up carpet on the floor. I thought at first that it was rather strange to play Chekhov sitting on the floor.

In the text, Liubov looks out towards the back of the stage to see the orchard. Peter said, 'No, you should look out front, into the audience.' When I got used to that it was absolutely extraordinary. Even though the audience is practically on top of you, you can still see and imagine things as if they're not there.

There was an extraordinary moment just after the play began, when we would stand in the corridor of the theatre behind the audience, improvising the excitement of the family's arrival at the house. We would build this up more and more, until suddenly we all burst into the acting space.

It was a very joyous production, and the feeling of the whole theatre, the café and its connection to the city, all of the entrance spaces, helped create the world of the play. However, I still can't do what Bruce and Yoshi do, which is to pop into the bar about

Niels Arestrup and Natasha Parry performing *The Cherry Orchard* in Paris

THE CHERRY ORCHARD

five minutes before they go on, for a drink or a sandwich, to chat with people, but I love the fact that the actors use the café in this way. I always have a feeling of coming home when I go into the Bouffes. Sometimes, after the performances of The Cherry Orchard, *people would spill out on to the acting area, all the elements of the play having been cleared away at the end. It seemed completely natural – like a party.*

PETER BROOK: *There isn't a* line of inquiry *in our work. There is simply an* inquiry, *a general attitude of interrogation. To keep an inquiry alive one must avoid getting stuck on one note. We like being able to do a South African township play and* Hamlet *in the same season. The vector linking the work is not descriptive or categorizing: it is a trajectory of meaning or quality, and is something that one follows rather than controls.*

Space has been an important reagent in this development. The Bouffes presented itself in 1974 like a beautiful instrument, and, like any instrument, the more you play it, the more you discover its possibilities. For years I had wanted to do The Three Sisters, *and in the end decided to do* The Cherry Orchard; *it seemed very natural, because the Bouffes lends itself to being a house, which is the soul of this play. We were led to do things for this particular piece that we have never done since, such as have Yasha climb up a ladder on the third gallery, through a trapdoor into the theatre's literal attic, to bring down some boxes, or have Varia walking rapidly round the back of the circle, using the inner staircases. (Although we used the stairs in* Carmen, *we have not so fully exploited the theatre in this way since.)*

Something we had until the time of The Cherry Orchard *was a central entrance in the middle of the stalls, through which the actors made their first entrance after starting to make lots of noise in the corridor outside. The scene went straight on, actors dispersing through the doors and up the stairs, immediately inhabiting the whole theatre; it was a very important moment in the production. But we were losing a lot of seats – and also the best seats – in this configuration, so we changed it after this production. It was marvellous when it was there, but we have never felt we needed this since.*

5 : *La Tragédie de Carmen*

Carmen at the Bouffes

In *La Tragédie de Carmen*, *The Cherry Orchard*'s expanse of carpets was replaced by a sea of loose earth – a sea whose organic qualities struck a chord with the time-worn walls and which reached right to the threshold of the theatre's doors and penetrated under the feet of the front row. (This front row was now more comfortably accommodated on curving benches with backrests.) There was no other 'scenery' used; the theatre was stripped of all embellishment (such as the walkway at the back), and a chamber orchestra with a piano was tucked almost out of sight behind both sides of the proscenium. Unlike the Ranevskaias' carpets, the earth lacked scale and did not denote a specific space: this natural ground stood for the sand of the bullring, the terrain of the mountain-top gypsy camp, and the city square where action takes place – suggestions which were aided by differences in lighting. It did not move towards a literal denotation of these locations. For those who knew Bizet's opera it did not deny them either; but the emphasis here was on liberating the story from its anecdotal details and revealing the tragedy at its core.

The earth had a corporeal beauty which constantly worked itself into the action of the opera. Characters tussled and rolled in it, and threw it in each other's eyes. They made magic circles in it with coloured chalk, and built fires on it, which would be brushed away in a cloud of dust when the scene ended. It could become a background, too: scenes were created within it by adding a zone of carpet (for Lillas Pastia's tavern) or by focusing the light on a limited area. While it touched the walls of the theatre, it did not draw them into the world of the play as intensely as they had been in *The Cherry Orchard* – with the one exception of the door in the left side wall, which served to communicate between the tavern and Carmen's bedroom.

Helene Delavault and
Véronique Dietschy
performing *La Tragédie
de Carmen* at the
Bouffes

PETER BROOK: *The productions that have come to us from the
outside have very often made the mistake of using scenery. The
strong thing about the Bouffes is that the entire environment is
complete in itself: one really doesn't need to tamper with it. Like an
Elizabethan theatre, it's an open space in which almost anything
can take place. It also has something that the Elizabethan theatre
needed, which is doors. In Greek tragedy the central door was a terrible expression of the unknown, the hidden; one sees how fundamental it is, and how close to situations of everyday life.*

*We've found in so many improvisations that the one prop we
really need is just a door. On a completely bare stage you can perhaps imagine someone knocking, but to feel that you're in everyday reality you have to be able to go through a door, slam a door,
open a door, and appear in a doorway. Carmen's lover takes her
into the back room, so all you needed was the possibility of going
through a door, and Don José going towards the door, the door
opening, and there! – the lover is caught with his pants down.
You can't do any of that without the existence of real doors.*

Maurice Bénichou was
Brook's assistant direc-
tor for this production.

MAURICE BÉNICHOU: *Most of the action takes place outdoors.*

Carmen's earthy floor
after a performance in
Copenhagen

The trick was to find something which would give the sensation of space without losing the scale needed for the most intimate moments – without creating the vacuous, lost space of some modern theatres. The earth gave a natural quality – it wasn't an artistic choice: it was just something that felt right. There were lots of people onstage: seventeen musicians had to cross the stage at the beginning, and because this was a bit chaotic it broke up any preciousness in the atmosphere.

The earth was fluid with meaning. It could give a hint of specific places (such as the bullring, denoted also by the traces of the red chalk circle which had been drawn around the lovers in the previous scene), or it could serve as the universal ground of a tragedy which reaches beyond place and time. Its extension into the depths of the auditorium served to embrace the public in the atmosphere of the opera. In keeping with the wholeness of this environment, the acting in *Carmen* was seamless and always in character; it was never 'theatre' set apart for consideration as such by the audience; gestures were natural and devoid of the woodenness and formality so often associated with operatic performance.

LA TRAGEDIE DE CARMEN

La Tragédie de Carmen was filmed for French television in the Bouffes du Nord without an audience. As with earlier films of *Measure for Measure* and *The Cherry Orchard*, the space was not presented as a theatre: rather, it was mined for locations appropriate to specific scenes. Sometimes the large expanse of the earthy stage was used (but without showing the balconies); the curving stair leading to the first balcony was the fateful access to Carmen's bedroom in the Lillas Pastia scene; the technical gallery high up under the arches of the dome became the arcade of the bullring.

PETER BROOK: *The basic idea was to strip* Carmen *back to its essentials, taking away everything that had been added to the very powerful but austere story of Prosper Mérimée. With Marius Constant [the production's music director] and Jean-Claude Carrière we worked and worked to take out everything extraneous, and in doing this one saw that there were very strong fibres going through the work. One thing naturally led to another: there were natural muscles and threads which revealed themselves. So we started to rehearse, and Chloé as always came and watched. With* The Cherry Orchard *fresh in our memory, we talked about carpets, or perhaps a completely neutral floor – such as linoleum – which just wouldn't have existed, which would allow all of* Carmen *to be evoked purely through the imagination. And then one saw that what the foot touched had a vital importance. We harked back to* The Ik *and looked forward to what was to become* The Mahabharata: *in this theatre the ground is of supreme importance, because almost all the audience is looking down. What the actors are standing on is the basis of the world of the play. In* The Mahabharata *what is under the feet and leads up then to the level of the ankle is totally naturalistic – no different from in a film. But, as you come up a little higher, the audience is then using its theatrical imagination. On this real surface Krishna comes in pushing one wheel representing a chariot, and the two make sense. The fact that we are in world of imagination, with a wheel becoming a chariot, would have been harder to establish if the action had taken place on a conventional stage or on a wooden surface. Many designers feel the necessity to make a complete unity – if one thing is realistic, everything else must be too. From the walls of our theatre, which present a funny mixture of realism and abstraction, we have been able to learn another point of view. The greater part of Jean-Guy's challenge when we left on tour has been to capture this paradox: the hardness of our* walls and yet their indeterminate nature. For Carmen *the walls (frequently made of planks) had a non-figurative character – they were what they were, but at the same time they fitted with the rough world taking shape on the stage.*

I had previously given up opera because I was never in a position to make the changes I felt were needed, but we found ourselves confronted with total freedom in the Bouffes: because it was ours, we could do anything we wanted. We changed everything: the administrative and financial character of the rehearsal pattern, the way the singers worked, every basic attitude.

The fundamental requirement was that I wanted the human being to be closest to the audience, and this created a spatial problem with the orchestra, even though we had a small orchestra, which we were able to define as a support to the contact between the singer and the audience, rather than the lead which the singer accompanies. How could we resolve this? Placed all on one side of the acting area the orchestra was too big, very prominent and acoustically too present, dominating the singers. We had a thrilling experiment with Marius Constant, putting them on the third balcony, which gave a brilliant sound, but a curious spatial gap between the action and the music coming out of the heavens. This could have been good for something else, but it allowed no marriage between music and performer – especially important as this music is meant to be carrying something intimate that the performers cannot express but that the music is expressing for them; it couldn't be cut away like this.

We had a very big discussion with the musicians as to whether we could split them in two. At first it was impossible for them to keep together; also, the conductor was stuck unseen in the corner, peering around so that he could see the singers. This meant that the strict contact with the singers that every star conductor insists on – being the the dominant person, holding all the tempi together – had to be replaced. This for me was a great advantage, which our conductors readily accepted: the orchestra in Carmen was not part of an ensemble in which the conductor was dominating everything as in an oratorio; the conditions changed, and it was like another beautiful form of music-making, which is when a singer has an accompanist. There are accompanists who have become legendary figures whom every singer swears by because they follow the singer. Alas, there isn't a single conductor who naturally does the same.

The impulses in opera must come from the singers, the human expression of vocal music. For us this meant that the accompany-

ing music – orchestra or piano – had to be going along with the singer, following carefully from behind the proscenium. This meant that the singers had to know their scores, and their partners' scores, much better than they normally would. Marius Constant invented an extraordinary exercise, which I think was unprecedented, which involved the singers learning the orchestra parts like a chorale. Through the experience of singing the orchestration, they knew the orchestra in a very different, organic, way from when they were used to hearing the orchestra coming from the pit below them. Because of that, the singers could keep their tempi without somebody reminding them, which allowed the performances to be in tempo freely.

JEAN-CLAUDE CARRIÈRE: *It's very difficult to analyse after the fact: at the time one does things without thinking, as best as one can in the given circumstances. But, looking back, it seems clear that the intimacy of the Bouffes – the capacity it gives to speak in a normal, unprojected voice, at very close distances to the audiences – has allowed me as a writer to use text in a more familiar, open and direct way than in a normal theatre; and this also goes for sung text, as in* La Tragédie de Carmen, *which I adapted with Marius Constant. The space rejects intellectual, literary or theoretical speech. Its 'popular' nature has always imposed on me a certain kind of writing. Over the course of a rehearsal one senses what kinds of speech come across better than others, and the space has an influence on a text which one senses only in an intuitive, empirical way. It has likes and dislikes, and one must be attentive, one must listen to the demands of the space. It imposes a certain kind of speech, a certain kind of acting, a certain kind of* mise-en-scène *which are in harmony with the spirit of the place. The great difficulty – which Peter has always brilliantly resolved – is to conceive a direction supple enough to be able to be transported to many other, very different, spaces. In a sense one has to take the Bouffes, or the idea of the Bouffes, along with us.*

Carmen toured almost continuously from 1983 to 1989, performing to more than a quarter of a million people, and involving a total of twelve different singers in the title role. It initiated and traversed the Centre's most fruitful period of spatial creation, which also included the world tour of *The Mahabharata*. It was performed in a vast variety of spaces. In response to its incarnation at the Bouffes, these all had to provide for at least three basic factors: the earth, the door, and an absolutely clear acoustic. The earth had to find a relationship with the existing architecture of a space (or a link had to be created); the door had to be built of solid material which seemed to be 'real', not a representational stage set (this usually meant building a wooden background around the acting area); and the opera's song – *mezza voce* over a chamber orchestra – had to reach every audience member with perfect clarity of communication.

New York: Resuscitating the Vivian Beaumont Theatre

The search for a base in New York was continued for *Carmen*. The La MaMa Annex would, at 300 seats, not have been adequate for the needs of this production. A different possibility was suggested thanks to the city government and various private developers, who had a project to restore some of the historic theatres around Times Square as a means of driving out the pornographic activity which predominated there. The New Amsterdam Theatre was at the centre of this plan: formerly the celebrated home of the Ziegfeld Follies, by the early 1980s it had become a rundown porn-and-gore cinema. Above the main auditorium was the 800-seat Aerial Gardens, scene of Ziegfeld's *Midnight Frolics* and of after-hours try-outs for the main house, which were frequented by such luminaries as George Gershwin, Irving Berlin and Fred Astaire. It was intended that both theatres be transormed at the same time, the upper house being readied for the New York run of *Carmen*. Architect Roger Morgan worked in collaboration with the Centre, preparing the space so that the basic construction would be complete for *Carmen*, the finishing touches of carpets, painting and upholstery being left until afterwards. Unfortunately, well into the building process, it was discovered that the steel supports of the rooftop theatre had degraded to such an extent that they could no longer be depended upon to bear the weight of the new construction. The project was abandoned,* and another space had to be found at very short notice. (This was June 1983; *La Tragédie de Carmen* was supposed to open in October.) Dozens of spaces were visited at this time, ranging from piers on the Hudson to a police station in Chinatown; that these researches were so varied and extensive is a testament to the courage and open-mindedness of *Carmen*'s producer Alexander Cohen.

The Vivian Beaumont Theatre at Lincoln Center was finally

*The space was in fact restored during the mid-1990s by architects Hardy Holzman Pfeiffer Associates for stage presentations of Walt Disney's animated films.

selected because it was one of the few large theatres in the city which was made to accommodate non-proscenium productions. It was built in 1965 to the designs of Eero Saarinen (the Finnish-born architect of Dulles Airport and the expressionistic TWA Terminal at JFK) and scenographer Joseph Mielziner. There were two principal motivations behind the design: the theatre should have a vast stage, in order to permit a fast changeover of the classic and contemporary plays it was destined to house (its original name was the Lincoln Center Repertory Theater), and it should strike a compromise between the proscenium and the burgeoning thrust forms of staging. Mielziner and Saarinen had different ideas about how this should be done: the former's experience was on Broadway, where he had built apron stages over the orchestra pit for productions of Tennessee Williams; Saarinen's allegiances were to the altogether new configurations of spaces such as the Tyrone Guthrie Theater in Minneapolis. The resulting design was a compromise between the two positions.

The space was used by the likes of Arthur Miller and Elia Kazan as something like an American version of Britain's National Theatre. Although it never fulfilled its repertory vocation, it stood somewhat outside the savage financial culture of Broadway, and was able to generate several classic productions in the late 1960s. It took its place alongside the other Lincoln Center monoliths (the Metropolitan Opera, the New York State Theatre, Avery Fisher Hall and the Juilliard School of Music) as a very 'official' cultural institution – a monumental box with a foyer which has the vacuous atmosphere of an airport terminal. Tucked around the corner behind the Met, it feels cut off from the grain of the city – a considerable feat, given the density and vibrancy of New York.

After twelve years of life, suffering under the weight of officialdom, and torn by the unresolved tension of its double vocation as a thrust/proscenium theatre, it closed its doors following the resignation of director Joseph Papp. It remained mostly dark for five of the following six years, until the Centre's visit.

La Tragédie de Carmen was put on in the middle of a battle between the boards of Lincoln Center and of the theatre itself. The Vivian Beaumont board had proposed a $5–7 million refit which would turn the space definitively into a proscenium theatre. Lincoln Center demurred, holding up money in an attempt to force the theatre to open before building work would be sanctioned. Various cheaper modifications were proposed, ranging from $250,000 to improve acoustics to $1 million to improve sight lines as well. Even those charged with the redesign were in dispute: architect I. M. Pei and project acoustician Cyril Harris had parted company, unable to agree about the modifications needed.

The Centre had an even smaller budget with which to effect the temporary modifications needed to revive the space for *Carmen*. (The funding came from the overall show budget of producers Alexander Cohen and Roy Somlyo.) The chief problems to be addressed were the abominable acoustics caused by the huge stage and flytower; the dead acoustic of the auditorium itself; and the ambiguous focus and sight lines of the seating (some seats were oriented parallel to the plane of the 'proscenium', so that their occupants stared at the profiles of the people sitting in front of them in the 'stalls' which occupied the area of the thrust stage when this was removed). For financial reasons, none of the theatre's 1,143 seats could be sacrificed, and new construction had to be kept to a minimum. There was an 83-centimetre step up to the stage from the front row, and in order to eliminate this threshold it was decided to bridge between the level of the thrust stage and the third row of the seating. Then, starting from the seventh row, a more gradual gradient would be established, finishing on the performance surface itself. This created a more natural acceleration of the slope away from the stage: the first rows were closely married to the playing surface, and the back rows were tilted up into a focused bowl. Two ramps were built leading through the public on to the stage; entrances could also be made on either side of the seating. The balcony was left untouched, every seat being used.

A trickier challenge was the 'scenic' treatment, the conjuring

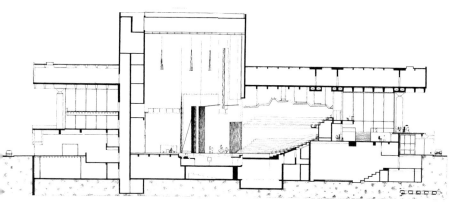

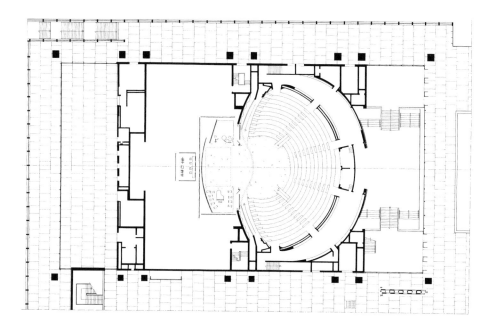

up of the world of the drama in relation to the building. Loose earth was strewn on the acting surface (as at the Bouffes) and continued on a new layer of doormat material through the aisles up to the entrance doors. The rough concrete side walls of the Beaumont had little presence and were unrelated in function and scale to the worlds of the audience and the stage. Grey, abstract, unsure of themselves, they stood detached from the seating in an indeterminate zone which would formerly have been closed around the stage by the balconies of the Shakespearean theatre or, in the case of a Greek theatre, open

Long section and plan of the Vivian Beaumont Theatre as transformed for *Carmen*

to the sky and the distant landscape. In order to unify this space, to close the circuits of energy more tightly around the drama, two high walls were built of rough planks daubed with grey paint (so that they at least chimed with the existing concrete). The new walls stood in front of the concrete, slightly reducing the volume of the auditorium, and closed down the opening of the stage to 9 metres (closer to the Bouffes' 8 metres). They had built in – on both sides – the 'permanent' doors which would be used in Lillas Pastia's tavern. Together with the additional focusing of the lighting, these walls

The Vivian Beaumont stage transformed for *Carmen*

formed a new, complete theatre environment within the shell of the Beaumont, extending off into the darkness of the auditorium beyond the world of the opera.

Acoustic, spatial and 'scenic' problems were resolved together by the installation of a curving wall set at the same distance from the first row as the great back wall in the Bouffes. Made from the same rough wood as the side walls, this cut off a vast part of the stage and, together with a low acoustic ceiling set just behind the proscenium, sealed the opera's music into the same volume as the audience. The choice of wood gave a warm quality to the sound (this would have been less sure with the original concrete).* But there was still something lacking in the auditorium's acoustic:

*A plywood wall was also added at the back of the auditorium, and the carpeting was removed from the risers of the theatre's steps to further crispen the sound.

JEAN-GUY LECAT: *Carmen's musical director, Marius Constant, still wasn't happy with the sound of the space: there was a dead reverberation coming down from the ceiling of the auditorium. Although we had engaged an acoustician to help us remedy the problems of this theatre, we didn't have time at that stage to study theoretical solutions, so I climbed up into the rafters and ripped out bale after bale of sound-absorbing fibreglass. Marius was conducting the orchestra down below; every once in a while he would walk around the auditorium to check the sound, and would shout up to me 'A bit less over there', and I would clamber over to correct the acoustic little by little, using the crudest – but ultimately most effective – of empirical methods.*

ROY SOMLYO: *Jean-Guy Lecat has never been given the credit he deserves for turning the Vivian Beaumont Theatre from what Joseph Papp termed 'unusable' into viable performance space. Working with technical director Arthur Siccardi under my very strict budgetary limitations, he had only twelve weeks to accomplish a magical make-over of the building's functional and cosmetic aspects. He managed to convince a sceptical stage crew operating under difficult union regulations to follow his lead; he worked endless hours, often by himself in a darkened space, in order to meet the deadline. His interventions (often destroying the work of acoustic 'experts') gave the Beaumont its first acceptable 'live' sound. Days before the first performance of* Carmen, *audio consultant Robin Liftin was called in to make whatever adjustments he felt were in order. He refused to touch a thing, proclaiming the renovations 'flawless'.*

Roy Somlyo was producer of the New York run of *La Tragédie de Carmen*

The Vivian Beaumont has happily been in continual use since *La Tragédie de Carmen* (which played to near-sell-out audiences for a whole season). Architects Hardy Holzman Pfeiffer recently modified the auditorium – lowering the ceiling slightly, installing sound amplification, and changing the colour scheme – and it has since been used for work as diverse as the musical *Juan Darien* and the solo performances of Spalding Gray.

Barcelona: The Mercat de les Flors

As in New York, the search for a space in Barcelona involved first seeing all the possible options. There were no municipal theatres; the city administration, who were producing the performances, therefore took the opportunity to seek out a new venue for themselves which would be opened by *La Tragédie de Carmen*. Biel Moll, cultural-affairs director for the mayor's office, was the guide. Various established festival venues were visited, such as the Grec, an open-air theatre on the Montjuic used for opera, theatre and music, together with empty spaces such as the North Station and a nineteenth-century market

hall. In every case there were spatial, acoustic and/or bureaucratic difficulties.

Moll had an ace up his sleeve, but hesitated to play it: it was
the best space available, but posed the greatest difficulty, as it
was being used by the notoriously obstinate city works department. A visit was nevertheless arranged and, as expected, the
space was wonderful. A vast empty volume, some 47 metres
long, 31 metres wide and 16 metres to the apex of the roof, it
had 10-metre high masonry walls all around with a plaster
covering which had accumulated a rich patina of weathering

and use. Natural light came from small clerestory windows, and the roof was supported by giant arches which looked at first glance as though they were made of deep steel I-beams, but were in fact composite structures made of hundreds of wooden planks. The ceiling itself was faced with wooden slats, which gave a comfortable sensation and a warm acoustic. There was a good scale to the existing structure, plenty of space in which to work, and a lively material feeling which could be conserved and integrated into the world of the drama. Furthermore, the building was in an eccentric position

with respect to the conventional theatres of the city: the Centre's production could perhaps attract an audience with an unprejudiced eye from the immediate working-class neighbourhood, and would oblige the 'mainstream' cultured public to step outside their normal habits and discover a part of the city they probably would not frequent – just like the audience of the Bouffes du Nord.

Carmen curtain-call in the Mercat

The space was built for the 1929 Exposition as part of a large complex displaying agricultural products and technology (Mies van der Rohe's seminal Barcelona Pavilion was also built

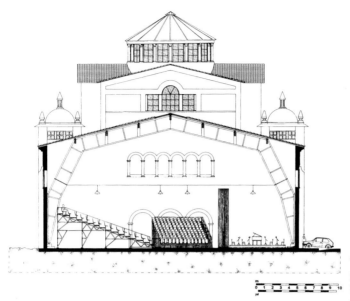

Transverse section and
plan of the Mercat de
les Flors as transformed
for *Carmen*

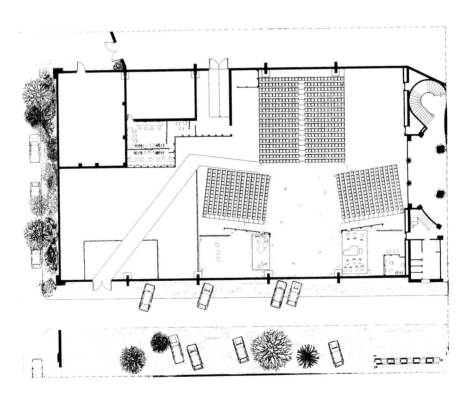

for this Exposition.) Since then it had been a flower market, but latterly had been in virtual disuse, serving only to house the floats from the city carnival. It fell to Biel Moll to persuade the works department to vacate the space and grant the necessary permits for the production. He describes what happened next:

> **BIEL MOLL:** *The days passed by, and I still had no agreement from the city. The negotiations with Mme Rozan had concluded easily, owing to her generosity and interest. Finally, with no authority to do so, I sent an 'official' letter to the CICT in my capacity as director of theatrical services for Barcelona, saying that all was resolved. This provoked a few raised eyebrows among the municipal leadership, but it also had the effect of making them aware of the importance of a visit from Mr Brook. After that everything was approved.*

So, only two and a half months after the first visit, construction work was able to begin.

The acting area was placed in one bay of the structure, and the slope of the wooden ceiling above acted as an acoustic diffuser aimed down at the bulk of the audience. Unobtrusive lighting rigs were suspended from the principal beams, and simple lamps hung elsewhere in the space were moved to provide the house lighting. The stained and fading paintwork of the back wall was left largely intact, but was daubed in places with a slightly warmer tone and the plaster was scraped off near the bottom to expose some of the brickwork and make a break between the floor and the painted surface. The earth here was of excellent quality (the same kind used for bullrings): supple and dense, it was spread very deeply (a total of 20 tons), giving an added sensuality to the setting. The 'scenic' side walls were built with planks taken from an old railway warehouse; they had a dark tint and a massiveness which contributed greatly to the acoustic. The elegant proportions of the 'host' space served as an anchor and guide for the new construction. The exposed back wall was a square with 10-metre sides (a smaller square was described below the base of the windows). The acting area, with its normal depth of 17 metres, therefore formed a shape close to a golden rectangle. The central scaffold of seating was extended so as to reach the opposite wall of the space; the two side blocks were continued for the depth of another structural bay. Finishing touches included the building of an alleyway to the entrance door a little way from the theatrical area. The modifications were inexpensive and rapid, and drew their force from the quality of the existing structure.

The production was a great success; powerful figures from the government and the cultural world were attracted, and it was agreed immediately afterwards that the space should maintain its theatrical vocation, under the name of the Mercat de les Flors. Contracts were signed for *The Mahabharata* to visit in two years' time (immediately after the opening run at the Avignon Festival), and other companies were invited to what became the first municipal theatre in Barcelona.

Düsseldorf

La Tragédie de Carmen was invited to Düsseldorf for a ten-day run in 1986. The city's Schauspielhaus, who were paying for the visit, could not make available their permanent space because it was locked into the high-turnover repertory system typical of German municipal theatres. After a search through the city's industrial spaces, a suburban train-turntable shed was chosen because of its inherent interest and correct proportions. (It happened, also, to have the same function as had

the Round House in London.) The shed itself formed a vast three-quarter doughnut around a train turntable. The outside was a rather austere 1920s concrete structure; the inside a diaphanous glass, steel and brick façade animated by the chance rhythm of broken panes. Taking an existing radial partition as a point of departure, a further wall was built to define the space of the theatre, which closeted off only a small slice of the overall 'doughnut'.

What gave this space distinction was its eccentricity, both in its use as a theatre and in relation to the city. A special train was laid on from the central station to bring the audience directly to this place which they would never have had cause to visit otherwise; the train became the theatre bar after the show. The state railway company (perhaps beginning to enjoy its unusual role) also provided two carriages for use as dressing rooms, which were shunted into an adjoining bay and fitted out with tables, lights and running water (one singer per compartment). A further carriage was gutted and used for meals and as a warm-up space. To ensure silence during the performance, trains that would have passed nearby were diverted and other engine manoeuvres were postponed.

Opposite: Train shed in Dusseldorf transformed for *Carmen*

Arles

In other cities the creation of space also provoked unorthodox actions on the part of the municipal governments. The city of Arles could not afford to convert a space on its own, so a consortium of Provençal towns (Aix, Avignon, Nîmes, Uzès, Alès, Montpellier, Marseille, Martigues and Salon-de-Provence) pooled their resources to have performances in a location somewhere between them. Each town would have one night to itself, its audience travelling there by bus. The space selected

Rice silo near Arles with sketch of seating structure

was a rice silo in the middle of fields near Arles, which was transformed by removing a section of wall to make way for seating and by spreading earth on the floor.

This was one of the rare occasions since the African and American trips when the Centre performed in a rural setting, and it was this that gave the venue its force. The audience parked a few hundred metres away from the building, then walked down a long avenue of plane trees accompanied by the sound of crickets; the music of the opera sounded out across the landscape.

Hamburg: The Kampnagel Factory

The Schauspielhaus in Hamburg already had an unorthodox space at its disposal: during restoration work on the nine-teenth-century baroque 'main' house (which would later host *Impressions de Pelléas*), the theatre took over and converted four spaces in the disused Kampnagel factory. *Carmen* opened one of these spaces. Later, the restoration work complete, the factory was to have been demolished; but Peter Brook pleaded (successfully) with the mayor to keep these

rough spaces for young companies and visitors who could not adapt to the overbearingly formal permanent theatre. The Centre has been back there with *The Tempest*, *Woza Albert* and *The Man Who*.

Copenhagen: The Ostre Gasvaerk

It was not intended that *Carmen* be performed in Copenhagen: a Scandinavian producer, Per Moth, proposed to put it on in Stockholm and Aarhus, and led the customary expedition to

find spaces in both cities. In Stockholm a circus was chosen; but nothing could be found in Aarhus. Determined that the production be seen in Denmark, the producer remembered at the last moment an abandoned gasometer in Copenhagen which Morten Grunwald, director of the Betty Nansen Theatre, was trying to save and convert into a theatre. The team agreed to make a detour to see the site on the way to the train.

The Ostre Gasvaerk is situated on the periphery of the city in an industrial area. It was built at the beginning of the twentieth century to the designs of Martin Nyrop (also architect of Copenhagen's town hall), who hid the metal gas container inside a brick cylinder supporting a wood and metal dome based loosely on the Pantheon in Rome. No longer in use, it had become an illegal rubbish dump. Grunwald and his team had flattened the accumulated debris and spread earth on the floor; when the team arrived at the site and parked with their headlights illuminating the interior, it was a bare volume seemingly primed for *Carmen*. The interior was paced out and, at the railway-station café, a preliminary scheme was rapidly sketched on a tablecloth. The principal problem was acoustic: the curves of the walls and the dome bounced sound around, giving rise to a 10-second echo. It was decided that a sound-absorbing material would have to be applied to the underside of the dome, but the theatre lacked the resources to do this.

Everything had to be decided within a week if the production was to be scheduled. Fortunately the city government stepped in at the last moment and offered to carry out the acoustic work and some repairs to the roofing, along with providing 200 tons of earth to finish the floor. The Betty Nansen Theatre paid for the wood for the seating; one of Grunwald's partners, Eric Lind, had a carpentry company

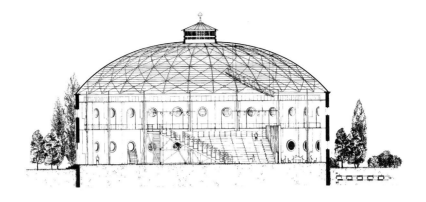

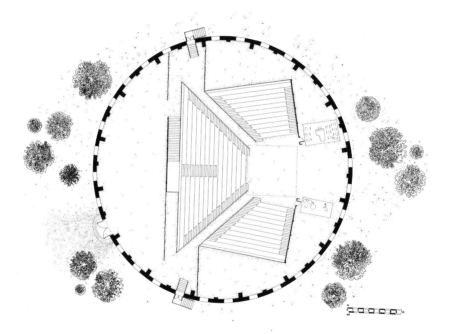

(Elindco); and his employees volunteered their labour to build the structures every day after normal working hours.

The 'theatre', which took up slightly more than half of the available area, was oriented towards a section of the wall whose idiosyncratic round windows became the backdrop for the drama. (Elsewhere the windows served as emergency exits.) The acting area, framed by wooden side walls, was positioned away from the geometrical centre of the space, to avoid the problem of sounds returning immediately to their source in an echo powerfully focused by the dome. A heavy tarpaulin was stretched on a frame above the stage and backed with fibreglass: sound was reflected down to the audience and deadened behind before it could resound around the dome. Any 'lost' noise was captured by heavy black curtains hung along the back of the three seating blocks (at 27 degrees, these were quite steeply sloped, their topmost level being aligned with a horizontal division in the building's wall). The reverberation time was reduced to 3 seconds – about the upper limit of acceptability for opera.

Improvised emergency exit through one of the windows

JEAN-GUY LECAT: *A theatre is a complex place: the auditorium and the audience and the stage and the performance confront each other, with the prospect of sharing their energies. At the same time, each of the two spaces needs to accommodate either the performance on the one side or the audience on the other. Space therefore has a twofold function: to accommodate and to relate. A too accommodating 'stage space' risks cramping the performance, instead of projecting it toward the audience, as happens in circular places (which is not a contradiction of the idea of the circle that accommodates living beings and is a constant of our work). In spite of everything, this form – so obvious, so perfect – is very restrictive and always creates difficult acoustics.*

Visiting a circular space such as the Ostre Gasvaerk can present a trap, as one is immediately seduced only to discover afterwards that the space does not fit in with the spirit of the show. At first I was unable to make up my mind about it, since I was under the spell of the sombre and silent void, which seemed immense under the headlights of the cars. The place obviously presented a problem: it was too big, too high, and round, with frightful acoustics (as is normal in a round place). But it had character – it was interesting and beautiful. I confusedly felt that we could

The transformed space
with acoustic reflector
above the acting area

play La Tragédie de Carmen *in it. But how?*

I went and sat in the middle for a few moments and noticed that, as in the Bouffes du Nord, the great height paradoxically created a kind of intimacy on the level of the ground. That was the point of departure.

Our intervention divided the place into two parts. In the first, the entrance space (approximately one-third of the total), the public had a total vision of the theatre space, the reflection of light from the stage illuminating just enough of the dark cupola to indicate the true dimensions. Then, through a set of black curtains, one penetrated into a second space, well lit and closed on three sides by tiered seating in light wood and on the fourth by two dark palisades revealing a segment of the existing wall (a section with proportions different, more elegant, from the rest), the ensemble being enclosed by the acoustic ceiling of approximately 100 square metres. In going against the obvious geometrical grain of the building, we managed to find a surprising space which drew on the force of the existing structure and allowed Carmen *to come to life correctly.*

The 'rule of luck' which Brook had discerned in the successful adaptation of *Orghast* to its setting had been the determining force in the selection of these spaces: there were no preconceived solutions, just a receptive, listening attitude towards what was on offer, and a slight will to create or provoke luck – a constant attention towards possibilities that other people might not consider. The fact that many of the theatres created for *Carmen* were former industrial spaces was due to a combination of factors (budget, timing, availability, ease of transformation), many of which were outside the Centre's control. For a later tour of Italy, when all the venues used happened to have some form of past or present theatrical vocation, chance again came into play. But this time the 'chance' factors were framed by a greater daring, a more precise control, in the strategies of transformation.

Rome: The Teatro Argentina

This was particularly true for the transformation of the Teatro Argentina in Rome, which was the Centre's first wholesale modification (for a tour) of an old theatre of high architectural quality – and, to date, perhaps the most successful, thanks to the harmonious marriage of the production with the reinterpreted building. Situated near the Campidoglio and facing a large square, the Largo Argentina, this theatre has long been one of the most important venues in Rome. Designed in 1730 by Gerolamo Theodoli, it was directly inspired by the Teatro di Tordinona, the first public theatre in Rome and the originator of the *théâtre à l'italienne* type. It is thus the direct descendant of Palladio's Teatro Olimpico and the theatre at Sabbioneta designed by Vincenzo Scamozzi, Palladio's assistant.

As in the Sabbioneta theatre, the auditorium of the Teatro Argentina was stretched away from the performer into a horseshoe, to favour the visual composition created on the deep stage. Originally destined for a mixture of dance, drama and lyric opera, the Argentina achieved an important operatic vocation in the nineteenth century (*The Barber of Seville* and *I due Foscari* received their premieres there under the direction of their composers, Rossini and Verdi), though in our times it has been largely dedicated to drama (Pirandello was artistic director for several years). It is smaller than the nineteenth-century opera houses we know: in fact, at 16 metres wide, 20 metres from the back of the stalls to the forestage and 16 metres high, its auditorium is not much larg-

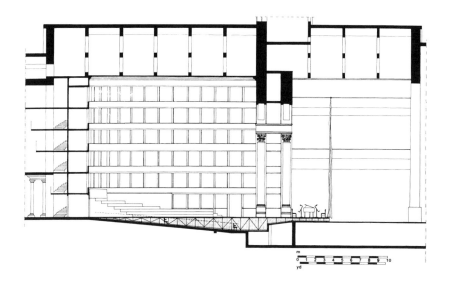

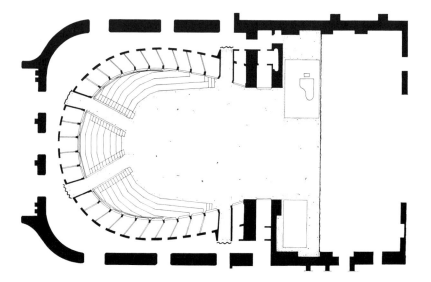

er than that of the Bouffes du Nord, though turned through 90 degrees. Its proportions and decoration are quite sober, the boxes all having the same square aspect. Architect Paolo Portoghesi, who restored the space in 1993, described it as having the most egalitarian disposition among the theatres of Rome. Its geometry is also simple compared to other horseshoe forms, with only one main axis and five centres used to generate the curves of the plan.

As elsewhere, the choice of the Argentina followed an exhaustive search through all the possible alternatives, taking

The Teatro Argentina as transformed for *Carmen*

in spaces as diverse as the Baths of Caracalla (an established opera venue), the Roman theatre in Ostia (which was too big), the Cinecittà studios on the outskirts of Rome, the Villa Medici, and the Odeion in Viterbo (where permission could not be obtained to play). The Teatro Argentina was chosen because of the fascinating possibility of making it into a temporary Bouffes du Nord-style arena space, advancing the stage into the circle of the auditorium and building new seats spilling on to this surface, thereby bringing the vertical balcony walls into the circuit of the drama. (Curiously, in the mid-1800s the thea-

tre was given a large 'thrust' stage somewhat similar in spirit for a pageant celebrating a royal marriage.)

Before transformation

One of the determining factors of this transformation was the need for it to be rapid: only five days were allocated for the installation of the new structure, the scenic elements and the lighting. Furthermore, the existing stalls seating could not be removed for what was a very short run (17–26 September): the new stage had to be carefully positioned on supports placed between the rows, and had to correspond to the level of the seats below. This last problem was overcome by making the new rake of benches integral to the playing surface, rising up just before it would touch the seats. The new seating was formed by 30-centimetre steps with a 10-centimetre-thick cushion placed all the way along the rim. The slope was contrived to arrive at the level of the first balcony, the heads of the spectators in these seats forming a continuous line with those on the new benches. The playing surface was positioned higher than the front of the existing stage because the latter was sloped and therefore would be difficult to join to the flat arena needed for *Carmen*. The final level actually corresponded to that of the

During rehearsals

foyer, giving the audience who walked on to the sand in order to reach their seats the strong sensation that it was in unbroken continuity with the 'real' world of the bar and the street.

The finishing touches were a black curtain hung a few metres beyond the line of the proscenium (to limit the space just behind the musicians' positions) and a beige carpet on the playing surface (to harmonize with the much-criticized colour scheme of the theatre, dating from a 1967 restoration), which was strewn with a few millimetres of sandy earth. Here there arose a point of ambiguity which had been more easily resolved in the rougher surroundings of the Bouffes: the earth could not be continued all the way to the baroque doors; it had to be 'faded out' on the carpets in the entrance passageways. As in the Bouffes, pebbles of increasing size were added towards the edge, forming a gradient to a smooth, dusty circle in the centre.

The resulting format allowed 700 people a very intimate relationship to the action. (The theatre normally seats 1,159. Besides the covered stalls, some seats were lost on the top balcony for visibility reasons, and some at the sides to allow lights to be put in new positions.) As at the Bouffes, the architecture was integrated into the circuit of the drama: the balconies,

looming over the action, gave a hint of the *corrida*. (Rich Roman ladies, perhaps inspired by the transgressive treatment of the space, casually hung their coats over the balconies, as if they were about to witness a bullfight in Seville.) The new benches focused this bullring down to the dimensions of the Bouffes' playing area. The two entrance passages towards the front of the auditorium took on the role of the side doors in Paris for the tragicomic comings and goings in Lillas Pastia's tavern. It would have been over-literal and excessively 'scenic' – not to mention bureaucratically difficult – to add *real* doors to these passages. The success of the transformation depended on its simplicity and its valorization of the existing space: there was a frisson from the theatre being experienced in an entirely new way, but it was the anchoring of this thrill to the demands of the drama and to the integrity of the space which gave it its real force. Some reviewers noted this: Paolo Cervone wrote that 'in this *parterre des rois*, with so many illustrious names crammed practically on top of each other as in an orgy, happy to perch on a bench with makeshift cushions, one feels the almost religious sensation of attending not a mere performance, but an unrepeatable event'.*

*Trans. Todd/Amedeo Petrilli.

Bari

Later in the tour an old theatre in Bari was briefly transformed from its current use as a cinema by building a bridge of seats spanning from the first balcony on to an extension of the stage. Once the cinema screen was removed, a fascinating back wall appeared: it was clearly part of the former street façade of a house, with doors and windows perfectly composed (by chance) for scenic use. The forgotten wall was painted and the openings boarded over so as to become part of the world of

the opera. Wooden side walls were made to close the proscenium opening a little and hide the orchestra.

Cagliari: The Roman Amphitheatre

The Roman arena in the capital of Sardinia was a long-established venue for summer concerts and opera: there was a wooden deck over the stone floor and the trenches which had once conveyed lions and gladiators to their fates, and seats were usually placed on this level to face a raised stage, behind which

was a panoramic view of the city and sea. The audience could barely see the performers, and the approach sequence obliged them to walk around the back of the stage in order to find their seats. It was therefore decided to build a new theatre on the wooden deck facing towards the opposite end of the arena, which was carved into the rock of a hillside. This configuration would also serve to contain the sound of the opera better.

The stage surface was covered with plastic and the customary earth. Scaffolding side walls were built to the same height as the three seating blocks and were covered with rough planks. The obtrusive metal gantries built to convey tourists around the site were covered with wood. A passageway was defined by lightweight partitions across the expanse of the arena floor, and these walls also hid the backstage facilities. The audience eventually approached the filigree of scaffolding supporting the seats from behind, climbed to the top and discovered the whole space, then descended towards the stage to fill the auditorium from the bottom up (seats were not numbered). Straight ahead, framed by the side walls, the edges of the arena steps were visible on either side of a deep entrance tunnel on the same axis as the theatre. The full length of this

space was used for long entries in the drama.

This new theatre sat at the conclusion of a long journey uphill from the city, at a natural resting point where the steep hill determined that civilization should go no further. This gave a special quality of 'background' to the drama: it was not just the aesthetic character of the rock and the poignancy of the ancient amphitheatre steps that counted. Rather, the conclusion of the *sense of the city* at this threshold gave a special force to the drama which emerged to confront the audience here.

Pompeii: The Odeon

The Odeon, or small theatre, in Pompeii is, like the Bouffes du Nord, a ruin. Its degradation was more sudden and more famous than that of the Parisian theatre: it was used from 75 BC until the day in AD 79 when a flash of heat and poisonous gas killed all the citizens and two waves of superheated ash vaporized anything wooden and buried the stones of the city 18 metres deep. The site was excavated from the end of the nineteenth century, and the adjoining larger theatre was put back in use for summer festivals; *La Tragédie de Carmen* was the first work to be performed in the Odeon for 1907 years.

Roman theatre form evolved from the Greek spaces (many of which were themselves adapted by the Romans). The classical Greek theatre had, like the Bouffes, a single floor extending from under the front spectators' feet to the columns and doors of the *skene* (a semi-permanent 'scenic' structure which represented the homes of the protagonists). The chorus, who stood for the populace, occupied the circular central area, or *orchestra*, and the principal actors remained further upstage, associated with the *skene* building. The Roman form repeated this

Pompeii before and after transformation

centre/scene dichotomy, but reinforced it with two thresholds: between the spectators and the *orchestra* (which was walled off to allow gladiatorial combat and nautical entertainments, but contained audience members for theatrical performances) and between the *orchestra* and a raised stage, which the actors occupied. The location of Roman theatres in an urban context (as against the ex-urban, 'festival' character of the Greek) meant that the structures were enclosed on all sides, rather than carved into the landscape; the free-standing *skene* became a complete *frons scaenae* wall. (There was usually a canvas roof for protection from the sun too.)

The Pompeii space has all these basic characteristics, with the difference that it was designed for speech and poetry (probably having a wooden roof structure), and is thus much more intimate than the neighbouring theatre. It is hemmed in by streets on both sides, and has an interior width of 26 metres and an overall rectangular perimeter. The curves of seating radiating from the orchestra are unable to attain a full semi-circular form within this width: the rows further back are truncated by the walls (in exactly the same way as in the

Carmen in rehearsal, Pompeii

LA TRAGEDIE DE CARMEN

famous theoretical theatre proposed by Sebastiano Serlio in 1545). There are the remnants of the nobles' individual seats and three shallow steps in front. By covering these front rows with a new surface of scaffolding and wood extending out from slightly above the level of the stage, the proportions of the Bouffes du Nord were duplicated almost exactly: an earth-covered acting area 13 metres across and 15 metres deep to the crumbling *frons scaenae*, with the back row of seats at the same height as the second balcony in Paris.

The 'scenic' elements for *Carmen* were easily created in this space. The 'cultural skin' of carved marble and statuary on the *frons scaenae* (which might have been too oppressive for the world of the drama) had been destroyed, leaving just raw brick with some ivy growing on it and three simple openings, which were used in the opera. The musicians were tucked just behind the arched entrance tunnels giving into the orchestra, which were ramped up to the new level and used by audience and actors. Other audience members approached along a torchlit street and descended from the top of the theatre. The Odeon is quite close to the Porta Stabia, the city's formal entrance (which also leads to the baths and the forum), whereas Pompeii's elegiac ruined houses lie further in, away from the Odeon, so for *Carmen*'s audience the lugubrious, highly personal museum-like quality of the city was hidden. In spite of the overbearing presence of the past outside, the evening therefore unfolded in the here and now, in relation to the fabric of a theatre conceived for human eyes and ears whose character has not changed in two thousand years.

Old and New

Why, among the theatres used by the Centre, should the Odeon and the Argentina (and indeed the Bouffes du Nord) provide a ready-made environment for the drama, but not the Vivian Beaumont? Why is there nothing in a modern space in which to anchor the reality of the play, everything having to be built up from zero? Peter Brook's sole prescription for the touring spaces for *The Ik* – that they should be 'full of life' – had the effect of casting modern theatres in a negative light, as few of them fulfil this simple principle: that of balancing a positive presence in the architecture of the building with the presence of the audience and the stage world.

Until now the problem of modern theatres had only arisen

for the Centre inasmuch as so many had been visited, rejected and occasionally modified. During the tour of *Carmen* the question became more acute, however: two cities decided to make brand new spaces to be inaugurated by the Centre, both of them (ostensibly) drawing on the Bouffes du Nord for inspiration.

JEAN-GUY LECAT: *When people enter our theatre in Paris, they say they are astonished at the beauty of the place – the walls, their colour, the intimate space, the cupola, the balconies. They ask when it was built (1876). They are sensitive to the void, the proportions, its verticality, its acoustics. Very often the same visitors (especially architects) wonder at the state of the theatre and ask, 'When are you going to restore it?' Are these contradictory reactions?*

In fact they demonstrate a fragmented and incoherent understanding of the place, whose beauty is elusive. In the end, when visitors want to put their impressions into words, they say the exact contrary of their previous celebratory comments: they talk about the cracks, the need for restoration. They fail to see that the beauty of this place lies partly in the essence of what they want to change. These questions and the contradictions they embody show that, above all, what is at issue is the spirit of the place.

These anecdotes conceal another issue: whether or not to restore places and spaces. Can we fix up a place and perhaps embellish it without losing any of the atmosphere which embeds the human beings who have lived there in time and their own culture? Isn't it precisely the incompleteness *of a work that stimulates the observer? This was even a philosophy at one time. Also it is necessary for each place to preserve its identity even in its modifications. By digging up its roots, don't we perhaps risk stripping the life from its walls, losing the essence once again? The question perhaps deserves to be asked of all ancient places before we start work on them.*

When visiting an old space, it is interesting to reflect on what has to be destroyed, altered, or preserved. The concept of preservation implies that the history of architecture should be understood as a collection of cultural experiences that need to be preserved. Any change has to respect certain rules.

PETER BROOK: *Why are new-built, architect-designed theatres inadequate? One must remember that the focus of the audience's attention in any theatre space is the human body. What should be the context of this body? If this body has the responsibility to*

conjure up a microcosm, a world in miniature for all those pre-
sent, what is the most effective support that can be provided by
the surrounding phenomena? Is it enough to have an abstract
space designed to receive the projected vision of a designer – a
backcloth to the microcosm? If we take away the artifice of the
backcloth, will the actor alone suffice to evoke a world through
the audience's imagination? Or is it possible that a living back-
ground – something which creates a sense of familiarity, a link to
real materials and everyday spaces – will help the imagination.
We must ask ourselves, Is it possible for man to exist without a
background? In film, in every shot, the person and the place are
inseparable. But theatre is not cinema. What is neither a set nor
an aseptic nothingness? What is warm, human, framing the
action, filling the imagination, yet imposing no statement?

Milan: Teatro Studio

Giorgio Strehler, who was director of the Piccolo Teatro in
Milan, wanted to create a smaller space as an annexe to his
headquarters in the via Dante. He sent his architects, Marco
Zanuso and Pietro Crescini, to study the Bouffes du Nord;

Curtain-call, Teatro
Studio

they were supposed to capture its spirit in the new space, which was to be built in the shell of the old Teatro Fossati. They succeeded in reproducing the basic configuration of the central playing area with balconies stacked around it, but these balconies had a rather antiseptic air, and the curving brick wall behind them was also rather scaleless and imposing.

The deep horseshoe shape of this space meant that it would have been possible (as it had not been in Paris) to put part of the audience on the stage facing the auditorium (evoking a sense of the bullring), but it was felt that it would be inappropriate to inaugurate the theatre in such a transgressive manner. Because the space was made almost entirely of brick (which was even used to make a vestigial proscenium arch), the scenic walls for *Carmen* were made of the same material – the only time this occurred.

Tokyo: The Ginza Saison Theatre

In 1984 Seiji Tsutsumi, president of the Seibu Saison Group, a powerful Japanese construction, hotel and shopping-centre company, invited the Centre to perform in Tokyo in a theatre that would be inaugurated with *Carmen* and designed to the wishes of Brook. Tsutsumi was building a new hotel – The Ginza Saison – in a fashionable centre-city district, and the theatre was to be part of this project, situated between the fourth and seventh floors. He requested that the plans of the Bouffes du Nord be sent to his architects, so that they could understand how this space conditioned the Centre's work and produce something which would be appropriate.

The Ginza Saison Hotel today

The plans of their first project were sent for approval to Paris in winter 1985/6. The design was that of a rather conventional modern theatre with a shallow gradient to the seating (an average of 13 degrees) and an extremely narrow, deep proportion in plan. The Bouffes had been only vestigially integrated: the curve of the seats around the Parisian stage was traced on to the rectilinear auditorium plan, and a few spectators seated on the ground were represented around the outline (and would have blocked the view for the people in the first rows). Unfortunately this was unsatisfactory. Brook demurred.

Tsutsumi sent a delegation to Paris, including the theatre's prospective technical director, Haruo Mitamura, and Kenichi Kinokuni, head of Seibu's powerful Cultural Affairs Department, to see if a solution could be found. The Tokyo building was already under construction, so significant changes to the structure were impossible, and stern constraints were imposed by the insertion of the theatre into the body of a hotel, with great difficulties of access and unchangeable height limits. After a frantic four-day burst of work, it was proposed that an entirely new space could be built inside the existing one with a shorter, steeper slope (22 degrees), a different treatment of the walls, and additional seating on the sides of the stage (which would be lowered so that the seating spilled on to it).

A visit to Tokyo was arranged for April 1986. The auditorium was inspected under construction; it would be finished according to the initial design, and the space for *Carmen*, which was designed in collaboration with Toshiya Kusaka, would be inserted afterwards and demounted after the run. Yamaha's acoustics laboratory produced a simulation of the acoustic of the proposed theatre, along with those of the Bouffes du Nord and Hans Scharoun's Berlin Philharmonie for comparison. Piano music was played through a headset and the sound was changed to represent different seating positions in each of these theatres. Of particular concern was the effect of the wooden 'resonating chamber' to be built for *Car-*

The theatre under construction

men, which would, as in New York, modify the sound of the predominantly concrete and metal auditorium. Different types and thicknesses of wood were simulated, and the Yamaha team also built test pads of damp and dry earth to factor this surface into the calculation. For *Carmen* there was the particular constraint that the musicians were behind the actors; it was vital to adjust the position and height of the wood so that the correct balance could be achieved with the singers throughout the auditorium. Other serious technical problems included the fires used onstage at two points in the

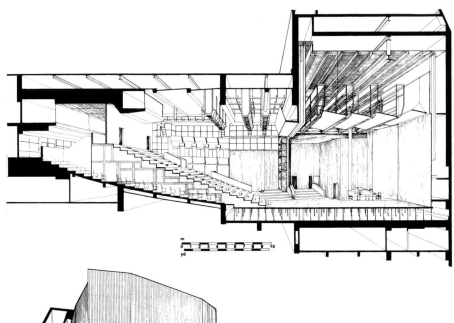

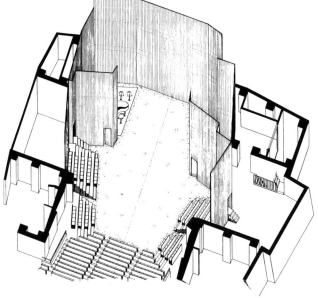

drama: fires were illegal in Japanese theatres. A lengthy meeting was held with the fire services to prove that the effects were safe and the proposed floor construction sufficiently flame-retardant. Stringent security procedures were imposed – all at Seibu's expense – and the national law regarding stage effects was specially revised for Brook's visit, so as to delegate final responsibility to local fire authorities.

The 'permanent' theatre was finished and dedicated with a Shinto ceremony. The next day work began on the Centre's space. A team of 160 builders brought 76 lorryloads of material up in the theatre's service lift. Structural elements, decomposed into small pieces, were bolted together inside the theatre. The existing cinema-style seats were left in place, covered in protective plastic; elegant benches based on those in Paris were installed on the new slope. Seating at the sides of the stage was made contiguous to this block, to avoid the need for intrusive guard rails, and the aisles created between the front and side parts were used for entrances at certain points of the drama. The safety curtain had to be accommodated by a gap in the middle of the seats; the wooden walls were erected fur-

ther back, closing down the stage opening to the proportions of the Bouffes. A wall was built from the top of the seating slope to close the new space (making it some 9 metres shorter, overall, than before), and four new entrance stairways were put in place, joining up with the level of the lobby. (Other entrances were continued through the block of seating from their level in the permanent theatre.) The wooden side walls were made of cedar (chosen because of its warm colour and resinous smell) in large interleaving sheets built using highly refined Japanese carpentry techniques. As in New York, the

The theatre before and during transformation

121

wood embraced the whole world of the drama; the deadening concrete of the theatre's side walls disappeared from the field of vision in favour of the new shell. (The raw concrete end wall had been proposed as a background at one point, but its appearance was later changed by the application of insulation to minimize the noise coming from the motorway which passed a few metres from the building.) After *La Tragédie de Carmen* the whole structure was dismounted, carried back down in the service lift, and stored (at great expense) in preparation for the arrival, a year later, of the English-language version of *The Mahabharata*.

Objective Sight Lines, Subjective Depth

Why go to such trouble to increase the slope of the auditorium? Why is this such a persistent problem with modern theatres?

Shallow slopes are designed on the assumption that a spectator will see the stage through the gap between the heads of the two people sitting in front (whose seats have to be positioned in plan such that this is possible – which reduces the freedom to change the curve of the rows of seats around the stage). The head of the person sitting *two* rows in front is therefore the height reference which determines the degree of slope, which can thus be very gentle. (In the professional jargon, this arrangement is known as 'every-other-row vision'). Various spatial (and financial) efficiencies result from this formula: by saving height in the stalls, more balconies can be stacked up within the possible cone of vision to the stage.

What is bothersome in this case is having the backs of two heads frame the distant actor. It is decidedly anti-convivial to exist in an intimate relationship with a part of someone's body which has no chance of communicating with us. (Brook: 'The back of someone's head is the least interesting part of their anatomy.') Furthermore, the 'frame' made by the two heads has a distracting effect (our peripheral vision is extremely sensitive to movement*), and creates a distancing threshold between ourselves and the action. Furthermore, our awareness of the group of people to which we belong is truncated.

A greater slope frees the vision not only of the stage as a whole, but of the audience as well. One can sense one's fellows – particularly those at the sides of the stage – and the focus can narrow to the action or widen to the whole public according to the currents generated by the drama. It also creates an emphasis on the surface of the stage as the 'ground' of the action, rather than the flimsy vertical elements of a 'set', and, as we have seen at the Bouffes, the joining of the audience with the ground of the drama is a marvellously flexible theatrical device.

* as biophysicist Ruggero Pierantoni has pointed out to us. See also page 243.

> JEAN-GUY LECAT: *The human gaze is naturally oriented downwards, whereas the first few rows of spectators in a traditional theatre have to crane their necks up to see the actor's face some 1.6 metres above them on the stage. Imagine if, in a restaurant, one were obliged to lie on the floor and watch people eating and waiters running about from this position: this is exactly what one sees in a traditional theatre from the front row. What is extraordinary in this affair is that no architect has a real reason today for putting people in such a bad position, except for habit and tradition.*

6 : *The Mahabharata*

The frantic touring of *La Tragédie de Carmen* overlapped with the preparation and early tours of *The Mahabharata* in 1985–6. Like *The Conference of the Birds*, this vast production (9 hours long, with 30 performers from 18 different countries) was due to have its premiere at the Avignon Festival. The nine-month rehearsal period (which included an extended journey to India for all the participants) was based largely at the Bouffes du Nord, and the material identity of the piece initially found its forms there.

After much experimentation with different types of clay, binding agents, colourings and proportions of water, the loose, fluid earth of *Carmen* reappeared as something more homogeneous and compacted for *The Mahabharata*. (It was combined with straw to strengthen it.) It was complemented by two areas of water: a small irregularly shaped pool downstage left and a long river upstage, parallel to the back wall. Two earthen platforms were added: on the audience's right for the musicians (one of whom, Mahmoud Tabrizi-Zadeh, also had a role in the play) and a smaller one on the left, which was where the old man Vyasa, the boy to whom he tells the story, and occasionally the demigod Ganesha/Krishna sat watching the drama unfold. The series of metal rungs which had been set into the wall for *Timon of Athens* was reinstalled for this production, and was complemented by a new series on the narrow side walls adjacent to the proscenium. A complicated array of fire effects was developed – many of them embedded in the earth – and, finally, padding was placed on the wooden benches built for *Carmen*, to make the audience more comfortable for the all-night marathon performances.

Once again the wholeness of the environment in the Bouffes du Nord served to create a strong, shared atmosphere: this was not theatricality in the quotation marks of an acting

Above and opposite page: *The Mahabharata*, Bouffes du Nord

area. The earth spread out over the whole floor level, meeting the walls and passing under the feet of the audience. The costumes, musical instruments, furniture and other objects used on this ground were consistent among themselves in that they all referred in a strong but not historically precise way to aspects of Indian and other Eastern cultures; they evoked a certain mood, but without shutting the door on our participation by being literal in the extreme. The earth became a vital bridge between this slightly exotic world and ours: it was a familiar, elemental substance, but used in this way, with these objects, it also carried a sense of the soil of India, creating a circuit which opened the possibility of communion between our place in 1980s Paris and the mythological Eastern world of the drama. As it touched the walls, it had the effect of bringing their identity into question.

> CHLOÉ OBOLENSKY: *The back wall of the Bouffes was very interesting and very powerful with its black rectangle, but we didn't think it could ever be a support for the world of* The Mahabharata. *So, with a lot of trepidation, we started to paint. We wanted something which recaptured the memory of things in India – something warm and all-enveloping; something vibrant, red. There was a tiny piece in the middle of the wall where someone had painted a view of a farmhouse in some countryside to be seen through the open door of an old set. It was a sienna type of brown-red, and we took that as the basis of the colour for* The Mahabharata, *as a kind of lifeline to the theatre's past. We wanted to change the colour without changing the body of the wall, conserving the past traces. We thought about covering the walls with a new surface to conserve the original colour behind, but this would have been immensely difficult just considering the area concerned – nearly 150 square metres on the back wall alone.*

The bridging from the ordinary to the extraordinary facilitated by these objects, colours and materials was crucially important for *The Mahabharata*. The drama begins with a boy being told by an old man (Vyasa) that he will witness an enactment of the history of mankind, which Vyasa will transcribe in a book to be given to him at the end of the play. The boy is thus a representative of the audience within the drama: we watch him watching the play from the platform onstage. Throughout the whole drama the links between us and the boy, the boy and the play, and the play and us remain elastic and open to redefinition, with the earth as its common ground and anchor. The characters are in a mythical past, but we have been told that they are our ancestors, and their behaviour (as lovers, warriors, brothers or mothers) is recognizable to us: in a way we are watching ourselves (particularly during the third part, The War, in which a terrible weapon threatens to destroy the world). The absence of a predetermined threshold between here and there liberates the flows of dramatic energy: the theatrical frame can include all of us; it can close down to become a mat representing a particular setting; or it can evoke specific aspects of our shared world (as with the swings suspended from the dome which made a momentary palace of the theatre).

PETER BROOK: *The first principle is to start on the level of the audience, very simply. If in* The Mahabharata *we had copied Indian forms, a god would have come on as in Kathakali, with long fingernails and fantastic make-up. However, even if for a second the physical beauty of it would engage the audience, the second afterwards it would seem remote and in no way connected with real life. It was quite clear that our job in* The Mahabharata *was to start very lightly with two actors of the country we were in, clearly amusing themselves and in league with the audience. Maurice Bénichou came wearing the mask of Ganesha and at once took it off; one saw that it was a humorous French actor clearly playing the game of being Indian. The audience sat back and gave their confidence to the actors, and an hour later we could go into all sorts of mysterious areas.* .

MAURICE BÉNICHOU: *For* The Mahabharata *I had difficulty at the beginning working with how to portray Krishna. I read a lot and absorbed a lot of images of him drawn from Hindu mythology – playing flutes, or with his 16,000 wives – none of which helped me. It's difficult to bring mythical characters down to earth, to relate them to things we know today. Peter gave me some excellent advice: he told me to think of Krishna as someone who intercedes here and there in a conflict, asking what's going on on either side like a real person, while actually knowing everything himself, like a god. If God invented Krishna, he conceived him as someone with a burning intelligence, with many special qualities – and if Krishna was invented by people they would see him the same way. The Bouffes helped me very much with the*

*character, because I always have the impression I'm playing nor-
mal people here, whether they're the patients of* The Man Who *or a god like Krishna or a drunkard in* The Tempest; *I never have
to make a tremendous effort to get things across. The* Maha-
bharata *is huge, epic, but at the same time it's the story of each of
us. The force of the Bouffes allowed us to be very strong during
the battle, with dust in the air, great violence of noise and movement; and then there'd be moments when Krishna spoke with
Arjuna as if they were alone, conversing normally. Sometimes I
was too quiet: even when you're speaking very softly you have to
have a great energy behind what you do here.*

Peter Brook: *If one supplies a world apparently complete
down to all its aesthetic details, a totality of information, a 'real'
image, the audience has nothing to do, accepts the illusion, and
becomes totally passive. If, on the other hand, one uses two pieces
of wood to suggest a forest, or a puddle to suggest a mighty river,
there is work to do all of a sudden – the immensely pleasurable
work of allowing one's circuits to complete the picture for oneself,
in the moment. This also serves to reinforce a sense of community in the audience – each member must use his imagination as an
individual, but, the picture completed, one senses a shared work,
a shared experience, and a genuine participation in the play
which goes beyond the simplistic 1960s notions of generating a
sense of shared purpose by encouraging the audience to run into
the performance space, taking part in the action so as to feel they
are 'participating'. When one appeals to the imagination, the
sharing is momentary and invisible. It is the ephemeral creation
of a common perspective without the imposition of perspectival
scenery, and it is all the more precious for that reason.*

*Every style, every convention has its limitations. Working
clothes, jeans and street corners are sometimes exactly what is
needed – and if any decoration were added there would be loss,
not gain. We explored* The Mahabharata *in tiny fragments, in
rough-and-ready improvisations in everyday dress. But for the
full nine-hour epic this would have been poor in a negative way
– threadbare. The myth demanded a special beauty, the excitement of colour. Unlike* Ubu, *this play needed to be clad – it could
not appear naked. This applied both to costumes and to spaces:
one could have a degree of roughness, but a certain serenity was
also necessary. In this way the drama became coloured and
defined by each different environment. We played in Avignon in
the open air, with sunset, sunrise and firelight. In the Bouffes we*

played on earth, in a much smaller space. The play was the same, but outside its exterior elements dominated, indoors it was the inner content that gained.

The Callet Quarry, Boulbon

While rehearsals were under way in Paris, a vast search for the space for the production's opening performances had begun. The Avignon Festival had a number of unusual existing venues at its disposal, and these were investigated first. They included the stage in the courtyard of the Papal Palace, which was felt to have a too-dispersed relationship between audience and performers, and the cloister used for the creation of *The Conference of the Birds*, which was too small. Both were also forcefully marked by particular historical periods, and therefore unable to nurture the universal character of *The Mahabharata*.

The performances of *The Conference of the Birds* in Adelaide in 1980 had revealed the advantages of quarries: generally flat floors; a contained acoustic; a high, vertical rock face against which to work. A search for such a space was therefore carried out in the Avignon region: a giant circle, 60 kilometres in

The Callet Quarry – first visit

The Callet Quarry
under transformation

THE MAHABHARATA

diameter, was traced on the map with Avignon at its centre, and all the possible spaces within that range were inspected (a total of sixty). Following a visit by the whole design, production and direction team, together with industrialist Jacques Callet (who owned a number of quarries in the area as part of his road-building business), a quarry near Boulbon, 12 kilometres south-west of Avignon, was chosen. It had good general proportions: 135 metres long and an average of 50 metres wide, narrowing as one advanced into the space, funnelling down into an increasingly intimate, enclosed volume. The

l–r: Jean-Guy Lecat, Marie-Jo Lhuillier (technical director of the Avignon Festival), Peter Brook and Chloé Obolensky visiting the quarry

theatre would be placed at the inner end, repeating the progression of Cagliari towards an unambiguously final destination. The entrance faced south – thankfully away from the 100-kilometre-per-hour mistral winds which peak during the summer months. (At other possible sites they were channelled directly into the quarry.) The colour of the rock (a crumbling limestone in small blocks) was good, and, unlike at other spaces visited, the walls did not discharge flows of earth when it rained.

This quarry, whose stone had gone into the building of the nearby Vallabrègues dam on the Rhône, had been disused for ten years. Callet enthusiastically accepted that it be transformed, and offered the use of his workers, equipment and materials at no charge for the grading of the floor. Two significant moves had to be made: the floor surface was uneven and collected water in large pools towards the inner end whenever it rained; and a large berm had to be made to close off the end space (this served to keep sound in, to keep out the noises from the valley below, to hide the seating, to direct the audience around to one side, and to create a pocket of stable air over which the mistral winds could pass). A second lower berm, split in two, would embrace the restaurant for the spectators and complete the form of a serpentine path leading from the entrance.

When an army of bulldozers had completed the basic work of raising the level of the theatre end of the quarry by 2 metres and adding the berms, it was time to determine the position of the seating. On the first visit, a longer than usual 24 metres to the front row had been measured away from the wall, but Brook had found this oppressively close to the 30-metre-high cliff. This impression had been reinforced by the presence of a mound of spoil at the base, which was covered in scrappy vegetation: the junction between vertical and horizontal was not clear, so the impression of distance was reduced by the mound. Now, with the grading work complete and the mound bulldozed away, the space could be appreciated more clearly.

The first few rows of seats were built to give some idea of the placement of the stage (which would have roughly the same shape as in the Bouffes, though a considerably larger size). The construction looked miserably lost in such a huge space: one still had the impression of being dominated. When the rest of the seats were built, however, the theatre suddenly seemed too dispersed, too expansive. At 15 degrees, the slope was gentle (the structure was taken from the old theatre inside the Papal Palace), and it formed a very broad continuous surround of the stage. Other dimensions were enlarged to fit the greater scale of the quarry: the opening of the acting area was 14 metres wide, compared to the Bouffes' 8 metres, the depth 24 metres compared to 17 metres, and the river was nearly 30 metres long. It was only when the space became living, infused with an attentive audience, that the proportions seemed right. Viewed when empty, the black chairs gave a false sense of scale: it was the act of inhabitation, the creation of a living focus on the occupants of the acting area and the consequent falling-away of the cliff in one's attention (it simply disappeared above the field of vision, like the walls in the Bouffes), which created a correct balance in the space.

There were many finishing touches. The level of the graded rock floor was built up with a layer of gravel, which would allow the whole space to drain in a few hours after the frequent late-afternoon storms. This was covered with crushed limestone of a type which hardened into a crust when wet. Then earth was strewn on top of this to give a good colour relationship with the rock face and a softer acting surface. When the

The Callet Quarry
before the performance

river was being filled with water it was found that there was a difference in level between one end and the other. (The driver who delivered the water was perplexed that one end remained dry, and kept trying to fill it up.) This had to be corrected. Also, a gentle ramp was built to allow the actors to walk on to the acting area in the dark. The actors' village (building-site cabins arranged around a 'yard' sheltered from the sun by a bamboo roof) was tucked behind the seating. An artesian well was dug to supply the company and the restaurant (which had to feed 1,000 people twice in the course of the all-night performances). A 150-kilowatt generator was positioned between the mouth of the quarry and the entrance to another (which was used as a car park); the electrical cables had to be fed through a hole between the quarries and buried under the public approach path. The French Air Force changed the timing and location of exercises to preserve the quiet of the quarry. Rocks were added at the base of the cliff and were built up into two side walls high enough to hide the actors before they entered. The flora of the site (including various bushes on the rock) was left otherwise undisturbed. But not so the fauna, in the shape of a fox living in a hole halfway up the cliff, who moved out until the commotion was over.

The audience either drove to the adjacent quarry or took a specially organized boat from Avignon along the Rhône; this docked a kilometre from the theatre, leaving a gentle uphill walk in the golden light before sunset. At the entrance to the quarry one saw only the face of the near and far stone berms, but during the course of the S-shaped path the rest of the space revealed itself, culminating with the sudden discovery of the bowl of seating capturing the space at the head of the quarry. (As at Cagliari, most of the audience climbed the stairs at the back and descended towards the acting area.) The setting sun caused a problem: French summer time had been adjusted that year, and the scrupulous calculation of the moment at which the back rows of spectators would no longer be in blinding light was wrong by exactly one hour. Brook gave an apologetic speech every evening, and the public had a little extra time to get used to each other and their unusual theatre.

The performance therefore began at twilight, with the playful first scenes merging into something stranger and stronger as darkness fell. Actors appeared on a wide ledge halfway up the cliff, and clambered to positions on the boulders which had been added against the cliff and to the sides of the audi-

ence. Any tiredness felt by 4 a.m. was jolted away with a loud explosion and a blinding magnesium flare (the all-powerful weapon belonging to Duryodhana) anchored in the cliff. The end of the war was heralded by birdsong and the gradual lightening of the sky.

Peter Brook introducing *The Mahabharata* and apologising for a delayed start (see text)

PETER BROOK: *In the theatre every external element is important, but nothing is irreplaceable. People who saw* The Mahabharata *in Avignon couldn't imagine that the play could work anywhere else. However, after we played in other quarries we brought the play to the Bouffes du Nord with the same elements of fire, water and earth. The scale was quite different, it was inside, etc. However, the people who saw it at the Bouffes said they couldn't imagine seeing it anywhere else. It was two sides of the same coin: in the open the external aspects and epic sweep of the myth were present, whereas in the Bouffes the experience was more internal, more emotional, and the audience found themselves naturally drawn into the more hidden aspects of the poem.*

JEAN-CLAUDE CARRIÈRE: *What really lifted the play at Avignon was the presence of the cosmos in the drama: the falling of* night at the beginning, the war in the depths of the night, the lightening of the sky, even, on one extraordinary occasion, a loud cry from a bird – the first before the dawn – immediately at the moment of Krishna's death. During the month's run this relationship changed, dawn coming two or three minutes later every night.

YOSHI OIDA: *It was hard here. It was so big you had to speak loudly – we had to force the play across. I felt as though the actors just decorated the quarry.*

MARIE-HÉLÈNE ESTIENNE: *There was a curious paradox at Avignon: although it was huge and there were a thousand people watching, from the standpoint of the audience it felt intimate, at just the right scale. It became immense, epic, in the open air; but when we returned to the Bouffes it had the same energy concentrated in a much smaller space – it was fascinating, extraordinary. The actors developed their gestures and their speech enormously between the two spaces.*

CHLOÉ OBOLENSKY: *You're in a different world. You have these*

The *Mahabharata* in performance

THE MAHABHARATA

*elements which are so strong that you have to readjust. It was
exciting to work at the same time in the Bouffes and at Avignon.
This was the best quarry for all sorts of reasons: shape, colour,
scale, distance. The important thing was just to follow this as naturally as possible, setting the river at the foot of the rock face, but
not make it naturalistic; keeping the relationship of the public to
the stage as normal, with the huge cliff as the back wall. People
behave differently out of doors: the eye roams, people slouch.
Everything had to be adjusted to the first principles given by the
space. These are very heavy tours, and we have to keep things
simple if we have only a week to adapt to each space. This means
that we want to bring to the fore the inherent qualities of the
space – the basic, stable elements.*

Bruce Myers: *It may seem paradoxical, but for me this was the
most intimate space for* The Mahabharata, *under the sky. It's not
literally a question of distance: it's a question of the finesse that's
possible in the acting – a question of relationships. Just being
under the stars moved people slightly towards the state of awe
that the whole legend can inspire: the relationship to the material was begun by the space, which shortened the distance we had
to cross with the acting. It was exhilarating to act there.*

Athens: The Petroupolis Quarry

Under the auspices of Athens's status as European City of Culture in 1985, the Centre was invited to perform *The Mahabharata* in the Petroupolis Quarry, a regular venue for summer
festivals, a month and a half after the opening in France. There
was already a space prepared for concerts, but it was vast and
flat, with some rows of seats perched on ledges on the rock
face. The German theatre director Peter Stein had also created
The Petroupolis Quarry

137

a giant scaffolding amphitheatre, arranged such that the audience had a view over the smog-choked plain of the city.

Between these two constructions there was a more intimate corner set against the highest part of the excavation (which was significantly grander than Avignon).

Transforming the site was a relatively simple matter of covering the running track there with earth, digging away a berm which obscured the base of the cliff, and installing the seats to enclose the acting area. (There was no hope of organizing the entire space as in Avignon, because this quarry was much too large.) The granite and seams of iron ore gave a red and blue pattern to the cliff – livelier than the regular, neutral blocks in the Callet quarry – and the earth used was cooler in tone to harmonize with these colours. The seating was arranged as continuous benches with long cushions in three blocks on a regular radius, with a slope of 25 degrees. It was a kind of miniature Epidauros: it had the same angle of slope, almost the same degree of encirclement, but, being scaled for eye-to-eye contact rather than for music, dance and chanted verse, it was only a fraction of the size.

Perth: The Hudman Quarry

The Mahabharata was invited to Australia in a co-production of the 1988 Perth and Adelaide Festivals and the Bicentennial Arts Programme. For the Hudman quarry at Boya, near Perth, a disposition of seating similar to those at Athens and Avignon was used, with straighter sections making up the embrace. The 20-metre-high quarry wall was lower than in Avignon and Athens, and the particular charm of this space came from its blue granite walls and the eucalyptus trees positioned around the base and rim of the rock face. The stone was more massive than in

Transforming the Hudman Quarry

the previous spaces (it had been quarried in huge blocks to line the harbour at Fremantle). During the intervals, the audience left the quarry to eat on a hillside facing out into the landscape.

There was a drawback to the beautiful trees: their dry leaves rustled noisily in the wind. The actors adapted their voices as well as possible, and, applying a more direct approach to the problem, Sotigui Kouyaté and the mother of actor Tapa Sudana (who had come from Bali) went into the hills one evening to perform a ceremony to calm the wind. Curiously, there was total calm for the first performance.

Adelaide

No research was needed for a quarry near Adelaide: *The Mahabharata* simply took over the space which had been inaugurated in 1980. Now, eight years later, the rock face had been scrubbed smooth and the surrounding vegetation withered by a fire. The red and white face (similar to the granite/iron-ore mix in Athens) was still beautiful, if bearing traces of artificial cleansing (a pathway halfway up had been sculpted very cleanly). The fire services extended this clean-

Adelaide

ing-up work into the landscape above, scraping the grass away in case one of the many fires in the production spread out of control.

The BAM Majestic

The Mahabharata saw the conclusion of the Centre's thirteen-year search for a suitable base in New York. As with *Carmen* and *The Conference of the Birds*, there was a frantic spin around the city to view possible spaces. This brought to more

The Majestic: exterior during the first visit (note the ladder for access)

than 200 the potential venues seen here over the years, incorporating every working and dark theatre in the city and just about every large-scale empty space. The Brooklyn Academy of Music's president, Harvey Lichstenstein, who had hosted the company back in 1973, wanted to find a venue which would live up to the *éclat* of the nine-hour-long drama; he was also prepared to take great risks:

> **HARVEY LICHSTENSTIEN:** *After we opened the Leperq Space with Peter, I of course hoped that he would come back with every subsequent production. When the English-language version of* The Mahabharata *was under discussion and Britain, Australia and Los Angeles had already expressed interest, I seized the opportunity. Peter said that the Leperq Space wouldn't be right, nor any of the city's proscenium theatres, so we went around looking at piers, warehouses and armouries (one of which we ended up using with Ariane Mnouchkine). We couldn't find anything that worked. We even thought of building a floor over the stalls of our opera house to create a more intimate space under the dome, but that would have been extremely difficult. Then, as we were going back and forth across the city, it suddenly crossed my mind that there was an old theatre about two blocks away from BAM which was boarded up, having been closed for about fifteen years. When I started at BAM in 1967 it was still functioning, but the owners left it soon afterwards and it was seized by the City of New York – apparently in lieu of taxes that were owed. We got into it by climbing a ladder into a broken first-floor window; we then had to walk down a corridor by flashlight, taking care to avoid floorboards that had been rotted through by water damage. The auditorium was badly damaged, rain was coming in, there were chairs piled up everywhere. Peter took a look around by flashlight and seemed to think it could work.*

Built in 1904, when the centre of Brooklyn had a thriving theatrical culture (twenty new spaces had opened in the preceding forty years), the Majestic had been the principal 'try-out' house for Broadway: Ethel Barrymore and Noël Coward had trod its boards. It had two deep balconies, packing in an audience of 1,828 – many of whom saw only a narrow sliver of the stage. The upper balcony had a separate entrance, with a single very steep staircase leading up directly from the street door. This was designed to keep the theatre's black clientele segregated from the whites in the better seats below. (There

THE MAHABHARATA

was also a small lobby for the Caucasian public.) Following the flight of manufacturing jobs from the city in the decades after the Second World War, the Fulton Street area became derelict and dangerous. The Majestic was transformed into a cinema. Then, in 1968, it was abandoned. The waterproofing seal around the roof line gave way, and soon there was a sheet of water flowing down the inside of the walls whenever it rained. This damaged and dislodged some of the plaster decoration, and began to rot the wood of the boxes and the stalls seating. The windows on the small street frontage of the lobby were smashed and the openings bricked over.

PETER BROOK: *It was with a terribly strong sense of déjà vu that I approached the uninviting façade of the Majestic. The space was just as much a wreck as the Bouffes had been when I first saw it: there were smashed chairs everywhere, pieces of fallen plaster, the smell of rotting wood and carpet. In spite of the fact that the asbestos safety curtain couldn't be raised (which meant that we saw only half of the space at a time), we were all charmed. It seemed terribly ambitious to want to transform this theatre just for our show, but after another few days of frantic searching we found nothing of comparable quality. We had to catch the evening flight back to Paris; a decision had to be made. I asked Jean-Guy to keep working while we had lunch and draw up a scheme in one hour, so that at our afternoon meeting we could commit ourselves to this adventure.*

JEAN-GUY LECAT: *I went around the theatre for a last time. The space itself would have to give me the solution. I went back into the auditorium, up to the first balcony. At the very moment when I entered I found that the stage was very far away, and I realized that in this space all the spectators were sandwiched between the immense balcony and the ceiling of the upper balcony.*

I had already noted on several occasions that, when walls or the ceiling appear within the field of vision, all that is beyond seems far away. I had therefore to find a way of giving each spectator the feeling of being with the others and within the same performance space.

These feelings of totally subjective distance are linked to shape, colours and materials, and also – fundamentally – to acoustics. Peter has said that 'When one sees properly one hears better', and we also know that when one hears well one feels closer. The 'presence' of an actor is almost always linked to his or her vocal pres-

The Majestic: during the first visit

143

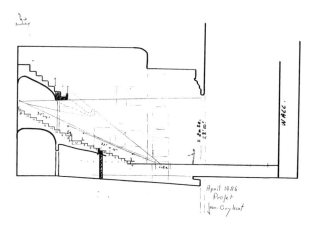

ence (which makes a theatre such as Epidauros possible).

*At that precise moment I did not yet have a solution. Then I
tested the acoustics (as I always do when sensing out a space): it
proved necessary to reduce the time of reverberation, and therefore the distances between performer and public. This was the
key. I set to work.*

The scheme, rapidly drafted out, involved the tactic first
used in the Teatro Argentina: of raising the level of the stage
(by 1.5 metres) and extending it out through the proscenium,
to be met by a prolongation of the slope of the first balcony in
a much more intimate, Bouffes-like, arena. In order to create a
sense of one shared volume – a volume of sound as much as of
sight – the second balcony would be cut back close to the line
of columns supporting it; this would also open up the view of
the whole proscenium frame to the back row of spectators in
what now became the stalls. A false wall would be built a few
metres from the existing back wall at the same distance from
the front row as in the Bouffes, and the new seating extending
the first balcony would close around the stage in exactly the
same shape and size as in Paris. The decaying fabric of the
walls and boxes would be made safe but otherwise kept as
found. The space would become the fourth venue of the
Academy of Music – a non-traditional space which was
thought of at the time as a catalyst for the revivification of its
depressed surroundings. (There was talk of a large arts complex to be built on adjacent land.)

Architects Hardy Holzman Pfeiffer Associates were given
the task of executing these basic modifications of the auditorium configuration, together with the addition of a new heating
and cooling system, the creation of dressing rooms and a new
lobby (in the back space of the former stalls), the installation

of up-to-date winching equipment in the flytower, and the renovation of the building's electrical system. The first budgetary calculations were not promising: $3.6 million was needed – $500,000 more than the City of New York was prepared to give. There were also questions about what would happen to the Majestic after *The Mahabharata* and the subsequent English-language version of Brook's production of *The Cherry Orchard* had finished. The City wanted to know that, if the configuration did not work out after these productions, it would be possible to return to a more familiar proscenium stage; fortunately, the scaffolding designed to underpin the stage would not be difficult to remove if necessary.

Budgetary problems were eventually resolved: the City gave $4.2 million towards the higher final budget, and BAM had to raise $1.6 million – an effort which was helped by the generosity of Lichstenstein's many Broadway and Hollywood contacts, and by a valiant stint by Brook on the gruelling 'chicken-and-peas' fund-raising-dinner circuit. The project was then developed in a flurry of drawings exchanged between Paris and New York. After many hesitations (particularly concerning the economic viability of cropping the top balcony by five rows), the original plan drafted out in an hour was eventually adopted, with the single change of the omission of the 'false' back wall. Instead, a new temporary surface would be applied to the existing scaleless cliff of bricks and painted in a similar manner to the Bouffes. Great care was taken with the calculation of sight lines, minutely adjusting the slope of the existing steps to give a total of three gradients. The rotting tip-up seats would be replaced with the same type of benches made in Paris for *La Tragédie de Carmen*.

By now it was March 1987. *The Mahabharata* was set to open in New York in October, so construction was started very rapidly. Much of the finished appearance had to be decided on site: it was hoped that the majority of the existing green and pink plasterwork could be preserved, but, as water had seeped in behind it and created the risk of pieces falling 13 metres on to the heads of the public, it was removed from much of the auditorium shell (with a zeal perhaps conditioned more by the litigious climate in America than by a desire for aesthetic integrity). Finally Chloé Obolensky and Ulysses Ketselidis came from Paris, and, together with a team of decorators from New York, patched up unpleasantly bald spots in the auditorium and painted the back wall. The old lobby towards the street

Section: before

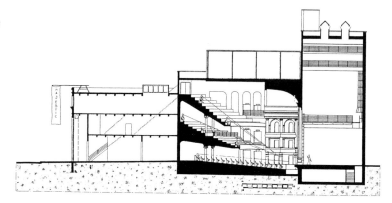

Section: after

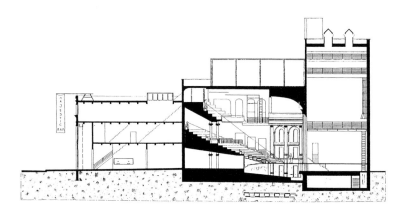

Plan of transformed
theatre

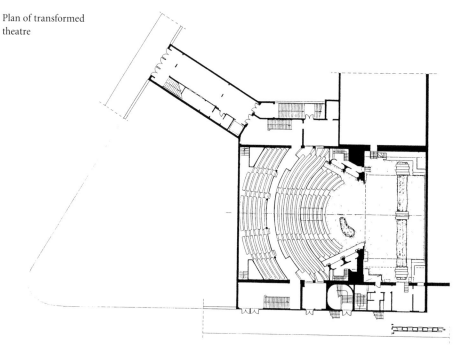

was also touched up in a rather playful manner by a false-marble expert in the decoration team (giving rise to accusations of postmodernist fakery in the architectural press). Where the steel structure of the balcony had been cut back, the foam-like fireproofing spray was left exposed; this was transformed by the decorators from a dull grey to a brown tone more in keeping with the rest of the space. Apart from the steps joining the old first balcony to the stage, the only altogether new elements were the steel gangways built at each side to connect the cut-back top balcony to its former entrance doors; the balcony also became a new lighting bridge.

The boxes on either side of the proscenium were shorn of their seats to create openings which had the same role of negotiating between play and architecture as the side walls and doors in Paris. They were not used for *The Mahabharata* (the musicians' platforms were built up in front of them), but during *The Cherry Orchard* they were put to constant use, together with an entrance through the middle of the arena, which was prepared in this first phase of construction work. All of the theatre's doors were removed and a decidedly non-traditional coconut matting placed on the floor in all of the front-

Former proscenium arch and new playing area

of-house areas; the theatre became a free-flowing, open space
both in and out of the auditorium, which the public appropri-
ated by sitting with picnics on the lobby floor (there were no
chairs) during the intervals. There remained one last hitch: the
earth spread out for *The Mahabharata* was mixed with grass,
which turned putrescent in the heat of a New York summer.
Brook tracked down Lecat on his holidays in the Alps and
urgently summoned him to New York to resolve the problem.
The whole stage had to be dug up, turned over and allowed to
dry so as to prevent a negative assault on the senses of the
audience.

The resulting theatre – renamed the BAM Majestic – has
900 seats (half the previous total) within a maximum distance
of 20 metres from the centre of the stage. Wider and less
focused than the Bouffes du Nord, it feels considerably larger;
but they are obviously sister spaces, with the same traces of
arrested disintegration on the walls, and the same eccentric
position with respect to the conventional theatres in the city.
But, even before it opened, this space had a very different
reception from that of the Bouffes in 1974. The copious press
commentary was ambivalent at best, and consistently criti-

Side wall of theatre
showing cut-back
balcony

cized the cost of the modification. The renowned director and teacher Robert Brustein wrote that 'This costly "poor theatre" begins to take on some of the bourgeois grandiosity (despite the atmosphere of feigned seediness) that made Nietzsche rage so rabidly against Wagnerian opera . . . Exquisitely transformed into an Etruscan ruin . . . the Majestic has essentially become an expensive colonial outpost for Peter Brook, created and outfitted for his personal use.'* Michael Kimmelman was a little more equivocal in *The New York Times*, praising the basic impulse to create an appealingly informal alternative to the prevalent proscenium theatres, and recognizing that the Majestic was perhaps not worth returning to its original cramped configuration. But, like Brustein, he felt very uneasy with the shifting temporality of the building. Singling out the retouches made to complement the 'ruin', he described them as 'an artificial impasto of time . . . the architectural equivalent of the intentionally worn look of a Ralph Lauren jacket'.* At the lower end of the spectrum of journalistic quality, the Majestic even made an appearance in one of the supermarket scandal sheets under the headline '$5 million to turn theatre into a dump.'*

*Cited in Albert Hunt and Geoffrey Reeves, *Directors in Prspective: Peter Brook*, p. 266.

New York Times, 25 October 1987

Weekly World News, c. October 1987.

The criticism of the BAM Majestic's cost neglects the realities of such work: any theatrical restoration is expensive, owing to the complexity of the form, the often ambitious structural configurations, and the sensitive security and fireproofing problems of a space made to contain hundreds of members of the public. Hardy Holzman Pfeiffer Associates recently restored the New Amsterdam and New Victory Theatres off Times Square – the latter at a cost of $23 million, which makes the Majestic look very reasonable. The fundamental changes of structure, roofing and auditorium form made for *The Mahabharata* cost only $2 million; the rest of the $5.8 million budget went towards new plumbing, electrical and air-conditioning systems to equip the theatre for longer-term use. This afterlife, which has been marvellously successful, has more than justified the initial investment: Brooklyn essentially obtained a new 900-seat theatre for a bargain price.

Financial concerns may in fact have been a screen to justify and quantify a deeper unease present in the commentary on the Majestic. A sign of this was the unprecedented demand by the City of Brooklyn for a certification of aesthetic warranty from the architects: Hugh Hardy had to swear that, in his professional judgement, it was acceptable to 'leave' the theatre like this. The implication behind the City's demand was that it was aberrant not to restore an historic building to something supposedly resembling its original condition. That this should be so in America and not France might have something to do with the paucity of architectural heritage in a young country. Ruins are the luxury of multi-layered civilizations, confident in the physical traces of their beginnings, bonded to the continuity of their heritage. In America, cultural origins are *there* and not *here*: whatever traces remain from the 200-plus years of post-revolutionary history are usually restored to the cryogenic state of a perpetual present-past, fictionally joined to today. Historian and geographer J. B. Jackson analyses this phenomenon in his essay *The Necessity for Ruins*. He describes 'reconstructed environments' (places restored to their supposed original state) as 'scenes of unreality, places where we can briefly relive the golden age and be purged of historical guilt . . . There is no lesson to learn, no covenant to honour; we are charmed into a state of innocence and become part of the environment. History ceases to exist.'*

The Majestic, like the Bouffes, can certainly permit us to be 'charmed into a state of innocence' through participation in a theatrical event, but its walls present something real (even tragic): a present, evolving past (a 'lesson to learn', perhaps also a 'covenant' with those already dead), against which this innocence finds its measure. If guilt is to be purged there, this is something that happens moment by moment in a body of people assembled there, not through the agency of an 'unreal' aura provided by the space itself.

Brustein was mistaken in claiming that the Majestic was 'transformed' into a ruin: it *was* one, and, as Kimmelman admitted, 'largely' remains one. What offended the latter commentator were the few completing touches made for *The Mahabharata* (such as painting the back wall): for him they brought a whiff of inauthenticity. But the wall was painted because in its 'authentic' state it was ugly and lacked scale; it was 'decorated' in the sense invoked by architectural historian Joseph Rykwert when he defines ornament as 'that which makes decent in supplying a missing essential'.* It was painted as if it had been found that way, but this is not an *as if* in self-conscious postmodern quotation marks: the point is that *it could have been so*. And, most importantly, the painting was yoked to the integrity of the world of *The Mahabharata*. It was not supposed to be experienced under the cold eye of the archi-

*J. B. Jackson, *The Necessity for Ruins*, p. 102

*'Ornament is no crime', in Joseph Rykwert, *The Necessity of Artifice*, p. 92.

THE MAHABHARATA

tecture critic in an empty theatre; it was made to be lived with as part of an ensemble which had unified sources of energy. Now it is already a part of the building's history, the token of its reopening, the significant trace of Brook's first visit, and will need to be reinterpreted itself as the building's history evolves.

Curtain call of
The Mahabharata

The three-month run of *The Mahabharata* was completely sold out; *The Cherry Orchard* enjoyed a similar popular success, and since then the Majestic has hosted a panoply of the world's most important artists in theatre, music and dance.

HARVEY LICHSTENSTEIN: *First of all the acoustic of the BAM Majestic is extremely good for music and theatre; but there is also a human quality and feeling to the theatre – it's welcoming and warm. It's certainly a unique theatre in New York, the only 900-seat house that is configured in that way. It's also one of the most interesting and attractive theatres the city has, in a human way. Most artists feel the same way, responding immediately to the warmth of the space, the relationships it sets up. People have complained about the benches, which had to be kept to a shallow depth to allow people to pass. I've never been bothered by them: I sat through* The Mahabharata *many times with no discomfort,* but perhaps that's just because of the way I'm built. Nevertheless we decided to replace them in 1996 with tip-up seats, so that there would be a larger seating surface. We kept the continuous backrest of the benches, which gives an elegant, unifying line to the seating, and raised it a little so that people would have a larger back support; we didn't put in armrests. Other than that, audiences have really enjoyed being there.

The artists that we have cultivated over the years have tended to be progressive and experimental; whenever they've had a piece that worked with the Majestic they've jumped at the chance to put it on here. We've had Steven Berkoff, Declan Donnellan, Pierre Boulez, Laurie Anderson, Martha Clarke and Philip Glass. Jonathan Miller did The St Matthew Passion here; he added a few rows of seats in the back of the stage, to make it more intimate and sort of in-the-round. He was so happy with the space: he said he'd been thinking of a church for the performance, but the Majestic captured that same quality – it became a spiritual place in association with that piece. And then, with his production of Monteverdi's L'incoronazione di Poppea – a completely different piece – this absolutely fit in, because the Majestic can take on a somewhat decadent character too. We've

Entrance of the theatre today

New lobby under the former dress circle

also been able to modify the space in various ways without changing the fundamental character. We can even put in a removable, moderate-sized orchestra pit. In general, artists enjoy being here. They feel energized by the space, and that means more to me than the words of any critic.

The audiences we attract are drawn firstly by the work, whether it be at the opera house or the Majestic. In general they're a younger, more diverse crowd than at Lincoln Center; the dress is much more informal. It has been hard to attract mixed-race audiences. A sister organization, 651 (the theatre's number on Fulton Street), was established in 1987 in conjunction with the opening, particularly to concentrate on programming and humanities projects, reaching out to the borough and the city's diverse population. The recent opening of the BAM Café (in what used to be the Leperq Space) allows us to have music (mostly jazz) before the show at the main house, and after on weekends. This, together with the Majestic and our new cinema complex (in the Playhouse) will get people more involved with BAM and hopefully give us a more ethnically varied audience.

PETER BROOK: We've never worked to a budget. Micheline used to say, 'Do what you want and we'll find a solution', and we would feel our way, try something, and if it was too expensive cut down on something else, and sometimes get into debt. For The Mahabharata Micheline got all the money she could out of the French government – which wasn't very much for such a big project: a special grant of £300,000. She was horrified to realize that we were losing great amounts of money every night when we were playing at the Bouffes, and – as her first principle was never to be in debt at the end of a year – she immediately organized a second tour of Carmen (meaning that two casts were on the road simultaneously) in order to dig us out of our hole. Sometimes newcomers from the outside can't understand our approach: they want to know what their individual budget is, how they can operate, but the process for us is a sort of jostle, negotiating things as we go along, arguing out priorities, rather like breaking in a horse.

One day, the Bouffes and the Majestic will be out of date. But if they still continue to be living spaces it is because they are 'open' or 'undefined'. In being anachronisms, they are not of yesterday, today or tomorrow. They are 'alive' because of their colour, their texture, their proportions and, above all, their humanity. They are open to many types of work, because they make no statement. This is what 'chameleon' means.

Frankfurt: The Bockenheimer Depot

The Festival of World Theatre invited The Mahabharata to visit Frankfurt in the autumn of 1985. Two possible spaces were considered: an urban former factory, which could have been accessed by boat along an adjacent canal, and an old tram works on the periphery of the medieval city. Both were initially rejected by the fire department; eventually permission was

Frankfurt: first visit

given to use the latter on condition that the structure be reinforced. (Some ancillary buildings were in the process of being
demolished, which weakened the central structure.) The principal space consisted of a 13-metre-high nave (the same height
as the arches at the top of the columns in the Bouffes du Nord)
with two lower side aisles. It was 75 metres long, divided into
fifteen equal bays of 5 metres. The central span of 16 metres
was formed by wooden arches (one per bay), which gave a
warmth and delicacy to the overall volume. There were two
trenches for servicing the underside of trams, and the spaces

Frankfurt: during
transformation

between the columns on the left side had been blocked with a brick wall.

In preparation for *The Mahabharata* this wall was demolished as far as the ninth bay and the rubble was used to fill in the trenches. A vast cistern at the far end was dismantled, and the stepped brick volume it stood on was extended to either side to form the back wall to the stage. (The lower ledge on the right side of the volume was conserved, as was a large door in the middle.) Two masonry side walls were built abutted to the third columns along (with short returns to give the impression

Lighting designer Jean Kalman and Peter Brook during rehearsals in Frankfurt

of thickness to the structure). Finally the seating was built in three sections: one filling the width of the nave and two smaller blocks on either side of the stage area. The central block was made from scaffolding with planks for seats; none of the sides were filled in, so it had a similar lightness and transparency to the building's wooden frame. It had a slope of 22 degrees, which was determined by the height of a reinforcing tie which traversed the volume at the base of the eighth arch. Lights were suspended from an unobtrusive secondary structure which stood in the side aisles.

The Mahabharata benefited from the inherent qualities of the structure: the warm acoustic of the wood, the rough quality of the back wall (whose lower ledge was clambered on to by the actors), and the satisfying basic proportions.

> **Maurice Bénichou:** *There were points in the drama when one's imagination could transform this exceptional – but purely functional – space into something magical, an Indian palace.*

The half of the space which the theatre did not inhabit was transformed into a restaurant for the hour-long breaks in the drama. The nearby university bought the building, and La Tragédie de Carmen was able to play there a year later with no modifications to the space other than the breaking of two doorway openings into the brick return walls. The producers widened the central block of seats, but these extra places were not suitable for use as they were cut off from the stage by the plane of the columns.

Madrid: The Studio Bronston

The Festival de Otoño invited *The Mahabharata* to Madrid during the first tour of the French version in 1985. As elsewhere, the existing theatres visited in the search for a venue were too small or lacking in quality.

> JEAN-GUY LECAT: *I was leaving town with the producers. I asked them if there were any other spaces we hadn't seen, even if they thought they might not be suitable. 'Absolutely no chance,' they said. Suddenly, off to the side of the motorway, I saw the vast bulk of what must have been a hangar or a sound stage. I asked them to turn off and investigate.*

Studio Bronston: first visit

The building in question was a suburban film studio. Recently bought by a bank, it was in the process of being demolished to make way for expensive houses, but could be preserved long enough for the three-week transformation and the six days of performances. Along with studios in Berlin and Munich (which themselves were transformed for performances of *Impressions de Pelléas* and *La Tragédie de Carmen*, respectively), it was the biggest of such facilities in Europe, having been used for Westerns and, recently, Antonio Gades's film of *Carmen*. The space was 20 metres wide, 65 metres long and 10 metres high, with a

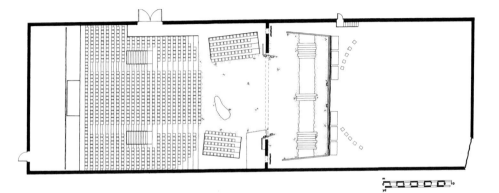

dividing wall roughly halfway down in which there was a 6-metre-square doorway. The walls and ceilings were covered in fibreglass, which was grey and dusty with age.

The space was transformed very simply by enlarging the opening in the dividing wall to 12 metres high by 8.5 metres wide; this became the frame of the 'side' walls. They were covered with rough wooden planks painted red, and a scaffold with a similar cladding was erected behind to form the back wall. A vast block of seating was built, filling the entire width of the space. It was formed into two slopes – gentle for the first

The existing door prior to enlargement. At right, Festival de Otoño assistant director Javier Lopez Reboredo and CICT agent Pietro Pagnanelli

nine rows, and much steeper for rows 10 to 24. The seats, appropriately, were from an old cinema. There were also the customary smaller side blocks. The stifling heat inside the studio was relieved by installing a ventilation system on the roof, which created a cooling current of air. While this was being put in place, positions to suspend the lighting from the ceiling were created, thereby minimizing the intrusion of the necessary theatre technology into the auditorium.

One of the strongest challenges of the space was its acoustic. It was vast and dead: any sound which managed to traverse the

huge volume simply expired on contact with the thick fibre-glass mat on the walls and ceiling. As the walls were parallel, it would have been unwise to remove the absorbent there: the result would have been a 'standing wave' of sounds bouncing back and forth like the infinite tunnel of images seen in parallel mirrors. But after removing the fibreglass from the ceiling an underlying structure of shallow terracotta vaults on a steel structure was revealed. These materials and forms, together with the diffusing wooden walls added for the show, created an exceptionally precise acoustic for such a vast space, proba-

The audience restaurant (at right) installed in the depot, with Gades' gyspy cabins from his film of *Carmen*

The finished space: the expsoed terracotta walls harmonised with The Mahabharata's colour scheme

bly thanks to the simple schema of the sound source (the actors) and the zone of first reflection (the wooden walls) being almost contiguous.

There was a little diplomatic tension created when the Queen of Spain's courtiers asked that a special block of seating with surrounding walls be created for her visit; this would have destroyed the essentially democratic character of the theatre, and she understood perfectly when this objection was relayed to her. Unfortunately her retinue was nearly two hours late for the performance; mortified, she made amends by coming to

The Studio Bronston today

see it again in Barcelona. Shortly after *The Mahabharata* the Studio Bronston was sold again and transformed into the Studio Luis Buñuel for the Spanish national television company.

Barcelona: The Mercat de les Flors

> **JEAN-GUY LECAT:** *One of the principles of our work has been that a certain lack of control – leaving room for chance – tends to be an enlivening factor. There are occasions, however, when it would be agreeable to have a little more control, more of a say in how the spaces we have created are developed. This became very clear to me one day when I was returning to Paris from the Madrid film studio used for* The Mahabharata. *I decided to stop by at the Mercat de les Flors, to refresh my memory of the space. There was scaffolding around the rotunda at the end of the volume: they had decided to carry out building works only a short time before* The Mahabharata *was due to come. Inside it was much worse: there was no longer a roof on the space, and a secondary structure was being built right in front of the wall surface we had used for* Carmen. *I telephoned Micheline immediately to say that there was no way the work would be finished in time, and in any case they had destroyed the aspects of the building we had appreciated earlier. We needed to find a new venue immediately.*

Following a call from Micheline Rozan, a meeting was arranged with the architects of the project, who agreed to suspend the building works after the roofing was rapidly completed. (They intended to build a low wall around the entire central space. This was put on hold until later.) A new steel structure supporting the roof interrupted the back wall used

The Mercat during reconstruction

Opposite page: Building the seating structure for *The Mahabharata*

THE MAHABHARATA

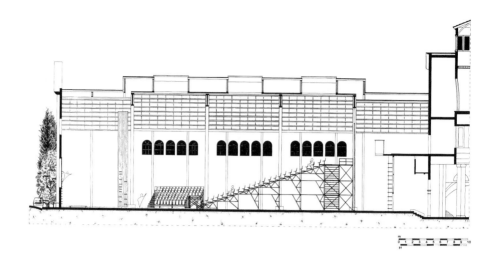

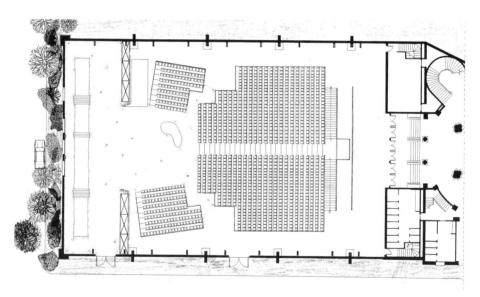

for *Carmen*, so it was decided to use the much larger end wall
and turn the audience through 90 degrees. As there was a gash
where an old dividing wall had been, with different colours of
paint on either side, a wholesale treatment of the surface had
to be carried out. Colours were sought in the surrounding
neighbourhood, and a warm ochre-coloured wall was discovered and adopted as the model. When a second coat of reddish
paint was begun from the base, the extendable ladder needed
to reach all the way to the top had been removed. With only a
day to go until rehearsals began, the red zone had to be left at

the maximum height of the smaller step ladders; in the event, this accident helped break down the scale of the wall and describe an 'earthly' lower zone. The three windows at the centre of the wall were covered with rough planks found nearby. Rungs like those in Paris were anchored into the back wall and on to the scaffolding which held up the side walls. These walls were faced with wood painted in a Cherokee red and were continued all the way to meet up with the profile of the ceiling, creating, again, a volume which took its lead from the existing structure. In this case it was a much larger space than before, with almost 1,200 people in the audience (the largest the Centre has ever played to). A new, more formal, entrance and lobby had been made from the old rotunda. This was used as a rest area and café during the two long breaks of *The Mahabharata*; and people also ate and wandered outside. The floor was treated with compacted earth as elsewhere, but this could not entirely mitigate the acoustic effect of having changed the original wood for a new concrete slab, and of replacing the wood surface of the ceiling with sound-absorbing material.

An interesting indicator of the limits of acceptability for the spaces was encountered here. The seating for *The Mahabhara-*

ta was built by the theatre, without too much input from the Centre other than the specifications of the stage size. Its maximum depth – 18.5 metres from the front to back rows – was the greatest used to date, and was felt to be too big. Moving back row by row, Brook and Lecat observed that an actor at the centre of the stage seemed dramatically to lose presence past a certain precise point. By the time they reached the back row the actor was more than 25 metres away and seemed somehow entirely out of reach. Brook ascribed this limit of presence to the ability to maintain eye contact with the actor in what he called a 'feedback loop' of mutual awareness.

The Mahabharata: a scene from The War

Zurich

For the premiere of the English-language version of *The Mahabharata*, in Zurich, an outdoor space was looked for in the first instance. The site of the municipal boatworks was suggested: there was a pier facing the lake, with mountains in the distance. After several visits during the day it was decided to test the acoustics at night. Police boats circulated in the lake to see how far away traffic would have to be kept so as not to

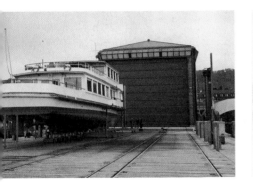

produce distracting noises. The answer was: Italy, probably. Sound travelled exceptionally well over the lake at night, and moreover a spectacle such as *The Mahabharata* on the pier could not fail to attract curious boaters.

There was another problem, in that the pier contained a hydraulic lift which was used to hoist boats out of the lake in an emergency. However, the boathouse itself could be used if the pier was kept free. It had a huge volume (72 metres long, 18 metres wide, and 18 metres to the apex of the roof). The outdoor space could be used for backstage functions. In order to

Above: The flotilla of dressing rooms

Zurich: first visit

165

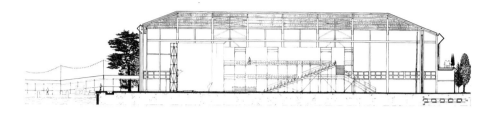

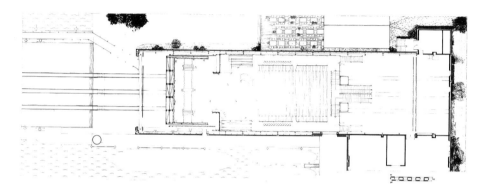

house the company village, a pontoon was hired and moored alongside the pier and builder's cabins were lifted on to the pontoon by crane. The pontoon was joined to the boathouse by a covered walkway in case of rain, and the rest of the pier became an area for warm-up exercises, meals and relaxation – it could be evacuated rapidly if it needed to be used to salvage a boat.

Inside, the space was as straightforward as can be: a metallic industrial shell with a lifting bridge spanning the width, rails in the concrete floor, and simple lighting. It was conceived to

Toshi Tsuchitori leading excercises on the boathouse pier

THE MAHABHARATA

shelter a precise activity with the minimum of pretension. Its twentieth-century materials made it different from the equally 'functional' spaces in Frankfurt and Copenhagen: it lacked the dignity and scale they gained from being hand-made, and had none of their solid, weathered surfaces against which the drama could find support. Its metal surfaces gave a bright, cold acoustic, and did not inspire the sense of well-being one felt in its older counterparts. It was therefore necessary to create an entirely new universe in the interior. The back surface was delimited by walls which, in keeping with the building, were made from simple scaffolding clad in a fibreglass gauze suspended a few centimetres in front. There was a 3-metre-high wooden wall at the back of the acting area to hide lighting equipment and actors as they changed sides, leaving the much higher top part translucent (of which more later); on the side walls the heavier material was continued all the way to the top. The gauze was suspended from the building's walls to the sides of the audience, to impart a unified feeling to the space and to dampen the too-bright acoustic of the metal. Inside this envelope the seating was built.

The functional seating used elsewhere would not suffice in

this neutral space: more 'life' was needed, and this was sup-
plied by designing a wooden structure with a strong presence.
A central rake of normal slope and size was bracketed between
two levels of balconies which followed the rectilinear form of
the boathouse. There were benches at stage level and one row
of individual seats on the two superior levels. Dark-stained
wooden handrails, vertical supports and six towers were integrated into a system of regular proportions (bays of 2.5 metres,
floor heights of 3 metres). The towers were designed to hold
much of the lighting. In makeshift venues the challenge is
often to support this equipment as unobtrusively as possible
with prefabricated elements. These structures have a habit of
breeding rampantly – and very obtrusively – as soon as a
venue is declared 'permanent'. Here there was a rare opportunity to give an expression of the necessary technical equipment as part of an integrated environment which included
audience, backdrop and actors. Indeed, this venue – which was
used for only two weeks – came closest of all the Centre's projects to the condition of a complete, purpose-built new theatre. Its form was inspired by a temporary theatre built for
Molière in the shell of a royal tennis court. This had the same

parallel balconies with rectangular openings, a very steep rake of seats at the back, and a two-level stage whose geometry was closely related to that of the 'auditorium'.*

*See S. Wilma Deierkauf-Holsboer, *Le Théâtre du Marais* vol. 1, especially plates VII-X.

Completed by the customary earth, this space became, in its form and proportions, a fine home for *The Mahabharata*. What made it special was the appropriation of certain aspects of its setting: the strangeness of going to see an all-night performance in a boathouse, and having a midnight meal on a boat moored alongside the pier (hired, like the pontoon, for that purpose). The summit of this intersection between the ordinary and the extraordinary came at dawn:

JEAN-GUY LECAT: *During a dress rehearsal I noticed that the sun rose over the lake on axis with the theatre during the final scene (the 'last illusion', when the characters have a meal together in a paradisaical setting). I suggested to Peter that we raise the huge rolling door at the far end of the building to let the audience see this. He said, 'Do it if you think it's right at the time.' It worked wonderfully well for the first all-night performance, when the world's press was in attendance; in fact, miraculously, the great orange ball of the rising sun was exactly in the centre of*

Mahabharata curtain-call with the sun rising in the background

the opening. Many critics commented on this, joking that Peter Brook was directing nature. On the second night, though, a cloud moved in front of the sun just after we opened the door.

JEAN-CLAUDE CARRIÈRE: *Peter is always changing things, such as allowing the sunrise to participate in the action in such an unexpected way. He sometimes asks an actor who has been used to entering from the right for two months suddenly to come in from the left, with all the implications that this has in terms of upheaval, apprehension, even fear. This underlines that what counts is not a fixed number of steps to get to a point in relation to a decor, but rather a relationship to the play. This relationship is constantly modified in terms of the very differing spaces that we have played in, and one must make an effort to remain supple and free of preconceptions.*

The wood for the theatre had been paid for by the city, which dismantled the structure afterwards and reused it. The benches were cut into shorter lengths and placed on the wide beach adjacent to the site. Had the boathouse been disused, this theatre could have remained in use quite happily (perhaps with a more fire-resistant structure). The square frames made by the balustrades and the uprights said (as did the similar proportions of the Teatro Argentina) that this was an egalitarian, equitable realm, and what provided the real interest was not so much the architecture but the way it brought people into relationship with one another. Furthermore, the lighting towers were an honest means of confronting the need for technical equipment (*The Mahabharata* was highly ambitious in this regard); the normal response in theatre-building is a kind of denial which usually results in the technological tail wagging the cultural dog.

Zurich: the wooden exit stairs

Copenhagen and Tokyo

These two spaces transformed earlier for *Carmen* were easily adapted for the new production. In the former case the curious wall with its giant portholes served well as a backdrop, but the acoustic quality of the space strained the actors to the limit.* In Tokyo a disposition of seating slightly different from *Carmen*'s was adopted to accommodate this larger-scale production: the side places were stopped at the line of the safety curtain, beyond which began the earthen platform on which

*This space has been conserved as a performance venue, with the recent addition of a sleek, minimalist bar of dressing-

sat the musicians, Ganesha/Krishna and the boy. The structure which had held the wooden walls was clad this time in burlap and red gauze; the river and pool were built in the same size and configuration, as elsewhere. Whole ladders were attached to the back and side walls, instead of the random arrangements of metal rungs used in Paris. A year's work was needed to convince the fire department that each of the sixty-five flame effects was safe. (Two officers learned them by heart and observed each one from different viewpoints as the performance unfolded, moving silently into a memorized position in a kind of invisible Beckettian sub-drama. During the entire run of *The Mahabharata* there were approximately ten occasions on which actors' costumes caught fire; in most cases the actors were able to deal with the problem unobtrusively by stepping into the river or pool.)

To aid the understanding of the drama, a summary of each scene was prepared in Japanese under the supervision of Brook and Yoshi Oida and was played through individual headphones in the auditorium at the beginning of a scene, so that the action could unfold without interruption or the distraction of surtitles. The production was a great success: the cushion places in

rooms and workshops (designed by architects KHS AS Arkitekter) beside the main volume and linked by a tunnel to the stage. The form of the performance space today is substantially as it was conceived for *Carmen*. However, when the building was published in the Danish architectural press after the renovations, there were no photographs of the auditorium and no mention was made of the building's genesis.

The Ginza Saison
Theatre transformed
for *The Mahabharata*

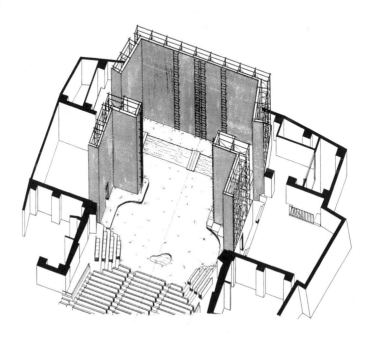

171

the front row (which were markedly less expensive than the other seats) were so highly sought after that people slept in a neat queue for up to three nights outside the theatre.

YOSHI OIDA: *We played* The Mahabharata *to total silence here. Miriam Goldschmidt told me that we were failing to interest the audience, and everyone was a little worried. It was only at the end that the audience applauded wildly and we knew we had communicated. When my sister, who knows nothing about the theatre, saw* The Mahabharata *here, she said that the space was completely transformed by the acting: it could be a mountain, a river or a forest, but it was all thanks to her imagination. The theatre itself gave nothing, which was good. If a space is too decorated you can't do anything with it: it stops the imagination.*

Tokyo: transformed for *The Mahabharata*

Peter says that when the people in our audiences change from one country to another we must adapt so that there is always the same result, so we change the acting all the time. Theatre is not like tinned food. Fortunately Jean-Guy manages to capture the same spirit in the touring spaces, so at least the building is never a barrier.

MARIE-HÉLÈNE ESTIENNE: The Mahabharata *was extraordinary here. The space wasn't particularly beautiful in itself, but it helped create a concentration, which was all that was needed with such an attentive audience: the people themselves made the space. I remember during the third part they didn't make a noise: in spite of the difficulties of comprehension, all 600 were weeping in complete silence.*

The Mahabharata: a scene from Exile in the Forest

Glasgow: The Old Museum of Transport

A possible UK visit by the English-language production of *The Mahabharata* received much publicity and discussion in 1986–7, and venues were sought in London. A printing works near Waterloo could have been suitable, but was snapped up for another purpose by a property developer; eventually, Warehouse K in the Royal Victoria Docks complex at Canary Wharf was chosen. In collaboration with William Wilkinson, financial controller of the Royal Shakespeare Company (and co-producer of the English-language tour), the London International Festival of Theatre (LIFT) had begun raising money for the production. Rose Fenton, director of LIFT, had received an undertaking from the London Docklands Development Corporation that it would fund a significant part of the overall £600,000 cost of the production and transformation; LDDC owned Warehouse K, and wanted to include it as a permanent arts venue in the rapidly growing Canary Wharf complex. The *Daily Telegraph* had also promised the revenue from £250,000 of advertising space to be used by the production's sponsors. Then a change in the schedule of the LDDC's funding was enough to throw the project off course: the transformation of Warehouse K was put on hold, but work needed to begin immediately for the run in a year's time.

> **ROSE FENTON:** *When the LDDC backed out, there was no one else for us to turn to in local or national government: the project just died. The Greater London Council had been abolished in 1985 by Margaret Thatcher's government. It had had an integrated, internationalist artistic policy, and could probably have helped us, but afterwards everything was fragmented across different boroughs and small-scale private sponsors with sometimes limited perspectives of what constitutes 'culture'. The last time we visited Warehouse K with Peter it had been temporarily transformed into an ersatz old-style English pub, as if to symbolize just the kind of nationalistic, parochial, backward-looking attitude which is diametrically opposed to the universal, heterogeneous character of both Brook's company and* The Mahabharata *itself. Fortunately London seems to have moved on from this period, accepting its multicultural, international character, and has begun to host more and more international companies.*

Robert Palmer, director of the 1987 Glasgow Festival (a warm-up for Glasgow's role as European City of Culture in 1990), had seen the show in Zurich:

> **ROBERT PALMER:** *My assistant Neil Wallace and I were absolutely stunned by the performance in this vast space on the lake. At breakfast after an all-night marathon we approached Peter and informed him that* The Mahabharata *was invited to Glasgow as part of the Festival. We knew that this was complete madness: we had no idea how to raise the necessary money, we had no idea for a venue, and Glasgow at that time was far from being an established centre for international theatre. Nevertheless, we made a pact that we would just have to find a way, no matter what the obstacles.*

THE MAHABHARATA

Glasgow: first visit

Combining funds from Glasgow and Strathclyde Councils
and the Arts Councils of Scotland and Great Britain, together
with private sponsorship from Renault Trucks, Palmer and Wallace were able to secure the budget for the production, which, at
£350,000, was significantly lower than elsewhere on the tour. A
search for possible venues was begun immediately: forty spaces
were visited, including shipyards on the Clyde, factories, and old
theatres which had become bingo parlours. None was suitable,
for reasons of scale, timing or money. The only space which
aroused real interest, the former Transport Museum, was in the

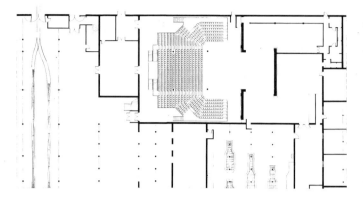

process of being demolished and would no longer exist at the planned time of the performances. Wallace and Palmer took the bold step of asking that demolition be halted until after *The Mahabharata*. (The building had been declared a 'dangerous' structure, and many administrative hurdles had to be cleared in order to neutralize multiple condemnation orders. Obtaining a theatrical licence was also particularly difficult.) As the space was being cleared, it was eventually accepted that it would be taken just to the point required to install the production, the rest to be destroyed afterwards. With the building work for the seats, new walls and some amenities, a budget from the city of £200,000 would suffice.

The Transport Museum had begun its life in 1893 as a manufacturing and repair works for the city's trams – initially horse-drawn, then powered by electricity. The space which would house the theatre was an erecting shop added on to the complex in 1898. A thousand people worked there, manufacturing 1,200 trams over the years, until in 1962 the tram system was dismantled and replaced with buses. The Transport Museum had been installed in the space to preserve the memory of the fabrication and use of these machines, and displayed several of them, along with cars and other vehicles. Having outgrown this space (which was also proving costly to maintain), the collection was moved to new premises near the Scottish Exhibition and Conference Centre in early 1987.

There were several immediately appealing features of the building: it was apart from the conventional civic institutions, close to the working-class Gorbals, and surrounded by a predominantly Indian community. The basic space was simple and solidly built: a 42 by 25 metres brick shell with arched entrance bays and a lightweight factory roof supported by two rows of columns roughly 8 metres apart. The walls were paint-

Chloé Obolensky and Ulysse Ketselidis painting the back wall

ed in a cream colour, and there were various ancillary spaces built at one end of the volume. Unlike in Frankfurt and Barcelona, there was no suitable 'end' wall against which to play. It was decided, as in these cities, to derive the proportions of the theatre from the basic structure of the space. A new wall would be built at the first row of columns from the back, extending a few metres to either side of each column and meeting the roof structure at the top. Slightly lower side walls would be built from the exterior shell to the next row of columns, which would be moved apart by a metre to give a better proportion to the opening. The stage area would be formed in the square between the four central columns, and the embrace of seating would be built around, filling the side aisles and extending upward to the following structural bay. The geometry of the 'host' space would be apparent, and the side walls would create a circuit with the existing brick, but the world of the play would be made up of added elements.

Dressing-room tables improvised from museum display cases

In spite of their absence from the immediate realm of the drama, the walls of the existing structure were sandblasted to remove their cream-coloured paint and reveal the hundred-year-old bricks, which had a pleasant patina. This markedly improved the overall ambience of the building. Three openings were bricked up to unify the space and shut out street noise. The new constructions were made from rough modern bricks. The back wall was joined with a partition salvaged from an ancillary space in order to form a storage area for props and to allow a passage for the actors from one side of the space to another; its visible surface was coated five-sixths of the way up with brown-coloured plaster, which was painted in the manner of the BAM Majestic wall by Ulysses Ketselidis, Chloé Obolensky and a team of local artists. The 688 seats were placed on a simple scaffolding structure, and the earth for the floor was brought from Greenock. (This being Scotland, not the South of France, the earth was very wet and had to be spread out and dried with hot-air blowers under vast plastic sheets.) Finally, lightweight wooden planks were placed across the base of the roof structure to mitigate the bright acoustic produced by large surfaces of glass. The whole transformation was carried out in three weeks.

Drying the stage earth

JEAN-GUY LECAT: *There is no building without a threshold, and whenever I visit a place one of the most significant moments is when I enter it. What I feel in the act of traversing this space,*

sometimes modest enough, is always important. A wall creates
two poles of energy, a boundary that marks the passage from one
state to another. An entrance is the passage between the outer
world, which we leave behind, seemingly known, and the
unknown forces inside.

It is interesting that we remember entering a theatre but rarely
remember leaving it. Therefore the first important moment is the
arrival, the crossing of the threshold. The true encounter with a
space begins when you enter it. We leave the city and penetrate
into that place, now half-derelict and deserted. In this precise
instant many things intervene, including the transition from one
kind of acoustic to another, and the atmosphere of the place. You
register these things spontaneously, even before analysing them.
The senses share in this perception, which is not merely visual, as
is often thought. A place is a set of concrete elements bounding
the space where life takes place and with its structure determined
by its original purpose. The forms, proportions, colours, materi-
als, scents, sounds, all taken together, define the first aspect of a
place, its atmosphere and its essence (the ancients spoke of the
genius loci – *the spirit of the place).*

The 15,000 tickets for *The Mahabharata* sold out within a few days. Sixty per cent of the audience travelled from England and Wales, and there was enormous attention from the London media. The transformation of the venue had received almost as much advance publicity as the production, so it was hardly surprising that the city decided to save the space as an arts centre for theatre, dance, music and exhibitions of visual art. (It was named 'Tramway'.)

Glasgow: curtain-call for *Carmen*

> **PETER BROOK:** *The whole of the* Mahabharata *tour, taking in so many different conditions and locations, was really a demonstration of what can only happen where there is a unique partnership such as I had with Jean-Guy. Without him these tours would never have been possible, and it was not just his technical competence or his experience that mattered. What was important was the intimate relationship that had been built up over the years with the real purpose of all the work we were doing, leading to his understanding from the inside what* The Mahabharata *needed. It was through this that he could go into such different spaces and not adapt them in the way that the word suggests, but modify them from the inside of a working and creative process.*

What matters is that the space has to serve the needs of the story one is telling. Furthermore, it has to become, in perfor-mance, a vital and glowing space. Some spaces already go halfway towards this, because they have something in their pro-portions and their texture that already lends itself to that; but some spaces are just dull and ugly. That is where the art of the person transforming the space comes in. This person visits a space and has a very simple choice. Either he can say, 'This is impossible, and the space cannot be used: the space has the wrong proportions, acoustic, texture or atmosphere, and I can't correct that' (and knowing this takes a shrewd and experienced eye). Or he can say, 'My work is partly done here already.' This was the case with the quarries we found for The Mahabharata; *three-quarters of the emotional content was already given, and it became a question of how to arrange it. Technique and art come together.*

At the end of *The Mahabharata's* tour the group gathered again in Paris to make two five-hour films of the drama (in English and French) at the Joinville studios. As soon as these were finished, customs officials claimed all the props and cos-tumes. (These had to be surrendered in order to avoid paying the huge duties which would have been incurred in travelling the world with fifty crates of material.) The last act in the jour-ney was then a huge bonfire in which every object and cos-tume the Centre had worked with for three years was destroyed.

PETER BROOK: *When we decided to film* The Mahabharata, *fate intervened in a very sympathetic way. The only studio that was available and suitable was at Joinville. It was due to be demolished a few months later. I remember entering it: its crum-bling walls were covered with photographs of Jean Gabin, Fer-nandel, Arletty, reflecting the golden age of French cinema. We knew we had stumbled on the cinematic equivalent of the Bouffes du Nord.*

7 : Return: *The Tempest* and *Impressions de Pelléas*

PETER BROOK: *Performance space – often thought of as a passive, neutral, mute, inanimate, subordinate thing, into which we 'project' our ideas – is actually something constantly needing to be brought back to life and into a fresh perspective, just like the text of a play. The evolving forms of our own work force us to reframe space at every turn. As society has changed, we have had to listen for fresh forms, movements and proportions which can enable the shifting union of performer, public and space. We have had to listen, and also intervene forcefully at times or very delicately at other times – or, sadly, not at all when it has been clear that authorities have misunderstood the nature of our spaces.*

By the end of the 1980s the Centre had seen just about every theatre and empty space in most major cities in the West. The supply of significant 'free' space was drying up, and the venues which had been created in Lisbon, Barcelona, Copenhagen, Frankfurt and Glasgow had all been made into permanent theatres – in some cases with significant secondary modifications to the fabric. In returning to these spaces, the tours of *The Tempest* and *Impressions de Pelléas* between 1990 and 1993 therefore involved a reconsideration of the work frantically accomplished for *Carmen* and *The Mahabharata*.

David Bennent as Caliban at the Bouffes du Nord

Both *The Tempest* and *Impressions de Pelléas* found their forms in the Bouffes du Nord, and drew strongly on aspects of the space explored in previous work. *The Tempest* continued the line of 'terrain' settings, but with a twist. The theatre floor was covered with red earth, and this was surmounted by a rectangle of white sand retained by bamboo poles, with a large rock marooned in the middle – a kind of Zen garden. As such it was a hybrid of the 'zone' of *The Conference of the Birds* and the whole 'environment' of *The Mahabharata*. The sand was a fluid symbol: it could suggest the island, or become the ship

The mimed storm sequence of *The Tempest*: (l–r) Pierre Lacan, Bakary Sangaré, Tapa Sudana, Jean-David Baschung

during the storm; but it never took on a slavishly literal meaning – it always relied on the audience's imagination to complete the picture. It was not marooned in the theatre as an acting area: when one of the characters stepped off it, he or she merely entered another realm of the drama, rather than returning immediately to the world of the audience. The walls were transformed dramatically for this production, being daubed with white at the back and green at the sides, the two key colours for this production.

CHLOÉ OBOLENSKY: *The way in which I work with Peter has always been not to embroider, but to suggest a different world; to excite the imagination of a spectator, but to let it free, leave it room to grow on its own. Very often we start by working on the shell – meaning the nature of the walls, the floor, whether there will be openings or things to climb on. If that shell is right in its dimensions, divisions and colour, you can start to experiment with putting objects into it. Sometimes they will just fall into place if the shell itself is correct, and that's all we need.*

If you work with the principle that all you can use are the walls and the floor, you feel the need to keep things free, so that you can play with them, find solutions which don't necessarily go back every time to the same conventions. Peter had shown me some Japanese screens which had a green oxide coloration – a very mysterious, very beautiful colour. We applied this tint to the walls on either side of the proscenium. I must say, however, that I eventually found that green in that volume became almost impossible to sustain. It gave a peculiarly aesthetic turn which didn't suit Peter's work, and also a certain coldness. A colour can function wonderfully for five minutes, but after half an hour or three hours it becomes something very different, and can work against the play. If we'd thought more freely we might have used paper or something like that: the surface of the walls has such a strong identity you can't work against it.

We put lines of broken moulding on the back wall for The Tempest, because I felt there was a need to stress the verticals. This would have been difficult with a free-standing structure in the Bouffes. They reflected the sandy area on the ground – one had a slight feeling of an invisible cube. The mouldings also happened to work well for Pelléas, because they gave the impression of an interior.

PETER BROOK: *In the two-room or proscenium theatre form, the audience is not in the same room and, more importantly, therefore not in the same physical space as the story. In all of our first productions one wanted the audience to feel that, although they didn't have to get up from their seats and walk down into the space to feel they were participating, they were actually in physical, realistic terms in the country where the story was taking place. This was a sort of realism; but realism in the theatre is not 100 per cent naturalism – it is a strong suggestion which is not carried through in every detail, like the real chariot wheel I described earlier in* The Mahabharata, *which stood for a whole, real chariot. Our backdrop – the ground of the theatre that the audience shared with the actors, whether it was concrete, sand, earth or carpeting – was the foundation for this realism.*

In The Cherry Orchard *the audience were invited into a house; in* The Mahabharata *they were invited into a real landscape which was a landscape of 3,000 years ago with real fires and real water. They had stepped out of the boulevard de la Chapelle, and were now actually sitting with the actors in a house in Russia, on a battlefield in India.*

But with The Tempest *this proved impossible, because there is no literal, physical island in the play. When, early in the rehearsals, Chloé Obolensky presented to me something following directly in the* Carmen–Mahabharata *lineage, which was the entire arena turned into an island, I thought, 'This would be marvellous were the play like* The Mahabharata – *epic, but taking place in a real land.' But the island in* The Tempest *is a mythical, symbolic island: it has no solid reality. If one really makes it, one is imitating naturalistic film technique – and this is a limitation, because the island has to be built in the imagination of the audience.*

We saw that we had to create an artificial division within the acting area, and allow the walls to sink into the background and become a shell – a shell that resonates and stimulates the imagination. Everything fell into place the moment we settled upon the idea of having a smaller rectangle of sand within the greater acting space, and the two elements present – the sand and the rock – became like two adjectives that a storyteller would use. We were no longer pretending to make something real: the audience's link to the story was through the imagination, supported by the qualities of the elements we had assembled.

Impressions de Pelléas was played in a style similar to that of *The Cherry Orchard*: carpets, a few armchairs, a fish bowl, a vase of flowers and costumes gave a taste of the *fin-de-siècle* world of Debussy's opera. The walls of the theatre were given the rich red accent that they have retained until today. Two slightly unequally sized rectangular pools of water were set into the concrete floor downstage, either side of the principal carpet. The pools were shallow, with decorative mosaics visible beneath their surface (not quite the bottomless well called for in the libretto: the audience's imagination was given some work to do when Mélisande's wedding ring remained clearly visible resting on the mosaic). As in *The Mahabharata*, the presence of water made possible a fluid transfer from inside to outside – the direct juxtaposition of water and carpet reinforcing this.

Here the setting did not encroach into the audience's space, but as an 'acting area' it was much less theatrically charged than the carpets of *The Conference of the Birds*. There was not the onstage/offstage dichotomy set up by the earlier carpets, and the actors remained in character except when leaning casually on the piano between scenes. The piano itself was not out of place in the mood of a nineteenth-century drawing room; its musical role (it and another piano were the sole

accompaniment for the singers) was therefore grounded in the world of the play. It was situated just beyond the crucial threshold of the proscenium. (There was also a second piano tucked out of sight behind one of the side walls.)

In order to go on tour, a new problem had to be addressed. Both productions relied on an environment with a precise geometry and atmosphere: the rough planks and earthy arena of *Carmen*, which nestled into the very different shapes of the Mercat de les Flors, the Ostre Gasvaerk and the Teatro Argentina, would have been too coarse for these pieces. Therefore, for the first time, a 'ready-made' background was designed, conceived in such a way that it could adapt to a wide variety of spaces – both existing theatres and the 'found' spaces opened earlier. It happened that the same basic structure would serve both *The Tempest* and *Pelléas*, with a change in the colour of the fabric and the addition of certain details for the latter.

> CHLOÉ OBOLENSKY: *The system we developed for* The Tempest *consisted of a series of uprights with net and material suspended at a distance behind, which kept the space as near as possible to what the actors were used to in the Bouffes but at the*

*same time provided an abstract frame, a space without particu-
lar architectural connotations. We provided the* volume *we needed, but without designing in a particular style.*

Braunschweig

The Schauspielhaus in Braunschweig presented a unique challenge: the main auditorium (a rather conventional turn-of-
the-century proscenium space) was closed for restoration;
however, the large volume of the stage and backstage could

still be used. This was just big enough, though interrupted halfway down by the beam separating the stage and backstage. Unlike the backstage walls of the Zellerbach auditorium in Philadelphia, which had the perfect kind of roughness to support the world of *The Ik* on the 1976 tour, this space was rather dead and lacked the purity of tone necessary for *The Tempest*. Chloé Obolensky designed a structure which would act as a frame for white fabric walls defining the environment of the drama. Entrance passages for the actors would be integrated, along with a space for the side seats of the audience; wooden beams above gave the effect of a ceiling to the space. For Braunschweig a block of seating was built on the stage itself, protruding lightly into this fabricated world, joining with the people sitting on the sides, within the space.

Antwerp

The decor devised for Braunschweig served for a similar installation in a space which lacked the right proportions and relationships in itself. The De Singel Theatre in Antwerp is a municipal space built in the 1980s. As the invitation came from

a company associated with a particular building (rather than from a city or a festival), it would have been costly and impolite to ask them to find another space – and there are, in any case, advantages to using ready-made theatres: dressing rooms, lighting, access and fire-safety questions are all taken care of, and new planning permission does not have to be sought. Here the problems were a pitifully shallow slope to the auditorium (only 9 degrees), a horizontal proportion to the volume (the proscenium, only 9 metres high, is 14 metres across), and a palette of materials (scaleless polished-concrete

Antwerp before and during transformation

cladding and orange-velour seats) which, applied to these proportions, lacked presence. A further handicap was provided by
a technical bridge which interrupted the volume of the auditorium.

All of these impediments were accepted and worked with to
the greatest possible extent. A new bank of seats at a slope of 24
degrees was built between the front of the stage and the technical bridge, which thereby became an emergency exit. This
changed the proportion of the auditorium, focusing energy
downward towards the stage and giving the deadly side walls a
greater vertical accent. Finally the 'box' designed for Braunschweig was inserted into the mouth of the stage, filling it
entirely and spilling out slightly at the sides. This created a
geometrical circuit between the existing walls and the highly
ordered space of the play, smoothing over the abrupt division
between proscenium and stage.

Tokyo

Exactly the same strategy was applied to the Ginza Saison
Theatre in Tokyo, which in its original incarnation had many

of the same problems as the De Singel space: the seating structure made for *Carmen* was brought out of mothballs again,
and the Braunschweig frame was installed in the volume of the
stage.

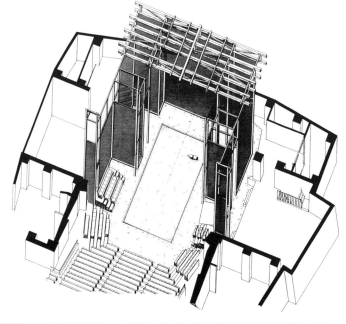

The Ginza Saison
Theatre transformed
for *The Tempest*

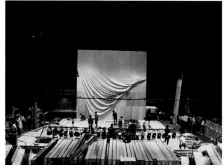

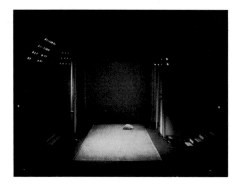

Barcelona

Impressions de Pelléas returned to the Mercat de les Flors to celebrate the tenth anniversary of the inauguration of the space as a theatre with *La Tragédie de Carmen*. The building works which had been interrupted for *The Mahabharata* were now complete: there was a permanent raised stage and seating, with a low wall running the length of the space to hide actors as they moved from their dressing rooms in the rotunda to the stage at the other end. A lifting bridge and a lighting grid had been installed, obscuring the elegant wooden arches. In short, everything that had been appealing about the space at its discovery had been compromised, masked by this new material. The only possibility was to play as if in any 'black-box' theatre, with curtains around the seats to screen off this chaos and the frame made for *The Tempest* built up around the acting area – this time with red fabric in place of the white, and added vertical elements cast in plastic from parts of the Bouffes du Nord.

The Mercat under transformation for *Pelléas*

JEAN-GUY LECAT: *Our work is singular in that we use the 'space*

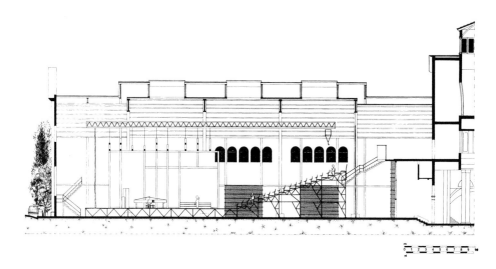

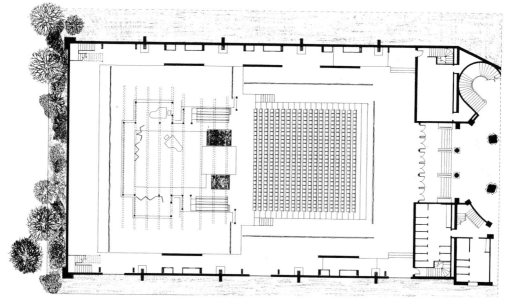

of the place' as the 'space of the show'. It is a space for words, a space for shared sight, a space both ordinary and civic, having as its only dimensions the imagination and the sensibilities of each person. We try to create a place of liberty – protected and enclosed.

What type of space is needed for this? What type of architecture? Can a space be a source of energy? Can it be a link, a factor of integration? Can it further dreaming and imagination? A poorly adapted architecture – stiff, clumsy or too slack – interrupts the exercise of thought.

Although in general the architecture of monuments and cities roots man in space and time, the architecture of the theatre – which is comprehensible only from the standpoint of life – retains a living presence only as long as it submits to continual modifications. That it is the responsibility of those occupying a space, those who give it life and use it to understand and develop their own space.

Frankfurt

In Frankfurt it was much the same story as in Barcelona: the wooden arcade at the Bockenheimer Depot which had made Maurice Bénichou dream of being in an Indian palace was now obscured by a plethora of lighting equipment, held in place by an obtrusive structure which was supported by metallic columns built around the original wooden ones. Fortunately this space was so long that one end remained relatively untouched, so the seating (which had been left in the space it had occupied for *The Mahabharata*) was demounted and rebuilt facing in the other direction, and the decor was installed with the addition of a red curtain taking up the profile of a whole arch. Here, for once, this point of contact was able to bring the imagination to bear on the whole space, whose columns and vault one could imagine as belonging to the house in which the opera is set.

PETER BROOK: *I think that the continued success of any theatre space depends on finding and maintaining a very delicate balance between a form and its contents. By 'form' I mean the quality of the vessel, the container, its capacity to accept or reject, to inspire or neutralize the different 'contents' – the events, the dramatic creation – with which it is brought to life. One is insepara-*

Pelléas in the
Bockenheimer Depot

ble from the other: they are mutually dependent. The contents
must be sufficiently vital to attract a lively public, to keep the
venue warm; and the form must be sufficiently generous and
accommodating to allow this life to take shape without impedi-
ment.

If one of the two parties is lacking, this will always lead to
something deadly and artificial. The legend of the Golem illus-
trates this well. An inventor tries to create a robot. He takes all the
right materials – metal, circuitry, bolts, and so on – and creates
an ingenious machine. But when he expects it to come to life he is
confronted with an impossibility: these forms do not suffice; they
cannot supply the necessary vital spark. Something essential is
missing – the robot remains a lifeless machine.

One sees, unfortunately, too many theatre spaces conceived of
by architects whose thought process mirrors that of the robot's
inventor. They see only as far as the vessel: they do not understand that what they do is necessarily incomplete in the case of a
theatre. In some cases there seems to be a rigidity, a fear, in the
spaces – a refusal to accept the need for openness in their forms;
a retreat into inflexible and deadening materials and structures.
As a consequence, there are many modern spaces that reject

almost all attempts to breathe life into them.

It is not just architects who are to blame for this: we must also face the fact that, far too often, the mayor of town X wishes to build a theatre (or a library or a museum) whose sense of permanence and monumentality will forcefully suggest the extension of his or her tenure beyond the next elections. In the case of a library or a museum this does not necessarily pose a problem; but politicians are by their nature reluctant to enshrine themselves in an ephemeral form, so they welcome a theatre built to last many lifetimes. Unfortunately the result is lifeless.

One must also consider the question of time in the creation of theatre spaces. I remember Peter Hall coming to see the Bouffes du Nord as we were transforming it in order to be able to play Timon of Athens *there in 1974 – a frantic process which lasted three months in all. He looked on wistfully, and explained that the National Theatre in London had just encountered another problem in its construction process and its opening had been postponed by another year after what had already been a ten-year wait. I remember thinking at the time that half of the eminent people assembled to form the steering committee for its design were already dead. In a similar manner today, even with accelerated construction procedures and streamlined forms of management, one sees that a theatre director who decides to build or seriously overhaul his or her space is rarely still there when it opens. The problem here is that, very often, the nature of the 'contents' has changed substantially before the 'form', which has been designed in their image, is finished. The trick is to find a way in which the ephemerality of the performance can leave a trace on the permanent character of the space. There has to be some kind of blending or smudging, some delicate cross-fertilization between the two at a certain level.*

Some people have tried to respond to this by creating 'polyvalent' or infinitely flexible theatres – contraptions as ingenious and as empty as the robot Golem, which can be by turns Elizabethan, frontal, in the round, or promenade. There are several problems which commonly arise in this situation. The first is that these spaces are extremely expensive to build and also very expensive to operate. (It is ironic that there will almost always be the extra funds necessary for construction, almost never for the functioning of the space.) The second is that these spaces are often designed in the image of the technology which allows all this manoeuvring; when used, this celebrates its own prowess rather than the character of the event which the theatre is ultimately designed to embrace. Even in the cases where there is a sensitivity in the design, it is extremely difficult to accommodate so many different forms and proportions in a harmonious manner. Ironically, we have found the Bouffes du Nord – small, poorly equipped, with great constraints regarding access – to be a marvellously 'polyvalent' theatre, perfectly formed to accept modern dance, classical music and jazz, and even wholesale transformations such as the giant box and balconies installed by Luca Ronconi for his Verso Peer Gynt *(or the small space for* Oh les beaux jours *described in the next chapter). Without changing the walls, the Bouffes can be a street corner, a temple, a Russian country house or a desert; its flexibility is legitimized by its strong, fixed identity. It is like rediscovering a familiar face from a slightly different angle.*

As far as our touring spaces are concerned, our opening of a new venue sidesteps some of the problems associated with theatre-building for several obvious and very practical reasons. First, we cannot wait five years for concrete to be poured and complex technical rigs to be installed. We always act in the heat of the moment. Very often venues have to be chosen even before the shape of the production is established – we have only a contour or a vague reference which I can communicate to Jean-Guy before he goes out into the world to try to find a suitable space. Given the scope of our tours, the quantity of work is enormous, and one cannot hesitate long before deciding on a venue and its disposition – work which becomes a form of improvisation not unlike that performed by the actors in their own creative process. Second, we have the advantage in our work of always leading with a notion of the contents rather than the form. The needs are similar to those that guide one when buying a new overcoat: it has to fit well and keep out the cold, and can also add some expression of one's character, without being so ostentatious as to distract attention from the person it covers.

At the end of the day we are not theatre architects. Our first and only priority is to find a space for our current project. Of course we are delighted if local artists or a city administration decide afterwards that they like a space and want to keep it, but it is then no longer ours. The challenge to keep the form in a responsive state, and to find the appropriate contents, necessarily belongs to the people who inherit the space and assume the responsibility for keeping it alive. Only rarely would one intervene – as I did in Hamburg, where it was touch and go as to whether the city would keep the Kampnagel-factory site, and I lobbied the mayor very strongly to keep the space as an alternative venue for young companies.

But, sadly, we have seen that over the years the balance between a form and its contents has not always been successfully maintained. Some spaces which were rough in a poetic and imaginative sense have gradually declined into becoming simply sordid and eventually miserable. Others have gone equally deplorably in the opposite direction and become more and more respectable and what the French call 'endimanché'– in their Sunday best – with the addition of comfortable seating, cloak-rooms and art galleries, and have gradually lost the character that made the space interesting and, most importantly, unlike any other theatre. But we have to be realistic about our role in this: one cannot control the future, and one mustn't try to.

Lisbon

The cloister/garage of the Convento do Beato António had a less unhappy fate than these spaces. At the time of the tour of *Pelléas* (thirteen years after *The Conference of the Birds*), hardly anything had changed. The whole place had been consider-

The cloister with new translucent roof

ably spruced up, but fortunately not to the detriment of its basic character. The terracotta tiles had been covered with a wooden floor, the cloister arcade had been sandblasted, the public entrance had been made permanent, and, while remaining in the centre of the factory complex, the space had been in occasional use for recitals and concerts. The impulse to recover the qualities of the cloister had spread into other parts of the former monastery, where the principal stair had been restored and was being used as a feature in the offices of the company.

The wooden flooring was easy to remove, and the basins for *Pelléas* were sunk directly into the tiled floor, which again became the basic playing surface. The carpets, chairs and screens from the Paris production fitted in well with the monastic architecture, which had a fluidity which enabled it to suggest both indoors and outdoors (perhaps assisted by the memory of having been a garden). Its depths and shadows

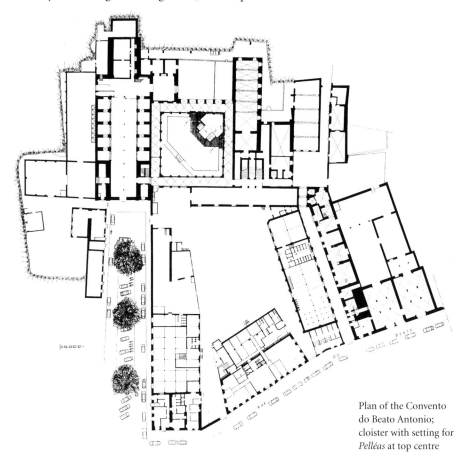

Plan of the Convento do Beato Antonio; cloister with setting for *Pelléas* at top centre

were exploited to great atmospheric effect by Jean Kalman's lighting. The owners of the space had stretched a blue cloth under the roof structure, but, like the wooden flooring, this was easily removed. The wise decision not to install permanent seating allowed the inexpensive reconstruction of the original configuration, except that this time the three blocks were joined up, adding an extra 100 places.

*Gaston Bachelard, *La poétique de l'espace*, p. 131.

*Ibid.

Jean-Guy Lecat: *A corner is a kind of semi-box, 'half wall, half door' according to the philosopher Gaston Bachelard.* To close the 'door' side here, we built a tier of seats for about 400 people. The stage and the public were on the same axis: one of the corners of the cloister. For Bachelard, 'in a corner you have the feeling of being at peace, an imaginary room extends around your body as in the centre of a house'.* The imagination is free to let itself go and extend beyond the reality of a situation. At the same time, the cloister's two walls contained and related the seating, making each spectator more present, more involved.*

But a corner can also become a space that is too self-enclosing, and lose these accommodating qualities. Luckily, in our case, the walls of the cloister were opened up by great vaults. Two of the

Pelléas in Lisbon

sides of the triangular walls were pierced with large vaulted aper-
tures that enabled the actors to penetrate the centre of the space,
creating permeable walls that thus avoided a disastrous effect of
concentration. The perspective effect in theatre gives the audience
the unpleasant impression that the actors diminish in size when
they walk towards a corner. The eye cannot make a measurement
in front of them and always needs some reference; in this case the
reference is perspective.

Glasgow and Zurich

Both productions visited Tramway in Glasgow and the Gess-
nerallee Theater in Zurich. The Scottish venue had kept the
red back wall from *The Mahabharata* unchanged; the space
was used exactly as it had been before (in the case of *The Tempest*, the only occasion on which a red background was used).
The Gessnerallee space – unused since it was opened with
Timon of Athens – had been cleaned up and transformed into
a permanent theatre. The walls were freshly painted and not in
tune with the worlds of either show; therefore the Braunschweig decor was redeployed.

The Tempest and *Pelléas*
at Tramway

JEAN-GUY LECAT: *Each time I am in Zurich (the city that invites Peter Brook more than any other) I revisit the Gessner-allee space and every time the same problem of the infiltration of street noise arises. At the time of* The Tempest *the city was planning to transform the building permanently to resolve this problem. The space, an old riding school, is apparently fine, even beautiful, with a good acoustic, but curiously we have never been able to use it totally empty with success. There is a question of proportion: it is too wide for its height and so gives the audience the negative impression of a large empty stage. For* The Tempest

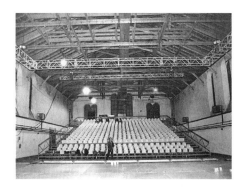

The seating structure in Zurich before and after transformation for *The Tempest*

we thought we could use the set that Chloe Obolensky had imagined for the city of Braunschweig. She had reduced the space and created very useful wings. One of the set's advantages is that its timber structure was built on site and we only had to transport the white gauzes. The transparency of gauze to sound (in contrast to curtains, which absorb sound and make a dead acoustic) allowed us to control the acoustics more easily with wood panels behind the decorations.

Madrid: *Impressions de Pelléas* in the Teatro de la Comedia

Two significant modifications of older theatres were undertaken for *Impressions de Pelléas*, drawing their inspiration from the temporary transformation of the Teatro Argentina six years previously. Unlike with *La Tragédie de Carmen*, however, there were specific objects and scenic elements to be installed in relation to the architecture of the different theatres.

In Madrid there was an excellent natural rapport between the theatre and the 'scenery'. The Teatro de la Comedia was

The Teatro de la Comedia before transformation

built in the nineteenth century with a Moorish decorative scheme. This chimed well with the ornate, eclectic ambience of the production's Persian carpets and Victorian furniture. This theatre is very intimate: only 13 metres across at its widest point, 12 metres high, and 15 metres from the balcony to the proscenium. As in Rome, new benches were installed which joined the first level of the balcony to the stage-side seats in a single slope. A new performing surface was built up over the stalls, marrying perfectly with the existing stage. Its wooden surface was painted black, with a finishing coat of red varnish. There was a comfortable joining between this new level and the side balconies: meeting at just the right height, the two elements looked as if they belonged naturally together. The elaborate metallic decoration of the guard rail and the first part of the proscenium arch worked in harmony with the pool, creating a circuit with the environment of the opera; the audience members in the box seats had an exceptionally intimate view of the action.

It should be noted that these elements were only *atmospherically* associated with the drama: as at the Bouffes, the building was not physically incorporated – it was not touched and penetrated. Unlike in *La Tragédie de Carmen*, there were few entrances and exits, and the only occasion on which another place was invoked during an entry was during the return from the hunt, when the singers came in through the audience; otherwise the focus was on the intense, limited world of the tragedy.

An acoustic reflector was installed just behind the proscenium arch, almost at the level of the opening: this served to bounce the sound of the pianos out into the auditorium, and

Madrid: as transformed

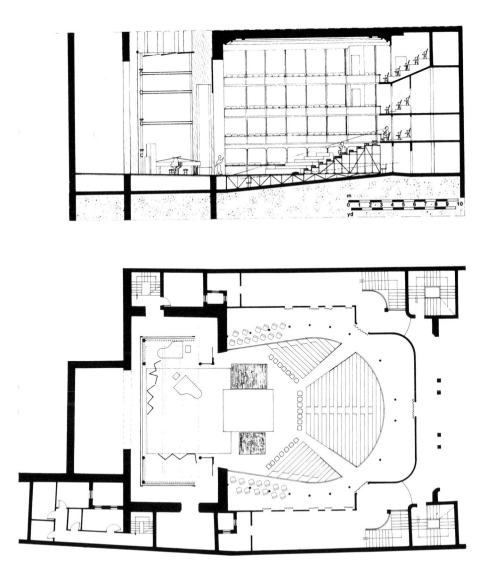

prevented echoes in the tall flytower volume.

This environment was shared by 500 people (rather than the normal capacity of 880). As in many other venues, the Centre had to resist the pressure from the host producer to install more seats and sell the places with a reduced quality of view in the new configuration (typically the higher balconies, which have a too-vertical view of the action).

Hamburg: The Deutsches Schauspielhaus

This installation was repeated two months later for a three-week run at the Deutsches Schauspielhaus in Hamburg. The differences here lay in the existing architecture (in an over-powering turn-of-the-century baroque style) and in the culture of the host theatre company (there was a huge technical staff, who transformed the auditorium in an incredible thirty-six hours). The space was bigger than in Madrid, and the proscenium opening particularly imposing. The 'faux' arch from the Bouffes had to be closed down to a somewhat uncomfortable extent, exposing more than 2 metres of red curtain at either side. Otherwise the marriage with the build-

ing was successful: there was a smooth union between the new seating and the deep first balcony, creating the sense of a single body of people. (The few rows of seats – amounting to 300 of the 1,000 places – which were suppressed were sacrificed not so much because of poor visibility, but because they felt out of contact with the mass of the audience.) Box seats, which had awkward sight lines but a very intimate relationship to the action, were sold to students for 10 DM – significantly below the rather high prices charged for the rest of the places.

As a general rule, a little room is left for the host city to express its qualities in the details of the transformation. Here the fearsomely efficient technical team used elegant, rigorous seats instead of the makeshift curves of cushion shared by the audience members in Rome and Madrid, and even the stage-side cushions were neat, firm cylinders, which, because of fire regulations, were attached to the floor.

The Tempest at Les Taillades

The line of spatial exploration carried out during the 1980s was, as we have seen, reduced in scope for these two produc-

Les Taillades before transformation

tions. There was, however, one important new transformation of an exterior space, which corresponded perfectly to the world of *The Tempest*.

This production had been due to have its premiere at the Avignon Festival in 1990, but an extension of the rehearsal period meant that these performances were cancelled: they were put off until the next year, at the end of a European tour. It was clear from the beginning that the Callet quarry would have been too vast for this tightly focused production, whose geometry, furthermore, was marked by right angles rather than the curves of *The Mahabharata*. Fortunately the researches carried out in 1984–5 had been so exhaustive that an immediate mental map could be consulted of all the quarries within a 60-kilometre radius of Avignon. At the south-eastern extremity of this orbit lies a tiny village called Les Taillades, nestled under the first ridge of the Lubéron mountains. The hill on which the settlement was founded in the Middle Ages had been quarried away when the population moved down into the plains to pursue agricultural activities. Thus the 'town centre' now consists of a square void roughly 26 by 26 metres, with the church and houses improbably perched on the rim,

The entrance to the quarry

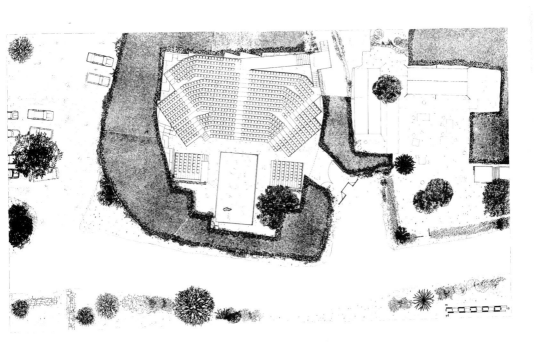

and new windows carved through from basements peering into the space. The accidental and the purposeful interpenetrate here in a lazy, relaxed way: there are a few steps leading to nowhere carved into the rock at the base of the quarry; at the top, a gracefully moulded corner of the rock sprouts a masonry wall which follows the lip around and springs into an arch over a gap in the rock face; the arch in turn carries a street above.

This urban curiosity served no particular purpose until the local mayor decided to attract tourists with concerts in the summer, and built a low concrete stage against one of the walls. The wall to the left of this presented a more auspicious background for *The Tempest*: it was framed by a fig tree on the left and by a lush spread of ivy which filled the right-hand corner. The long rectangle of sand could extend under the tree, some of whose branches would be tied back to permit passage beneath. The whole of the facing side of the quarry was filled with a broad rake of seats, with two smaller side blocks framing the acting area and forming a zone for the musicians. Side walls were built from the kind of stone found in the quarry; electrical services were buried in a trench, and the lighting was

Opposite: The last performance of *The Tempest* (Jean-Claude Carrière at centre with light coloured trousers)

suspended from behind the rim of the quarry and concealed as much as possible within the ivy. Drainage could not be regulated as in Boulbon, because there was only one opening through which water could leave the space. (A late-afternoon storm once left parallel streams of red earth and white sand tracing this path.)

The approach sequence consisted of a pathway winding uphill around the quarry, giving a glimpse of the whole before one stepped over the rim and descended the aisles to fill up the auditorium from the front. The acoustic was naturally intimate, and the manner in which the stone tightly embraced the world of the play and the audience further concentrated the sense of togetherness. As in the Callet quarry, the evening began in the shared light of sunset, before focusing down at nightfall to the brightly lit sand defining a zone at once apart – a launchpad for imagination – and present, indistinguishable from our world, materially united to the Provençal stone and sky.

JEAN-GUY LECAT: *For some of our performances we have deliberately chosen places that embody the twofold presence of man and nature:* The Conference of the Birds, The Mahabharata *and* The Tempest *were set in quarries. We were in a space which was both enclosed, since it was circumscribed, and open, because you could see the sky above. We had just what we wanted: the reality of being both inside, with the intimacy and the acoustics needed for a play, and outside, so that the audience had the sensation of freedom given by this opening.*

We noticed that the actual presence of the sky and earth were extraordinary supports for these performances. Before every performance of The Conference of the Birds *a flight of swallows would flit across the stage to encourage us. In* The Tempest, *Ariel and Caliban became the brutal embodiments of the elements that had generated them. In* The Mahabharata, *the primitive presence of the four elements (air, fire, earth and water) restored the fundamental dimensions of the complex battles between men, demigods and demons.*

The presence of the earth – source of life and foundation of existence – as well as the walls of stone, satisfied the desire of the people in the quarry for protection. And yet this nature needed human intervention to become natural once again, to revert to a more authentic meaning. We used artifice – going so far as to change the position of the trees and rocks, and alter the level of the ground, to achieve a 'natural' balance.

8 : The Acting Island:
From *The Man Who* to *The Tragedy of Hamlet*

> If there is an art to the theatre, it is not an aesthetic art,
> which is secondary, but an art of concentration.
> PETER BROOK

Works from the last half-decade, such as *The Man Who*, *Je suis un phénomène* and *The Tragedy of Hamlet,* have seen a shrinking away from the architecture of the Bouffes du Nord towards a pure, abstract, self-contained world of precise theatrical gesture.

The production which initiated this line of research was *The Man Who* (inspired by Oliver Sacks's book *The Man Who Mistook His Wife For a Hat*), in which patients suffering from neurological disorders are questioned and examined by doctors. The play consists of a series of 'sketches', each lasting a few

Sotigui Kouyaté and Maurice Bénichou: the Man from La Rochelle sequence in *The Man Who*

minutes, which resume a medical consultation. In the text these 'cases' are generally identified as belonging to specific medical categories such as autism, but not so in performance: we are simply confronted with human beings who are mysteriously detached from our received way of viewing the world, without a trace of psychological disturbance (other than that provoked by the crippling effects of the neurological disorder). There are cases such as a man who is unable to perceive the left-hand side of objects, spaces and himself; a man whose memory recalls only the last few minutes; and a man who, unable to see because of an injury to his optic nerve, is nevertheless able to grasp, as if he could see them, objects placed in the space in front of him. The clinical atmosphere initially established built up into a meditation on the mysterious nature of our sense of being in the world. It required an acting ability of enormous precision, absolutely devoid of 'effect': the aim was to show the histories of real patients in an almost documentary, transparent manner.

The natural materials – earth, water, clay, sand – with which the theatre had been filled since the early 1980s clearly had little to offer to the world of a play such as this. The play required a certain kind of naturalism, but not something so strong as to make us forget that we were observing an act of theatre. The actors performed in unobtrusive contemporary dress, with the addition of doctors' coats and pyjamas to denote specific roles in a simple way. The sand and compacted earth of *The Tempest* was cleared away, but one element of that production remained: it was found that the acting area defined by the bamboo poles and rock had proportions which suited the new work perfectly. For *The Man Who* this zone (roughly 6 by 7.5 metres) was filled with a simple industrially made wool carpet set into a wooden platform some 17 centimetres high (the height of one step in a flight of stairs) which was placed on the black floor of the theatre. (The rectangle was longer in depth to give the illusion of a square shape when seen from the middle of the auditorium in perspective.) Upon this island, detached from the material world of the Bouffes, there were a few chairs (made specially for the production to an austere, modern design – but without a self-conscious 'style'), a table and two televisions. The televisions and a video camera operated by one of the 'doctors' were used to show what the play's 'patients' were drawing on the table, to show the patients their own actions, and to present at the end a series of images of the brain.

The platform presented as neutral a playing surface as possible, but this neutrality was carefully crafted with respect to the colours and shape of the theatre. The carpet was clearly taken from a roll, unlike the Persian carpets of *The Conference of the Birds*, *The Cherry Orchard* and *Impressions de Pelléas*. But the hand of the director had 'cut' the carpet to give it its identity in the theatre, framed by the border of the platform: it was not an imported object with a life of its own. Nevertheless, it remained a flexible frame for the drama, a launchpad for the imagination. It gave a specific hint of the antiseptic world of a

The Man Who at –
The Bouffes du Nord

The Odeon in Vienna

The Berliner Ensemble
Theatre

Qui est là? at the
Schaubühne in Berlin

doctor's surgery, but, when 'doctor' Sotigui Kouyaté took 'patient' Maurice Bénichou to look at the sea (in the section entitled 'The Man From La Rochelle'), the edge of the platform became the edge of the ocean.

> **BRUCE MYERS:** *This was fundamentally different from the other work, in that the platform is a* decor. *The platform represents nothing other than the desire to install the actors in a world which is absolutely clear and clean, and to have a certain image of the hospital environment. One knows that, having taken the step up on to the platform, one is acting: you don't step off until you're finished. It's completely different from drawing a square on the ground with chalk: one would then be freer, closer to improvisation.*
>
> *Despite the separation of this world, the walls of the Bouffes still count: they exist by themselves, not in relation to the modern world of the platform with its television screens. Everything counts – each detail, each staircase, the colours – in forming the 'shell' in which it is appropriate to insert this alien zone.*

On Tour

> **PETER BROOK:** *A platform serves to pinpoint an action, and the moment you have a platform everything around it becomes pure space. We've almost always found that the best equivalent to the walls of the Bouffes on tour is the black-velvet curtain: in other words, indeterminate space, the focus on the boxing ring. The Bouffes is black velvet in a superior version – a nothingness which is full of life. But this is what makes it unique. To imitate Bouffeness with some red-painted flats, roughened up and ageified, would be hideous.*
>
> *We found after a long search that real hospital furniture wouldn't work in this environment. We had to invent our own chairs – chairs which had the characteristics of being purely functional, certainly imaginable for sale (and therefore not merely 'theatrical'), and at one with the piece in that their severity gave them more in common with a hospital than with a salon. Linoleum would have been over-realistic. Wall-to-wall-style carpeting was just enough to suggest an interior, and to deny ever so slightly the obvious hospital associations.*

The Man Who undertook a tour which was as extensive as that of *The Mahabharata* (over 500 performances in Europe,

Asia, South Africa, and North and South America). However, the nature of the production did not require ambitious spatial transformations, and this permitted a more flexible itinerary which took in conventional theatres in the provinces of England and France. (In fact the tour was the first which took place almost exclusively in purpose-built theatres.) There were, however, still basic conditions of intimacy and acoustic clarity to consider – not all of which were met successfully by the host spaces as they were found.

Much of the tour used the kind of neutral modern theatres which would never have been appropriate for *The Mahabharata* or *La Tragédie de Carmen* – including relatively anonymous spaces in Lausanne, Rennes, Buenos Aires and Tokyo. In each case the quality of the host architecture had little importance, as long as the basic conditions of intimacy were satisfied. In the dullest of spaces the placing of the audience around the same level as the acting platform, with a few rows forming the customary embrace at the sides, was all that was needed. Curtains were suspended wherever necessary to create the right proportion or to kill a too reverberant acoustic.

Lacking strong material presence, these spaces saw an exclusive focus on *human* relationships. Minute differences in attentiveness, tone and response took on great importance, especially in a tour of the British provinces.

> MARIE-HÉLÈNE ESTIENNE: *People laughed out loud almost everywhere during the tour of England, which amazed us. But in Manchester (at the Contact Theatre) there was complete silence – the only place in Europe and America where this happened. It was disturbing at first, but one has to accept the audience*

> BRUCE MYERS: *Now there's an almost unconscious shared ability to adapt the playing to different spaces, in spite of the great precision of a show like* The Man Who. *One makes a tiny modification in intensity or energy, but not in gesture: it's a mysterious thing, not objectively apparent.*

The Centre had not performed in London since a very brief visit of *Ubu* to the Young Vic in 1978. That the performances of *The Man Who* should be at the National Theatre made the run doubly auspicious: Brook had served on the committee which oversaw the design of this building in the 1960s and '70s. The Cottesloe, the National's 'experimental' studio theatre, was packed to bursting for the Centre's performances, and the scale of the space gave rise to an intimate, attentive atmosphere.

For a return visit a year later the Cottesloe was not available. Richard Eyre suggested the Lyttelton: its stage was built on hydraulic lifts, so the traditional step up could be eliminated. The stage had never been lowered, however, and it was quickly discovered that there was a major problem: the sight lines from the balcony had been calculated for the raised position, so nobody behind the front row would be able to see the action of *The Man Who* clearly. In the event this didn't matter: the overall volume of the theatre was too big, and the balcony was closed off with a curtain (the front row being kept for latecomers).

Spaces opened earlier were revisited. The back walls of the Gessnerallee Theater were covered with black curtains. The BAM Majestic was screened off like the Lyttelton, the balcony closed off entirely and the stalls seating reduced by half. The back wall – still painted as it had been for *The Mahabharata* – was left alone, but black curtains were suspended at the sides to reduce the volume and close in the acoustic. Some new seats were added at the sides of the platform to create an even greater intimacy than before. In Glasgow, Tramway's red wall was, for once, covered up with a black curtain:

> ROBERT PALMER: *Tramway has proved itself to be a marvellously flexible arts centre over the last fifteen years: in the space opened for* The Mahabharata *and the other space we were able to conserve adjoining it, we've had art exhibitions and installations, concerts, dance, rock music, children's shows, social gatherings, even weddings. People like Robert LePage and Patricia Brown have been happy to take the space as it is: they like the warm atmosphere, the solidity of the back wall.*
>
> *There have been times when the venue has become a political issue: during the lean years of the early 1990s it was used as a symbol of elitism identified with Pat Lally, the council leader who had originally approved its creation. Now, happily, it is undergoing a thorough re-evaluation. This has brought up all sorts of interesting questions. There is now a vibrant younger generation of artists who were too young to see* The Mahabharata, *and they are uncertain what to make of the 'Brook' wall. Perhaps they will change everything. One of the key stipulations we gave to the architects of the renovation is that their space*

should 'inspire but not impose'. It should be flexible, and it should not lose the presence of the old industrial space. Whatever happens, I hope that Tramway will never be 'finished'. It's sad to note, though, that regulations concerning fire safety and access have tightened to such an extent in the last ten years that it would be out of the question to create another space like this today.

Woza Albert

JEAN-GUY LECAT Woza Albert *was created at the Bouffes du Nord with almost no set, just a painted floor and four lighting masts 5 metres high forming a square around the acting area, illuminating the centre as if they were street lights, and a pallet serving as a table, a shop front, etc. Working with Peter, I have observed that the lack of a set gives the actors great freedom; they have minimal elements as a starting point to connect with the imagination of the audience, and using objects against their normal function seems to increase their power.*

Woza Albert at the
Bouffes du Nord

Our tour took in an ornate nineteenth-century theatre in Seville with balconies, boxes and a slightly raked 1-metre high

217

Seville and Milan

stage. We never play on a stage; but here the lights created a space which was an extension of the box fronts, as if they were part of a street with a square at one end; and the stage, as an obstacle, disappeared. In Milan, later, an abandoned theatre wrapped itself around the lights as if they were part of a rough cityscape.

It's quite simple: if the space can help the play, we have kept it; if it is too strong, we have transformed it or hidden it. There are no fixed rules why this should be so in either case. If I can conclude one thing from twenty-five years of working with Peter Brook, it would be this: 'The more we show, the less we say.'

Oh les beaux jours

Brook's production of Samuel Beckett's *Oh les beaux jours* (*Happy Days*) was not created at the Bouffes du Nord. When it played there as part of its tour the theatre was completely transformed. The play required a frontal relationship to give coherence to the *tableau vivant* of Natasha Parry's Winnie buried in her earthy mound, with her taciturn husband, Willie, hidden behind. Their world was delimited by a white

THE ACTING ISLAND

cyclorama, and the ground-level banks of seating were rear-ranged into a single unified tier stretching from the proscenium up to the level of the first balcony (which thereby became part of a single, continuous slope of heads). The theatre as we have known it as a rich presence seemed to disappear: the side walls were unlit and had nothing to do with the world of the play, being out of the active field of vision of most of the audience; the back walls were masked by the cyclorama; and the theatre's sense of height evaporated with the direction of all the gazes towards one stationary point.

NATASHA PARRY: *The Bouffes gave extraordinary intimacy for this performance. But one thing which didn't work at all was the curtain: it didn't fit either in front of or behind the arch (where it wouldn't go up far enough). The theatre didn't seem happy about it at all. So we had what felt at first like an awkward business of me walking on in the dark and getting installed in the mound in front of the audience, then flopping forward and waiting for the lights to come up. After a while, however, this felt perfectly natural. Everybody knows the play, so the surprise given by the curtain rising on this extremely memorable* tableau vivant *has rather lost its force.*

On tour there were some spaces which were extremely difficult, where you felt immense separation from the audience. Very few spaces, in fact, helped the play, though one of the exceptions was the Riverside Studios in London – a space which was dear to Beckett – where the steeper than usual slope of the seating gave a greater intimacy and helped me feel that I could be in contact with everyone. It's very hard in this play to look down at the audience from a raised stage; you feel like you lose the audience. The theatre I found most difficult was a big old space in Marseille, which was so vast I felt I was on the stage in Covent Garden, with the audience watching through opera glasses. It always takes a few days to get to know a space. In Marseille, rather than reaching out, I had to learn how to draw the audience in, how to be aware of all the space. In this sense the acoustic, the ability to sense one's own echo back from the audience, is perhaps the most important thing for establishing a link, an exchange. Even at the Bouffes one has to work on this, being careful with the ends of lines.

The Bouffes is a theatre which tends to demand movement and energy in order to share the performance around the circle. In Oh les beaux jours *the scope for this is obviously limited: one* can only move at first arms and upper body, then only the head, and in both cases only when Beckett says to do so!

JEAN-GUY LECAT: *A very strange acoustic effect occurred during the rehearsals. The large volume behind the proscenium is very reverberant, and we had suspended curtains around this space to diminish the echo. This made the sound so dead that Natasha couldn't hear herself. I proposed adding wooden panels behind the set on either side and facing her way. She said the effect was a little better. Next day we needed one of the panels and so removed it. That day Natasha told us that the acoustic was perfect. In each city on the subsequent tour we added this panel at the same place, without ever being able to explain why only one panel was better than two.*

PETER BROOK: *Although it was a tour de force to transform the* Bouffes *for* Oh les beaux jours, *I don't think we'd do it again if we had the opportunity to perform it another time here, because something about the theatre was lost. Many people regretted coming into the space and it not feeling like the Bouffes, all the attention being focused on the decor. If we did it again I would put Natasha in the middle of the acting area with the earth spreading out from the mound in every direction as far as the walls – a real desert!*

Don Giovanni

PETER BROOK: *One is always looking for reality, which is the exact opposite of what is known as operatic realism. The problem with operatic realism is that it is totally unrealistic. There are certain works – such as Janácek's – which seem naturally to take place in a solid world, but most operas take place in the imagination. In Mozart there is one work which has to be set concretely, which is* The Marriage of Figaro. *Every element is palpable, and a* Figaro *that took place in no man's land would be utterly flat. Even if there's no scenery, there has to be a high degree of realism through the props, the costumes, the acting.* Don Giovanni, *on the other hand, is a myth which takes place in a nowhere which is like the nowhere of* King Lear *or* Hamlet *– in other words, a storytellers' background. In the same way that the Egypt of* The Magic Flute *does not exist, the Italianized Spain of* Don Giovanni *is also something which can exist only in the imagination.*

From the very start I wondered how one could evoke this with

Don Giovanni in
rehearsal at the Théâtre
de l'Archevêché in Aix:
Peter Brook at right,
Claudio Abbado con-
ducting

*the simplicity and pureness that responds to a musical event. I
thought of doing everything with lines, with posts, sticks that
folded, space defined purely by lines within a rigidly defined
musical idiom designated by classical rules, which Mozart always
followed strictly but with a certain playfulness. What could be
both strict and playful? We thought that brightly coloured lines
could do this, being rigorous and vibrant at the same time. Used
in different dispositions, they could articulate the space, create
situations for people sitting in different positions, going behind,
and so on. Unfortunately they became technically cumbersome
as we developed them. We tried having them collapse and fold
up, or flown in, but they became too much of a burden on the
theatrical energy of the piece. We ended up using simply poles,
which could be manipulated to define areas, used playfully as
lances, and so on. The most technically complex effect involved
having a 'forest' made from the suspended poles slowly rise into
the flytower to represent the descent of Don Giovanni into hell.*

In Carmen, *on our own territory and with a small chamber
orchestra, it was no problem to divide the musicians and place
them at the back. We made many experiments for* Don Giovanni, *putting the orchestra at the back and the side, but the sheer
number of musicians required by Mozart's score made this
impossible. We tried making the orchestra really visible, right in
the middle of the stage, but the conductor would have his back to
the audience, or be out of contact working through closed-circuit
television. In the end there was no way around for a fifty-piece
orchestra, so we accepted the pit and jutted the acting area out as
far as possible, leaving the conductor just enough room to see the
whole orchestra and the stage. On tour we had better luck than at
the open-air theatre where we played in Aix-en-Provence, where
the stage was very wide; in Brussels we played in a vast circus
where we could bring the platform and the orchestra out into the*

space, with the audience a little on the sides, and this was as close as we could get to the sort of relationship that we like.

Qui est là?

For *Qui est là?* – a research work taking the text of *Hamlet* as a point of departure – the furniture from *The Man Who* was simply painted dark brown and was manipulated to form different settings in the play (a bed, a throne, the stage for the players). The carpet itself was literally folded into the action: it was wrapped around a fallen chair to denote Ophelia's grave. The only objects which imported an outside 'style' were two large brass candlesticks standing behind the acting platform: these served to delimit the space of the theatre behind the acting area, declaring the back space as 'elsewhere'.

> PETER BROOK: *People have remarked that the proportions of some of our spaces and objects are canonical – a rectangle with sides in the ratio of 1:√2, for example, for the screen used during the players' scene in* Qui est là?. *In reality these forms are arrived at through intuition and practical constraints: in this case we were recycling a table from* The Man Who, *and asked the actor who would appear behind the piece of furniture how high we should put the frame so that it was comfortable for him. Proportioning systems such as Le Corbusier's Modulor, based on the golden section, are fascinating in as much as they take the human form as the root (and, in a way, metaphorical) structure for relating things in space to our perception and presence, and I understand the value of such systems when creating new spaces at a large scale. In the theatre, however, we see that the force of a human presence is linked to myriad factors, some of which are extremely subjective and shifting. For this reason there can never be a Modulor for the theatre. If one applies a formula or a scheme of any sort, one imposes a straitjacket on the living event. But if one goes about it the other way, using intuition, followed not blindly, but by trial and error, then sometimes a miracle occurs. At the end of the process, a specialist arrives and says, 'Bravo, you've made a golden section!'*

As with *The Man Who*, the aim here was to create a neutral theatrical ground upon which the craft of the actor would have the full responsibility for evoking a given world. In *Qui est là?* the scenes from *Hamlet* were interspersed with state-

ments by great dramatic thinkers of the past (such as Zeami, Artaud, Stanislavsky); acting itself was the preoccupation (as it is throughout *Hamlet*), and the 'scenic' elements of the production served to place the actor on view – alone, without support – completely clearly.

Yoshi Oida as the Player King is *Qui Est Là?* with (*l–r*) Bakary Sangaré as Hamlet, David Bennent, Mahmoud Tabrizi-Zadeh and Bruce Myers

On tour it was found, again, that 'neutral', 'black-box' spaces were often congenial to the show, but they almost always required some reconfiguration to create a more intimate atmosphere in both acoustic and social terms. The acting 'island' demanded a certain disposition, a certain set of proportions to be formed around it, and this shape was rarely provided automatically: seats had to be moved; new rows were placed on either side of the stage to form an embrace. For all that the setting was 'neutral', the essential factor in such a work – the relationship with the audience, their ability to share the intricacy of the gestures, and to add their own attention to complete the event – was something that had to be negotiated in each venue every bit as carefully as the gestures of the actors themselves. In fact the spaces themselves were never neutral – each had its biases and peculiarities which had to be confronted and worked with to create the right balance. One minor but revealing difference in the staging between the Bouffes and the touring spaces was the addition of an extension of the acting area's white carpet on the the two sides, reaching under the feet of the front row of the public. (It was therefore on the level of the floor, not the platform.) The curves of the Bouffes had provided a sufficient sense of unity; rectilinear modern theatres lacked something by comparison, and an extra bridging factor had to be added in these spaces.

Je suis un phénomène

Je suis un phénomène – written by Brook and Marie-Hélène Estienne – followed in this line both in spatial terms and with regard to subject matter. The theme of the play was once again the mind – in this case the mind of the celebrated Russian mnemonist Solomon Shereshevsky, and in particular his relationship with the neurologist Alexander Luria. It was as if one of the case histories from *The Man Who* had become the subject of an entire play, which went beyond the rigour of the examination room and began to look at the cultural and philosophical ramifications of a neurological 'problem' – in

Je suis un phénomène at the Teatro Trindade in Lisbon

this case, the inability to forget anything. The staging followed closely the 'island' line described earlier, this time with furniture with a slightly more domestic accent (the *Man Who* chairs with padded backs and familiar domestic objects such as table settings). The televisions were still present, but were used in an altogether different manner. They were turned on end to give a vertical format, and, instead of projecting images of the drama, they presented a visual commentary on Shereshevsky's feats of memory. Using the language of interactive computer displays, with animated text, fades between images, playful displacements of objects and photographs, they provided a correlative for his descriptions of mnemological methods, of improbable acts of recall of series of numbers etc., and also served to prompt notions of different settings (clinic, home, and, in a present-day coda, New York).

Le Costume

The South African domestic tragicomedy *Le Costume* was presented in the same staging format as these works, but with a certain added colour to bring home its specific cultural setting. There was no raised platform, just a recognizably African patterned carpet in the same format and position as the neutral wall-to-wall style flooring used in the *The Man Who* and *Je suis un phénomène*. The carpet corresponded roughly in size to the tiny Soweto apartment in which much of the drama takes place, and, apart from a fateful bed which was present throughout in the centre, all other settings and activities (washing, cooking) were evoked through mime rather than through actual props or objects. In a manner reminiscent of earlier works such as *Ubu aux Bouffes*, accessory objects such

The setting for *Le Costume* at the Théâtre de la Place in Liège

as a coat-hanging rail were subjected to '*détournement*' and employed imaginatively as other elements: the coat rail became a window, or, leaning against the bed with three men sitting inside it, it was an impromptu bus shelter, outside of which the rain was pouring down. The theme of inanimate objects taking on a life of their own was in fact central to the piece, in the form of the eponymous suit left behind by the wife's fleeing lover, which was conserved by the jealous husband as a 'guest', a torturing reminder of the wife's infidelity.

On an extensive and rapid tour, *Le Costume* played in several cities for as little as two nights, thereby making modifications of theatre auditoriums impossible. Performed on an 80-centimetre-high stage in a conventional, frontal configuration, the play lost almost all its force and charm: its subtle effects of mime and play with objects depended absolutely on a banishing of the threshold between viewer and performer, and on the presence of the audience on three sides, sharing in the creation of the piece.

> PETER BROOK: *The degree of transformation that we could do for* The Mahabarata *or* Carmen *is much harder to obtain today. This conditions our work – we need to produce things that fit into a wider range of spaces, that are more adaptable themselves, which is why the concentrated area has worked well. We played* Le Costume *in Montreal in a very intimate space on a little raised platform with the audience on a slope facing down. In Toronto, though, we were very unhappy indeed because we were put at the very last minute, against our wishes, into a really big American-style conventional theatre where the seats weren't banked at all and the stage was high. There, with the best will in the world and no theoretical prejudice against such forms, and the actors doing their best, the basic relationship that carries the play was impossible to form.*
>
> *There is an enormous social and psychological difference between the actor on a platform, like an orator or preacher in a superior position, and the opposite condition, where the audience is not so much looking down as warmly encompassing the actor. Doing* Oh les beaux jours, *Natasha Parry found it extremely difficult to establish the relationship with the audience when she was on a raised stage – to say nothing of the odd idea of looking up at a desert. Also, as the audience goes up, people tend to lean forward in an attentive posture, whereas in the stalls of a conventional theatre one tends to slouch and lean back into a sleep-inducing posture.*

The Tragedy of Hamlet

The Tragedy of Hamlet was staged on a simple orange carpet (again, the same size as in the previous works) placed on the stage floor. Costumes were just slightly less neutral than the everyday dress used for *Qui est là?*: colours and cuts were restrained, and presented a faint suggestion of being from the past – possibly medieval or renaissance. Whereas Sotigui

Kouyaté had donned a loose red cloak to identify himself as the ghost rather than Claudius (whom he also played) in *Qui est là?*, Jeffrey Kissoon had a slightly more 'complete' tailored gown with a raised collar to permit the same effect here. Only the text was used to distinguish explicitly between inside and out, night and day, bedroom and salon. There were a few cushions and seats on wheels, which were manipulated by the actors to form different configurations representing changes of scene. The Elizabethan simplicity of this setting put the actor's craft under the microscope in exactly the same way as *The Man Who*, but with a vastly different subject and scope. There were lighting effects for some scenes – a shadow-play at the beginning of the players' scene, for example – but in general the tone was extremely level and anti-aesthetic. At the same time, at the Bouffes, the theatre could not help but be drawn into the drama. The mind's eye searches for correlatives, for accents with which to anchor the drama, and the lugubrious, 'rotten' nature of the Danish court chimed strongly with the disintegrating, eschatological side of the theatre's character. Also, more universally, the heavens, the ground and hell below – the vertical axis often referred to in the drama –

The Tragedy of Hamlet
at the Bouffes du Nord

were made palpable by the solid, shared floor, the soaring columns, and the unifying, overarching dome above.

PETER BROOK: *In* Qui est là? *the aim was to enter into an imaginative discussion about something which has no place, which is the theatre experience. In* Hamlet, *the essential aspect of the play is not that it is taking place in Elsinore. If one looks at all the realistic period films of* Hamlet, *the essence of the play is not helped at all by the presence of a real castle.*

During rehearsals for Carmen *we tried many kinds of floor surface – including carpet and linoleum at different times – and eventually through these researches we arrived at the sense that the work was taking place not in the never-never land of opera, but in real places, and this was part of the guts of the piece. Therefore we played on earth. With* Hamlet *we followed the same process, but the other way round. We tried in rehearsal our big ornate Persian carpet, just the stage floor, simple 'wall-to-wall' carpeting in white, brown, beige, and felt that it was all overworked and inappropriate. Persianness imposes something foreign to* Hamlet. *Wall-to-wall carpet, which was ideal for* The Man Who, *was miserable – too poor for* Hamlet. *Then Chloé had the idea of using a concrete platform cracked like a pavement – to fit in with the walls of the Bouffes – but this we found to be too cold and also physically too hard, and it took away from the liveliness, the playfulness, that we wanted to bring out. Also, from a purely practical perspective, the actors couldn't comfortably kneel, sit, do somersaults or fall on concrete. And, curiously, it did something else: the strength of concrete in the particular context of the Bouffes made it in fact become a naturalistic set. If we were doing* The Trial of Joan of Arc, *or Janácek's* The House of the Dead, *this would have been splendid, because it had something cold, slightly forbidding. But it didn't work here, as it was pushing* Hamlet *into something we wanted to avoid, which is a dark medieval drama. I didn't want* Hamlet *to be a gloomy play. It is a tragedy, but a radiant tragedy.*

Out of that work came, by trial and error, the realization that the playfulness we were looking for would be supported by brilliant colour. We had a vast piece of Indian material which was white, and we dyed it red and this fulfilled the whole purpose. In rehearsal we experimented with taking this carpet away for the final duel, to bring a note of finality into the tragedy; but this introduced a scenic effect (with the cumbersome, time-consuming task of physically removing the carpet), and the play worked better when there was a unity to the space.

Although we did nothing to the walls of the Bouffes for Hamlet, *they were mentioned in almost every review. There was an appeal to them, obviously, in the carpet, but the walls themselves seemed to want to be drawn into the peculiarly entropic atmosphere that surrounds the court at Elsinore.*

For the costumes, the brief I gave to Chloé Obolensky could only be expressed in negative terms: modern-dress costumes are a cliché; acting in jeans and casual 'street' clothes is a cliché; smart modern dress is a cliché – the marvels that come from designers such as Yohji Yamamoto today are so stamped with a fashion association that, although I love them, one is always conscious of their style, which is generally alien to the theatre event. Other clichés, which seemed dangerously fresh when I started working fifty years ago, are to use modern military uniforms, evening dress, period costumes from recent times. So what Chloé has to do is is to find her way between these traps: not something neutral; not modern clothes; not something linked to a particular period. Because her natural tendency is always to go into black, white and grey, we thought of making the costumes simple shapes, very functional, just evoking the fact that this is not the present day, that there is a suggestion of being in some time from the past, just as when one tells the story of Hamlet *to a child one begins, 'There was once a prince . . .' Then all the visual vitality the play needed came from the objects, the carpets, the fabrics, rather than the costumes.*

A soliloquy can be played straight out front, very simply, but the moment there are several people onstage one has to create the relationships between them. If a space is absolutely bare, one finds that the choreographic possibilities for theatre are very rapidly exhausted. For dance this is not a problem, because there is no limit to the shapes the body can take on, but with acting the range is much smaller – actors can't just make pretty pictures in the way that dancers can. If you just use a square of bare boards, the actors can move to the right, the left and the middle, and then it rapidly becomes boring because nothing renews itself visually. In Hamlet *we found we needed objects in order to articulate the space, to bring in diagonals, circular movements, so that people could be close together, further away. The best way of exploring this at the start of rehearsals is to work with simple furniture such as chairs. We found with* The Man Who *that all one needs to do is have someone move a chair or turn it around to completely change the setting, indicating that we are in another space. In the case of* Hamlet, *chairs were too cumbersome; but it seemed to me that if* we had nothing but cushions it would have been necessary to do something very cumbersome, which is lift and carry them to denote changes from one scene to the other. We therefore made four cushion-like objects on wheels which could be easily pushed around into new shapes. Editing down, we found that everything could be done with two of them, filling two and a half hours with changing patterns which nobody really noticed, but whose absence would have become glaring, because the same lines and shapes would have had a tendency to repeat themselves. (In America there used to be a Broadway cliché saying, 'This is a very bad production because they all stand like firemen' – meaning that the actors all stand in a line facing the audience as if they're holding a hose.)

I don't work watching myself working and saying, 'What is your tendency?' Only after the fact can one discern a set of pre-occupations, if that is even worthwhile and interesting, as with a painter who works with a particular palette of colour until, without analysis, it is felt to have lost its relevance and needs to be changed. When one begins the process of rehearsal, absolutely everything must be possible. With Hamlet, one idea was that we use the whole space, with no acting area defined: what happens if there is absolutely nothing, somebody walks on into this vast space, and bit by bit one brings on whatever one needs? It is clichéd to see vast Shakespearean plays as needing vast spaces to illustrate the grandeur of the play. Productions all over the world have tried to create Eisenstein-scaled vastness to represent Lear's solitude, for example; but what happens with Shakespeare is that one creates enormously long entrances and exits which cut the natural rhythm of the play. When the Johannesburg Market Theatre's production of The Island was at the Bouffes, I remember thinking that one could do Hamlet on the same tiny platform that they used – about a quarter of our eventual carpet – because this created such enormous concentration. When we started rehearsing Hamlet, we began by using a slightly bigger space and tried to see how much we could do on it. It was very exciting for the first scene, but of course it didn't work for two and a half hours. With a bigger carpet we were still able to work outward, opening up from the minimal, intimate inner space. The advantage of the bigger area in Hamlet is that it can be used non-stop: Bruce Myers, playing Polonius, leaves Ophelia, walks around the stage as the King comes on from another side, and we're already in the next scene. This transition would be comical with a platform only 2 metres shorter on each side – everything is a question of proportionality, balance and common sense.

For about fifteen years I wanted to do Hamlet *with the audience on the stage, facing into the theatre, which would have meant doing it for a cast of forty on the balconies, even a hundred appearing and looking down during the players' scene (we went as far as to see how this could be done practically with students), the battlements on the third level, the sword fights going along the balconies, people falling off. It would have been a spectacular production, which fifteen years ago was tempting – a wildly extravagant, romantic thing. But Jean-Guy could never get more than 150 seats on the stage, which seemed like pushing things too much economically. Also, in terms of a basic balance of the audience size to the size of the show,* Hamlet *as we have finally done it is, I think, truer to today than that extravagant version would have been.*

To have a high stage would not be appropriate in the Bouffes: it is a question of centimetres, or even millimetres, when one decides to build a threshold in the space. Had we done Hamlet on the 17-centimetre-high platform of Qui est là? *it would have been a completely different play, with a much more self-consciously theatrical character. This was the issue all the way through rehearsals for* Le Costume, *where we also ended up with the mat simply on the floor. Its intimate story needs a concentrated area, and yet the surrounding hardness and darkness of the concrete recalls the night of township life. One needs both the darkness and the simple enough but bright interior, so that the audience is in the space in a double world. A platform would have cut off the ambiguity of this relationship.*

Endpieces

Jean-Claude Carrière

Peter takes care never to fix the meaning, the structure of a performance. Over the course of a tour one must remain open to outside events, political changes, natural disasters, which can change the sense of a play from one day to the next. I remember one time when we were touring in Switzerland he gathered the actors for rehearsal and told them that they had a special exercise to prepare for that evening's performances: simply to go out into the town and sit in cafés and public spaces listening to the local people, trying to attune to their rhythms and habits.

Very often, at the beginning of a show, after a few hesitant previews for friends, then some members of the public, then the critics, then playing to packed houses for two weeks, Peter will call a meeting and announce to the very buoyant, satisfied cast, 'It's clear that there's an enormous amount of work that needs to be done.' And he is always right: the work is never finished; the capacity for discovery is endless.

After twenty-five years of experiment and activity, the one thing that Peter has never lost sight of is that the theatre itself is part of the action, whether it has been transformed, reduced, reversed, or changed in colour: it has its own story, and when people enter the theatre, before anything has happened onstage, there is already something to contemplate, something to look at. It calls to mind the famous story of Leonardo da Vinci exhorting his students to pay attention to old walls which have been drawn on by the rain and wind, for when carefully looked at they can seem to reveal images of things, of horses, of clouds.

Jean-Guy Lecat

I have spent a lot of time travelling around visiting spaces (perhaps more than 2,000 over the years), and so one might think I have a lot of experience, have become accustomed to doing this. But every visit has unique features.

Discovering a new space first of all means going to encounter a place and the human being who conceived and constructed it. The first thing to do is to try to recognize what was aimed at and done by someone else in another period and another context: to seek to understand through the filter of culture, so as to avoid destroying the fragile equilibrium which remains after that place has lost its original function.

Let's take the Théâtre des Bouffes du Nord as an example. Today this building, in its bareness, has an architecture in which the allusions to the nineteenth-century bourgeois theatre for which it was constructed have disappeared. All the same, the essential things are still present, even though this faintness of specific historical reference points often leads some members of the audience to ask questions about the origin of the building.

When I visit any space I take the time necessary until the space itself comes to me. I sit in silence and I wait. It was in this way that I had the intuition of how to transform the Majestic Theater in Brooklyn.

But there is no good space without a good project, or a good idea behind it which subtends the action; otherwise we create a beautiful space for no reason, no idea, without sense, at the end of the day we have a space which is good for *nobody*. But a space well done can have several lives.

In the beginning there was the action. Not the actor. Not the character and certainly not the author. The event. And behind the event, behind that, this fact, what one had to get before anything else: the commission, the brief.

The rest, the characters, their appearance, their costumes, the passions that motivated them, the author himself even with his imagination, his memories, his intonation, his distinctive language, all this is part of the category of the means.*

*Paul Claudel, Hommage à Jacques Copeau, 1949

The question of the commission of the project is for me essential. During all my searches for spaces for Peter Brook I never doubted what I sought because I had a direction. The project was a play, a story to be told and shared, with these two questions asked by Peter: where? and how? It is necessary to have much humility and to recognize that without the project

233

of Peter Brook I would never have sought these spaces.

Recently a Japanese architect, Tadashi Saito, built a new theatre in Tokyo. I had the opportunity to visit it, and found it remarkable – rich in meaning, full of character and charm, even though it is brand new. Above all it has the right proportions. I asked the architect what had inspired him most, and he replied that some years ago he had seen our theatre in Paris and that it had deeply impressed him. But he built a formal proscenium-arch theatre which has the form of the Parisian theatre, but not the spirit. He had seen the walls, not the work

The Setagaya Theatre in Tokyo

of Peter Brook, who has his actors play in front of the arch.

There is not one history of the theatre but many different ones, and most have used the circle. Let us choose, for example, three theatre spaces over 2,500 years: the Greeks, the Romans and the Elizabethans, they all played inside a circle. The Italian theatres during the Renaissance started to build their decorations outside the circle. During two centuries the actors also followed the set, moved slowly outside the circle, and the form of the theatre became fixed.

Peter Brook, in his theatre in Paris, came back to the circle. This is essential, and this is what the Japanese architect didn't understand.

In a workshop I do around the world for young architects and theatre directors, we visit all the theatres in their city. It is very interesting: they think they know them all, but they realize they have never looked at them carefully. In each theatre we try an experiment: I go on stage and I walk from the front of the stage to the back wall, and the participants everywhere in the auditorium have to stop me at the moment they feel my presence has disappeared. They always stop me a few metres behind the proscenium arch, at the point where an imaginary line would close the ovoidal form of the threatre. (It is worse in rectangular spaces.) It is as if I cross an imaginary wall. The proscenium arch is like a theshold, everything behind it looks far away.

We had confirmation of this when we did *Happy Days*: the play was trapped with the decor inside the original stage. Half of the spaces we have used around the world were theatres, and the same question came up.

Creating a space is not an objective in itself. A new place must first of all have been willed by someone, and it is this that endows it with significance.

Sotigui Kouyaté

I did not follow Peter on the first journeys through Africa; I came to the Centre at the time of *The Mahabharata*. If you ask me what the Centre is like, what the character of our journeys has been, I have to say that I can only speak for myself – as an actor and, above all, as a West African. I can't dissociate myself from my roots, my culture.

Joining Peter Brook's group was not a disorienting experience for me, but quite the contrary. In our part of Africa we live in community; we share. I also belong to the caste of griots, who are mediators and conciliators: their role is to bring people together. One is born a griot: it's transmitted from father to son, The griot is in a certain sense an artist from birth, but not really in the European sense. One uses words to tell stories, and also to communicate people's history, their origins, and their present and future. One needs artistry to do this, and speaking is a difficult art. One must know how to transport and make a vehicle of speech, which we say is the weapon of the griot.

My theatre work is similar: it is a school based in life. I've learned everything through practice rather than through any school, and I'm still learning every day. A wise man – if such a thing exists – is someone who knows that every day he has something to learn from others. The prerequisite of this is listening, and listening is a capacity we are losing more and more.

I found with Brook a regard for others, both as actors – professionals – and as human beings. Simply put, there is respect and mutual consideration at every level. There is no privilege or hierarchy between older or newer members of the group, between older and younger actors. At our discussions during *The Mahabharata* there was no hierarchy: the children spoke up just as much as the adults, on the same footing. Peter was open to everybody. He made a point of asking people's opinion if they were shy. For those who don't understand, it could appear that what I say is some sort of eulogy. But this is not true: I'm just stating facts, and one must not shy away from the need to do this.

When I joined Brook I was agreeably surprised: having been invited to France, I expected to find myself in a French company, but instead there was a real mixture – people from eighteen different countries for *The Mahabharata*. This corresponded perfectly with my nature as a griot, who goes in search of contact and meeting with other peoples. I immediately felt at home in this theatre, which has become for me a family. I don't feel better anywhere than at the Bouffes: this place is good for you. It's rare and beautiful to find oneself in a group where no one looks at the colour of the skin, pays attention to the language you speak, or asks what religion you practise.

Universality is the first principle for Brook, I think. No one is reduced to their national or local identity. There are no barriers between people – and that goes for the relationship with the audience too. I cannot dissociate the theatre from life. Peter has always been searching for a space to nurture these qualities. I have no idea what the Bouffes du Nord is, why it is the way it is, but as soon as one encounters it there is a pleasure, an openness, a spirit circulating through the space.

I'm not qualified to comment on the touring spaces in depth, because I simply use them, but I see when I arrive in a place on tour that Jean-Guy, Peter and Chloé Obolensky have a genius for finding or creating the spirit of the Bouffes in many different forms. This must demand enormous research. To create a space where every time I have been able to find my place easily, to feel at home, demands a great deal of sensitivity, openness and a listening attitude. The world at large seems to be losing these capacities; but for an artist they are fundamental, and it is one of our responsibilities to demonstrate them in our work. When all the factors are balanced, one is carried by the space: it does part of the actor's work.

It is perhaps my African sensibility to find that the outdoor environment is infinitely richer than any interior space, however wonderfully conceived. One is always contained by four walls. In Mali our national theatre, the Koteba, has been institutionalized, put indoors, thanks in part to academic colonial ideas of art coming from foreign teachers – particularly from France. In the past we simply closed off a neighbourhood about a hundred metres square, and the people formed a circle around the action. In Africa the circle serves for everything – every ceremony from birth, baptism and marriage to funerals, festivities and meetings. We find this circle all the time with Peter, for meetings and exercises. It is the most natural form in which humans can meet, communicate and contemplate.

Deborah Warner

The Bouffes opened the door for a whole generation. It stamped its identity on all of us. It gave us freedom. I saw everything there from *The Cherry Orchard* onward, and it's not an overstatement to say that I went into theatre because of Peter. When I directed *Titus Andronicus* at the RSC in the late 1980s, I wishfully saw the Swan Theatre as a kind of Bouffes du Nord, so much was this a part of our imaginative world at that time. It was thrilling that we got to take the show there later.

Peter's unique showmanship, taking us on pilgrimages, forcing us outside our theatre-going habits, has underlined how everything about theatre needs to be an event, an unrepeatable experience – which is the antithesis of the repetitive, repertory notion on which many of our big institutions are based. He has shown us that one is directing space just as one is directing people. The audience's entrance into the theatre is every bit as important as Hedda Gabbler's first entrance onstage. That's what excites me, and I've been teasing out the implications of this in my own work for ten years.

In Beckett's *Footfalls*, with Fiona Shaw, we tried to find a way to rediscover the Garrick Theatre, to see it afresh, using the auditorium itself as an elaborate set for the piece. This approach fell foul of Beckett's literary executors, who insist on embalming his work in the 1970s experimental aesthetic in which it was conceived, and the show was cancelled. Unfortunately, always giving an audience what they expect is to sow the seeds of a dead theatre.

The Waste Land, also with Fiona Shaw, was played in all kinds of spaces, most of them not theatres – or at least not working theatres. The idea was to inhabit a fresh space where

Deborah Warner is an associate director of the Royal National Theatre. The theatre, opera and fine-art-related 'performance' works she has directed include *The Turn of The Screw*, *Richard II*, *Journal of One Who Disappeared* and *The St John Passion*.

there would be no expectation of what the show would be. To prepare people for 600 lines of dense poetic text, one needed to open their ears, to jump-start them through an unhabitual journey to and through a space. For 'settings' we used only things which were found on site, giving rise to an aesthetic of the 'turn-around', the time when the crew is working onstage between shows, a moment of irresolution, with cables hanging down, rigging on the stage – something quite anti-romantic. The idea was not to boil everything down to some notion of underlying space, but rather, like stripping insulation off wires, to try to get back to the rawest properties of the space. This is an architectural matter: a space which is half-dressed may, exactly like a human form, be provocative and exciting.

This way of working has allowed the design to come about very late – something which theatre managements would not normally tolerate. (What Peter has achieved very brilliantly at the Bouffes is to design as the show is rehearsed, destroying and re-creating everything up until the last minute if necessary.) This has proved to be possible even in larger institutions – even with opera. I was very apprehensive about doing *The Turn of the Screw* at the Barbican, until I saw the hall under reconstruction, absolutely enchanting without a proscenium and in a certain disarray. I just asked them to stop where they were and let us tinker with their work in progress. The acoustic was fantastic, and the audience saw what they thought to be a familiar space in a new way.

For the Euston Tower Project – a *dérive* through three floors of an empty office building, without text or 'action' per se – the space *was* the event in many ways, and one had to listen to its truth very very carefully, which was extremely difficult and uncomfortable in this case. The atmosphere of buildings is just as strong as that of people – just as noisy, individual, moving and infuriating.

In all such cases – and I think Peter's work on space bears this out too – you're in a honeymoon period so long as things can't yet be named, while they are being opened. This period is very short-lived, very special. The danger comes when you decide that you have found something that works. The audience must never have their expectations met, but there comes a moment where things become familiar and something has started to die. The problem with established spaces is that people think they know what they are going to get. For a short period of time – say four or five years for me in recent times –

one can keep mining the same seam; but then one needs to move on. How one does this, how one snaps away, is crucial. One must change – it's part of our responsibility – but one must do so without throwing away valuable things, important lessons from accrued experience.

I think just at the moment it's a mistake for architects to design theatres. I have a feeling we're all about to rush back into the old spaces, the ones we've all rejected for ten years. Perhaps we're going to find a way to revivify what we now think to be the most banal, dead spaces. In any case, as Peter's work has shown, space for theatre has to be responsive, alive and varied in order for it to be useful for us. It's very difficult to design such a space. Unfortunately, however, it's very easy to design deadly spaces which kill creative possibilities.

Andrew Todd

Grounding

How can one attempt to bring a sense of unity to a heterogeneous, randomly gathered contemporary theatre audience? What, if they exist, are the essential forms, the fundamental proportions, of theatrical space without which basic relationships break down? What combination of spirit and matter needs to be added or isolated in order to bring to life such a gathering? How can a space feed and free the imagination without stopping it at a particular image or association?

We have seen Peter Brook's International Centre addressing these questions throughout a thirty-year inquiry, by means of the very particular inner worlds of the Centre's various productions. The productions themselves have not been formed in the abstract: we have seen how, in particular, *Orghast* and *The Mahabharata* achieved their initial forms thanks to an anchoring in a particular place, and all the productions have grown as they have encountered the immensely varied outer worlds – East and West, rich and poor, city, suburb, village and country – on the Centre's itinerary.

Although this has rarely been a stated intention, the work has also, in a haphazard way, achieved a grounding in the context of the history of theatre space (despite the original intention being to leave behind the moribund forms and manners of conventional theatres). There are concrete traces: eight original venues exist as a by-product of this work. Coming ostensibly from a marginal position in architectural culture, they have certainly disturbed the 'mainstream' balance in New York, Barcelona, Glasgow, Lisbon, Frankfurt, Zurich, Copenhagen and Avignon. But this work has also thrown into relief existing theatres from almost every period of history from ancient Rome to the present. It has revealed the circular nature of history: a space conceived for Pompeiians two thousand years ago can be more alive and relevant than something built yesterday; a bourgeois baroque auditorium can reveal its latent potential for fostering a sense of union. What are the common features of these extraordinarily diverse spaces? What essential qualities in them have been brought out by the Centre's work? What threads unite their different positions in time?

Universal and Unique Forms

To begin at home, as it were, we have seen that the Bouffes du Nord's unique balance of qualities could have occurred only through the agency of accident, a collaboration of chaos and order – something wholly appropriate in our discontinuous tapestry of a society. The 'ordered' part of this hybrid contains the ghost, the echo, of the antique forms – the Greek and Roman theatres – which were surveyed for the first time in the modern world by Andrea Palladio. Unlike the Bouffes, these forms were hardly open to chance: because of the homogeneity of their society and the intense currents of religious belief in everyday life, it was possible to build theatres of stunning simplicity and permanence, which contained literally the whole of free society* for the duration of the dramatic festivals. The balance between participation and observation was perfect: the dramatic festivals were rather like religious ceremonies where everyone knows the moves; there were very few original storylines outside the universally known mythological canon.

*The citizenry of Athens – i.e. no women or slaves.

These pure forms resounded in the entirely different context of Elizabethan London. Palladio's drawings of the ancient theatre made their way to England in 1570: the edition of Vitruvius that he illustrated was owned by the Elizabethan magus John Dee, who paraphrased many of the Roman writer's ideas in his preface to the first English edition of Euclid's *The Elements of Geometry*, a sort of theoretical treatise on building aimed at a readership of craftsmen and artisans. Dee knew that the wealthy court had little interest in the ideas of the

Renaissance (which was all but over in Italy by this stage). He sought, therefore, to communicate the mystical understanding of spatial proportion offered by Vitruvius to the class of people who were most directly involved with construction. One such person (and a friend of Dee's) was James Burbage, who in 1576 built The Theatre, the first purpose-built structure for presenting drama in England. It seems highly likely that the subsequent London playhouses – the Rose, the Hope and Shakespeare's Globe – were also influenced by Vitruvian ideas,* as well as by these playhouses' antecedent inn-yard theatres and animal-baiting arenas. They were rough, mongrel forms, but structured by a pure, cosmic geometry. They shared with the ancient theatre the permanent backdrop of the tiring-house wall (equivalent to the Roman *frons scaenae* and the Greek *skene*) – a stable ground for the sudden shifts of scene which Shakespeare used with such fluidity.

*Cited in Andrew Gurr, *Playgoing in Shakespeare's London*, p. 228.

The diversity of Shakespeare's audience was such that 'Stinkard' and 'sweet Courtier' were united in the same space. It is unlikely that they would all have been able to understand the metaphorical frame of reference of the theatre – the association of the geometry of the building with the zodiac (which Frances Yates, in *Theatre of the World*, suggests was painted on the 'heavens' or roof over the stage), and its expression of the man-centred cosmos of Renaissance thought. The capacity to read specific symbols would have been restricted to only an initiated few; but there was a fundamental democracy enshrined in these numinous ideas: Vitruvius and the Renaissance thinkers who followed him took the human body as the point of departure for their systems of proportions. There was a moral as well as a metaphysical concern for man's stature, for his nobility as the embodiment of divine proportions. The theatres were thus made to a human measure, to be the right size for people's ears and eyes as they followed the drama. A contemporary observer (perhaps John Webster) described a Bankside audience in the following way: 'Sit in a full Theater, and you will thinke you see so many lines drawne from the circumference of so many eares, whiles the *Actor* is the *Center*.' This is a beautiful image of a virtual unity, of the communion of myriad points in their momentary attention on a common focus.

Our observer muddles the senses in an interesting way: he thinks he sees lines – but they are lines of sound, not of sight. This reminds us of the pre-eminence of the aural in the Shakespearean imagination: Elizabethan theatres were sound-spaces designed to foster lightning changes of scene painted only by words, attuned to the stimulation of the imagination rather than the fixity of the visual image. The imaginary circle formed around this focus is held within the natural extent, the correct measure of our aural sense. It is therefore no accident that the Bouffes du Nord, whose basic plan was conceived by Cochin precisely for its acoustic intimacy, should be exactly the same shape and size as the Rose, the theatre where Shakespeare and Marlowe's early works were first performed. (As soon as the site of the Rose was discovered in 1989, Peter Brook was highly curious to see the archaeologists' survey of it superimposed on to the plans of the Bouffes.) History, apparently advancing in logical, measured steps, once again shows its capacity to turn back upon itself and reach out across voids of time.

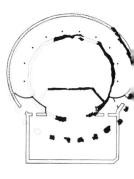

The plans of the Bouffes du Nord and of the remains of the Rose Theatre at the same scale

There appears to be no continuity between the form of the Bouffes and the volumes of the 'found' spaces made for the tours: these vary from the infinitely grand (Avignon and Persepolis), through a middle range of similarly proportioned industrial spaces (all much larger than the Bouffes), to the more intimate shells of Caracas and Lisbon. The link to the fundamental form of the Paris space occurs through the way in which relationships have been limited in these volumes. Except in the quarry spaces, where a different scale was dictated by the host environment, the Parisian acting area (about 10 by 10 metres, of which 6 by 6 metres is most heavily used) has been taken as the template everywhere. (In fact, when visiting spaces, Jean-Guy carries cardboard cut-outs of the stage of the Bouffes at various imperial and metric scales to try out on plans.) From this area outward, a balance has been found between the limits of acceptable visibility and audibility and the presence, proportions and character of the space. The most satisfying cases are where there are direct points of co-incidence between the human and spatial limits, as when the horizon between levels in the building gave the suggestion that the seating end at just the right distance and height in Lisbon, Copenhagen and Frankfurt, and when the structural grid determined the plan form in Frankfurt, Barcelona and Glasgow. Because of this jostle between fixed forms and discrete circumstances, the forms of these spaces are all unique.

The 'fixed' forms given by the limits of vision and audibility have been found empirically by Jean-Guy, Peter and Chloé Obolensky in almost every case. As far as hearing is concerned, the behaviour of spaces in relation to the very subtle processes of auditory perception makes it almost impossible to generalize: each case is highly individual. In the case of vision, however, the 25-metre distance from centre stage which was felt to be a little too much for the 'feedback loop' of eye-to-eye contact to be maintained in Barcelona has a certain objective quality, confirmed by other examples. Ruggero Pierantoni has reflected upon the insight that contemporary biophysics can bring to bear upon this experience:

> From cortical physiological studies, it is well known that we have in our visual cortex a certain number of cells specialized in what can be called 'visual contact' or 'eye-to-eye contact'. These electrophysiological units, which are located in the infero-temporal cortex (or ITC), have the basic function of presenting knowledge about the presence of a facing specific individual. These cells are very sensitive to pupil size, pupil contrast against the facial background, and pupil movements. If the dimension of the image of the pupil projected on the interior of the retina does not reach the minimum perceivable dimensions, the 'eye-to-eye' cells cannot do their job.* Recognizing the human face, reading its expressions, recognizing familiarity, and interpreting facial 'messages' are all strictly based on the perceivability of the pupils. (This eye-contact parameter also represents a critical step in the perceptive and cognitive maturation of the newborn.)*
>
> If we take an average pupil of 4 mm in diameter, its image projected on the retina will be 4.5 microns (4.5 thousandths of a millimetre) at 15 metres, 3.7 microns at 18 metres, and 3.4 microns at 20 metres. The classical data from visual-acuity studies state that 4.38 microns is the limiting value for the 'comfortable' detection of a bright point against a dark background. The threshold of acuity for the recognizability of a pupil is therefore reached somewhere between 15 and 20 metres.†

*See De Simone, 'Face Selective Cells in the Temporal Cortex of Monkeys', *Journal of Cognitive Neurosciences*, 3 (1991), pp. 1–24.

*See C. A. Samuels, 'Attention to Eye Contact Opportunity and Facial Motion by Three-Month-Old Infant', *Journal of Experimental Child Psychology*, 40 (1985), pp. 104–14.

† There are other factors which affect the reception of this data: at lower levels of luminance visual acuity will be reduced – to objects occupying 7 microns on the retina at a luminance of 1 candela per square metre, or 12 microns at 0.1 candela per square metre. Also, contrast against the facial background and iris can change the degree of acuity. For someone with a dark iris, the pupil/iris complex can be 'read' together as a larger surface (12 mm in diameter) in contrast to the white of the eye (the sclera); this can increase perceived eye-contact distance to up to 45 metres. Furthermore, the complexion of actors of African origin creates a double contrast of black–white–black, which can also have the effect of increasing acuity. In general, with a normal contrast between the pupil/iris complex and the face/sclera, the former is detectable at 20 metres, but much greater degrees of contrast are necessary at larger distances.

Bruce Myers has said, rather beautifully, on this same subject:

> When you can maintain eye contact there's more care; you
> sense the responsibility for someone's imagination – espe-
> cially in the case of children. One is in a vulnerable position,
> and therefore has more responsibility; one forms a moral
> contract with the audience. You look at somebody and you
> don't want the violence that you have to play as part of your
> character to be real, in the naturalistic sense; but you do
> want the story to be real, shared, convincing. Film is com-
> pletely different. No one can care for a camera; you care
> only about yourself.

The Centre's journey has very often involved the challenge
of returning 'double-space' or proscenium theatres to the unified, one-room, form of the Bouffes and the Shakespearean
and ancient theatres. As Charles-Nicolas Cochin pointed out
more than 200 years ago, it makes sense to put the actor in the
same space as the audience if he is to be heard better. This intimacy also has its obvious visual correlative: one sees better the
closer one is. What is different, however, in the sense of sight –
and particularly exaggerated in the case of a proscenium theatre – is what happens to our perception when we observe an an
actor 'framed' by a foreground presence. Ruggero Pierantoni
explains how contemporary science has thrown light on this
phenomenon:

> If two objects of identical size are placed at different dis-
> tances from the eye, they produce images on the retina
> which are a precise function of their absolute size and their
> distance from the observer. However, our cognitive faculties
> tend to distort this 'absolute' geometry and ascribe to the
> further object a much greater distance from the eye than is
> actually the case. This phenomenon – known as the 'size
> constancy effect' – was measured experimentally by Holway
> and Boring in 1941. At a fixed position from an observer
> they placed a white disc whose diameter could be adjusted,
> and a further disc of constant size was placed at various
> positions behind the first. For each of the positions of the
> second disc, the observer was asked to change the diameter
> of the first disc such that it appeared to be always the same
> size as the further one. The relative dimensions of the fixed-
> size and adjusted disc gave the surprising conclusion that
> the viewer perceived the further disc to be approximately

four times further away than it actually was in relation to the foreground object. Objects such as the proscenium arch in a conventional theatre, which impose a foreground presence, therefore have the effect of radically distancing – to our mind's eye – the actors on the stage beyond.

The Imaginary and the Real

The Elizabethan example has a prime importance to the Centre for many other reasons in addition to its proportions. In the first instance, Shakespeare's dramatic work remains *the* reference point: four of his plays have been performed or adapted by the Centre since it arrived at the Bouffes – nearly a third of the Centre's work. The heterogeneous population of London in his era is a microcosm of the global mix the Centre has engaged with its work. The 'permanent decor' of the tiring-house wall which anchored the rapid imaginary shifts of scene in Shakespeare's plays reappears in the Bouffes du Nord, the Mercat de les Flors, the Callet quarry, the Bockenheimer Depot and many of the other spaces that the Centre has used. There is also the rooting of this architecture in everyday life: the 'impure' associations of animal-baiting and eating and drinking could never quite be forgotten in the Shakespearean theatres – the drama always had a measure against which its imagined reality could find proportion, a rich, dirty soil in which to grow towards something purer.

The International Centre has built its theatrical worlds upon a rich mosaic of life: rocks, gas, biscuits, trams, trains, monks, lorries, flowers and rice have preceded Carmen, Krishna and Prospero. These ordinary entities serve as the ground, the earthing-rod which the imagination needs if it is to have its full range and force; one only knows how high one has climbed if the point of departure is still visible. These things have been allowed to retain their aura and their independence in the transformation of the spaces; they have never been framed or put on a pedestal as if to say 'Here is reality, captured for you to admire.' Their currents of life would be extinguished unless one admitted a certain weakness before them, and accepted that the random forces controlling them can bite back. But 'free' space, when kept as such, has a tendency to be demolished or modified for another use. Where it has not been appropriate or possible for the Centre to retain a controlling interest (which is very often the case), the sad fact is that these spaces have tended to lose their charm. Politicians seem to dislike the idea of leaving a space empty, incomplete and open to interpretation: it has to be filled with *their* imprint, *their* benevolence. There are only the rare examples of Lisbon and Glasgow where not too much damage has been done.

We usually think of buildings as solid, resistant things; but all architecture is susceptible to continual modification. Uses change constantly; society redefines even the most monumental structures; nature slowly degrades things. The frantic pace of human progress is played out against a gentler increase in entropy and renewal of the physical world. In theatre buildings this clash of time frames is at its most acute: we witness the creation of a world in the space of one evening, and the nature of a theatrical 'world' (such as the Centre's) can change rapidly from year to year, as its only irreducible building block is the human body. For this reason the evolving life of the spaces described in this book should be invested with the same quality and richness as the precedent time present upon their walls. This has been achieved in the Bouffes du Nord: there is a beautiful union of the evolving memory of Brook's tenure – its smeared layers of cream, white and red – with the pits, cracks and burns which betoken the earlier, unloved, period. There is a gentle balance between the currents of living and dying on these walls, of decay blending with renewal. (The walls have already seen the disappearance of Mahmoud Tabrizi-Zadeh, Douta Seck, Ryszard Cieszlak and Vittorio Mezzogiorno, and the emergence of the latter's daughter Giovanna as a young actress of talent in *Qui est là?*.)

Building for the Social, Spiritual, Physical Body
The Shakespearean theatre, we have seen, was universal *and* marginal, a perfect mix of high and low which seemed to emerge naturally out of the soil of Elizabethan culture. In the gulf that separates Shakespeare's time from ours, the way we think of theatre space has changed fundamentally – most significantly in that theatres are usually built as special 'other' places where we retreat to sample a carefully concocted tonic known as 'culture'; and, in general, we go to these places to look rather than to hear. As we have seen in Tokyo and Antwerp, today's architects tend to conceive of theatres as adornments to their cities – like special jewellery worn only for a meal in the best restaurants – with a little extra money spent on the fittings, handrails and furniture of the foyers to

let us know that (whether we will actually feel it or not) we are beginning a precious, out-of-the-ordinary evening.

Inside the space, everything is arranged to favour the one-dimensional relationship of the sight line to the two-dimensional image presented beyond the threshold of the stage. We are in thrall to the captured reality of perspectival vision; as with cinema and television, we are passive witnesses of a self-sufficient other world whose independence is enforced by the space. The sense of hearing, however, is circumferential rather than linear; sound invades and vibrates our bodies, whereas vision keeps us at a distance. Other issues – notably that of the *presence* of the architecture in relation to the stage world – do not arise within the logic of these spaces, which results in the energy-absorbing, deadly side walls, the uncertain moves to form these into a frame for the stage, which we have seen in the Vivian Beaumont and Antwerp theatres.

A veneration of functionality and technicity as ends in themselves is the principal cause of this confusion inherent in these spaces. The great geniuses of the modern movement have a large degree of responsibility for promoting this attitude: architects such as Le Corbusier (whose own work on a small scale is powerfully personal and irrational) justified their early experiments by appealing to their logical derivation from structural, constructive and functional imperatives – things which, like the framed image on a stage, can be controlled, their quality measured. The specialized disciplines which the modern era has produced (particularly relating to technical know-how, guaranteeable knowledge) have seized upon this culture of logic, have carved out their own terrain, and have thereby imposed a certain institutional inertia on any interdisciplinary collaboration: we talk today of acoustics and visibility rather than listening and seeing, the former being quantified and controlled by experts, the latter being simply what the rest of us do naturally (perhaps immeasurably). This conflict is often particularly clear in the theatre, with the 'technicians' and the 'artists' suspiciously delineating the boundaries of their respective worlds, resisting any movement beyond their professional pigeonholes to engage in open collaboration (a battle which has been conspicuously 'won' by the technical camp in the Frankfurt and Barcelona spaces).

Peter Brook's work on theatre space suspends all these categories and puts all these ossified relationships into question. It is as if, back in the 1960s, he asked an ostensibly 'functional' question – What is a theatre for? – and has since pursued it to its logical extremes, such that any quantifiable, formulaic solution disintegrates before much more serious matters of spirit, space and society. If a theatre's 'function' is – as Brook suggests at the beginning of Chapter 3 – to gather people and open the pathways towards the possibility of a transcendent sense of communion, it is impossible to imagine the search for a space in which this can happen being satisfactorily concluded at the level of sight lines, seating angles, fire exits and so forth. It involves, rather, a listening attitude – an attitude which is sensitive to the balance of every detail. This involves the acquisition of a great deal of practical know-how, an ability to improvise solid, workable solutions in greatly varying contexts; but this practicality is built upon an attunement to factors which are linked to the invisible. Each plank of wood correctly positioned in *Carmen*'s walls, each earthen floor in *The Mahabharata* so well made that it blends with its context and we think of it as something real, is a building block towards the intangible realm, the 'rising to another level' which Brook speaks of as the ultimate goal of theatre.

Over the last thirty years, the actors of the International Centre have devoted enormous energy to the cultivation of their bodies as performing instruments, as whole systems which participate in a much larger whole. Ultimately the spaces within which they work are another form of body work: they are addressed to, devoted to, the contingencies of Japanese, American or Spanish bodies – contingencies which are related to our physical make-up, the position and movement of our eyes, ears, legs or feet, but also related to the way in which our frames embody social identity, personal memory and individual spirits which are both unique and universal.

Peter Brook

We had a special performance of *Hamlet* in aid of Aids and cancer research, and I came onstage with a friend – a professor who runs a research unit which does very important work in the field. I discovered that he and I not only are friends but also have something in common in our work: I work on the principle that an audience coming into the theatre should leave feeling better than when they came in; the doctor in the hospital has exactly the same ethic. That is the one ethic that I have.

I don't think the space necessarily has to create the improve-

Peter Brook contemplating the Majestic Theatre from the original first balcony

ment – on the contrary, one can take the most barren, miserable space, and the actors can for a moment transform it so that the audience feel united and more alive. I think of all the sordid school gymnasiums we have played in, the children coming from a smelly canteen into a gym which has no charm and nothing to give to their imagination; the depressing African and Portuguese hostels we still visit . . . The point of performing is for everyone to feel that they are in a living space and that they feel better. If you go into a theatre and afterwards feel worse – go back out into an already rotten world feeling more angry, more depressed, more frustrated – then the performance has not had its only possible benefit, which is to make you feel better, consoled, relieved, or, ideally, more courageous, given new vitality. Beyond that, a very rare case can give one more insight, more understanding. The movement of a performance must be from something less to something more.

Although space cannot create this movement, it can support it, and we gladly seize upon such support whenever the opportunity arises. Some spaces are 'good' by nature, and help to raise the level of attention before the performance has begun. The 'goodness' of a space is an architectural matter: from Stonehenge through ancient Egypt and Greece and the Renaissance, on to the Grande Arche de La Défense, architects have found positive principles embodied in geometry and proportion. Certain types of space are beneficent because of their shape: there isn't a human being walking into Chartres Cathedral who doesn't recognize it as a good space, and you feel infinitely better than in the best theatrical experience by just walking into Chartres or the basilica at Vézelay.

However, this form of space-making cannot be carried too far for the theatre. One has to say that a theatre cannot be and must not be considered as a temple: a theatre is a temporary, practical place, which should also have the capacity to inspire and to be uplifting. For an architect to be carried away – as Denys Lasdun was with the National Theatre – and so try to build a theatre as noble and as permanent as a temple is going too far in one way. If, however, someone says, 'This is just a working space, so let's just follow the requirements and nothing should go beyond basic functionality', then the architect won't have done his job in the other direction.

One of the main justifications for the theatre is that it reminds us of something fundamental, which is that in human life nothing lasts. This is something obvious – one doesn't need to be a Buddhist to know it – but it is easily forgotten, and human beings try to go against reality by holding on, fixing, blocking something, rather than accepting that the whole of life is a coming and going, that everything is in flux and everything is changing.

There are certain basic forms that everyone knows and responds to – and even if you don't know them you can't fail to discover them – and one of them is the circle. The circle is one of the first symbols that the whole of humanity lives with, and, just as with other basic forms such as the cross and the triangle, no one needs anyone to draw their attention to it. I think that one doesn't need to analyse why people are impressed when they go to Egypt and see the Pyramids – one just sees the triangular forms and recognizes them as very powerful.

Many people of my generation never had the experience of seeing people outside theatres begin to gather of their own accord in a democratic curve instead of being arranged in straight lines. The moment you see that, you begin to understand that a circle of people is something more living than a row of people. On that level, if the circle comes constantly into our work it is because we would have had to be unusually insensitive not to have found it naturally. The circle is a natural thing: it is an abstraction that is concrete and human.

One must work from the Modulor principle that in the theatre the proportions must come from a living appreciation of the human being – of the relationships between the human beings performing and the human beings watching. Out of that – again experimentally – one opens the question of how high, how far away, the audience can be; and eventually one can arrive through experience at a very precise notion of the point at which there are too many rows: that up to that number everything works, but if you add another five rows the experience is broken. All that can be analysed to a degree, but, the moment that this is applied like a formula, something in the living experience is very likely going to be broken or occluded.

Certainly, working the other way around by asking first 'What is the ideal proportion?' can be used for building a temple, because there you work downward from the abstract: whether you call it God, the universe or the Platonic world of ideas, there is an abstraction which begins to take on a reality by entering into mathematics and geometry and proportion. So the house that is meant to remind you of what is beyond normal human life starts with proportion. In the theatre, however – and the Elizabethan theatre always reminds me of this – one is dealing with not just the heavens, but also the living marketplace where everything can happen. The gaze can go up or down or laterally, freely around the audience and the whole environment, unlike in a space made for a linear ritual. In the theatre one can arrive at notions of abstract truth, but the process for getting there is the reverse of that undertaken to build a temple: one starts in the dirt of everyday life, and if one is lucky one can rise above it for a moment. The great danger comes when the architect proceeds either from practical considerations or from purely abstract ones.

Inasmuch as it has a value, our experience is accurately and fully explained in this book, but ultimately people must discover the relationships that apply in theatre spaces at first hand in order to understand them properly. What one does today depends on one's understanding of the past, seeing that today is different, and intuitively sensing something of the future – which happens without thinking. When a space is made, its meaning changes constantly, because the present time is constantly changing. There used to be in English advertising for clothes and furniture a cliché which in fact has a lot of truth to it as far as theatre spaces are concerned: 'This will last a lifetime' – which I think is absolutely just, because a good space shouldn't last more than that, or less! One life is plenty.

Destroying the earthen floor of *The Mahabharata*

Bibliography and Filmography

Films

Stages (documentary charting the Centre's work in Adelaide in 1979)
By Peter Brook
Lord of the Flies (1964)
Meetings with Remarkable Men (1979)
King Lear (1953 with Orson Welles)
King Lear (1972 with Paul Scofield)
The Mahabharata (French and English versions, 1989)
Mesure pour mesure (1979)
La Tragédie de Carmen (three versions with different casts, 1983)
Tell Me Lies (1967)
Une expérience théâtrale en Afrique
Les Secrets de Carmen
The Beggar's Opera (1953)

Books and Articles

Blau, Eleanor, 'Revival on 42nd Street: New Amsterdam Roof', *New York Times*, 11 May 1983
Bohigas, Oriol, et al. *10 Anys de Mercat* (Barcelona, 1993)
Bradby, David, and Sparks, Annie, *Mise en Scène: French Theatre Now* (London, 1997)
Breton, Gaelle, *Théâtres, Theaters* (Paris, 1989)
Brook, Peter, *The Empty Space* (London, 1968)
– 'Espaces pour un theatre', in *Le Scarabée international*, no. 2 (Paris, 1982)
– 'Les Lieux du spectacle', in *Architecture d'aujourd'hui*, no. 152 (Paris, 1970)
– 'Pour des espaces indefinis', in *Techniques et architecture*, no. 310 (Paris, 1978)
– *The Shifting Point* (London, 1987)
– *There are No Secrets* (London, 1993)
– *Threads of Time* (London, 1998)

Brown, Georgina, 'Why London Missed *The Mahabharata*', *The Independent* 25 April 1988
Cochin, Charles-Nicolas, *Projet d'une salle de spectacle pour un théâtre de comédie* (Paris, 1765)
Deierkauf-Holsboer, S.Wilma, *Le Théâtre du Marais* (Paris, 2 vols., 1954)
Dumur, Guy (ed.), *Histoire des spectacles*, Encyclopédie de la Pléiade (Paris, 1965)
Fowler, John, 'Indianisation of a Tram Shed', *Glasgow Herald*, 9 February 1988
Ghyka, Matila, *The Geometry of Art and Life* (New York, 1946)
Hancox, Joy, *The Byrom Collection: Renaissance Thought, The Royal Society and the Building of the Globe Theatre* (London, 1992)
Harries, Karsten, *The Ethical Function of Architecture* (Cambridge, Mass., 1997)
Heilpern, John, *Conference of the Birds: The Story of Peter Brook in Africa* (London, 1989)
Hunt, Albert, and Reeves, Geoffrey, *Peter Brook* (Cambridge, 1995)
Illich, Ivan, *Tools for Conviviality* (New York, 1973)
– *Towards a History of Needs* (Berkeley, 1977)
Jackson, John Brinckerhoff, *The Necessity For Ruins* (Amherst, 1980)
Jomaron, Jacqueline de (ed.), *Le Théâtre en France*, Encyclopédies d'aujourd'hui (Paris, 1992)
Laguepierre [to be completed]
Leacroft, Richard, *The Development of the English Playhouse* (London, 1973)
Leacroft, Richard, and Leacroft, Helen, *Theatre and Playhouse* (London, 1984)
Leatherbarrow, David, *The Roots of Architectural Invention: Site, Enclosure, Materials*

(Cambridge, 1993)

McHugh, Fionnuala, 'Gods and Heroes in the Tramshed', *Mail on Sunday*, 10 April 1988

Mackintosh, Iain, *Architecture, Actor and Audience* (London, 1993)

Mielziner, Jo, *The Shapes of Our Theater* (New York, 1970)

Oida, Yoshi, *An Actor Adrift* (London, 1992)

Palladio, Andrea, *The Four Books of Architecture* (London, 1738)

Patte, Pierre, *Essai sur l'architecture théâtrale* (Paris, 1782)

Rykwert, Joseph, *The First Moderns: The Architects of the Eighteenth Century* (Cambridge, Mass., 1980)

— *The Necessity of Artifice* (London, 1982)

Sennett, Richard, *The Fall of Public Man* (Cambridge, Mass., 1977)

— *Flesh and Stone* (New York, 1994)

Smith, Anthony, *Orghast at Persepolis* (London, 1972)

Tirincanti, Giulio, *Il Teatro Argentina* (Rome, 1971)

Vitruvius, *I dieci libri dell'architettura*, trans. with commentary by Daniele Barbaro, 1567; reprint edition with introduction by Manfredo Tafuri (Milan, 1987)

— *On Architecture*, trans. Frank Grainger (London, 2 vols., 1970)

Williams, David (ed.), *Peter Brook: A Theatrical Casebook* (London, 1992)

— (ed.), *Peter Brook and* The Mahabharata: *Critical Perspectives* (London, 1991)

Wittkower, Rudolph, *Architectural Principles in the Age of Humanism*

Wright, Allen, 'Epic Space Wins Brook Approval', *The Scotsman*, 12 April 1988

Yates, Frances, *Theatre of the World* (London, 1969)

Performance and Tour Dates of the CICT

Legend: (*th*) theatre, (*w*) warehouse, (*g*) garage, (*out*) outdoor, (*q*) quarry, (*big top*) circus, (*m*) riding school

Timon of Athens, 1974–1975

Théâtre des Bouffes du Nord: 15 October–31 December 1974, 22 April–10 June 1975

French version on tour October–December 1975 (total *c*.50 performances): Thonon (*g*); Dijon (*w*); Mâcon; Strasbourg; Villeurbanne (*th*); Évry; Le Havre; Toulouse (*th*); Grenoble (*th*); Nice (*th*); Pontoise (*w*); Zurich (*m*); Bordeaux (*w*); La Rochelle; Douai (*w*); Brussels(*th*)

Les Iks, 1975–1976

Théâtre des Bouffes du Nord: 12 January–8 March and 26 April–21 May 1975

English version on tour 1976: London (*the Round House*) 9 January–28 February; Berlin (*TV studio*) 13–19 May; Vienna (*slaughterhouse*) 25–30 May; Venice (*cloister*) 14–16 July, (*Campo*) 18–22 July; Belgrade (*unfinished cinema*) 17–19 September; Washington (*th*) 5–15 October; Philadelphia (*th on stage*) 16–21 October; Chicago (*gymnasium*) 22–27 October; Minneapolis (*th*) 28 October–3 November; Berkeley (*th*) 4–8 November; Los Angeles (*UCLA cinema studio*) 9–14 November; Houston (*th*) 15–21 November

Ubu aux Bouffes, 1977–1978

Théâtre des Bouffes du Nord: 23 November–31 December 1977; 10 January–25 March 1978

On tour 1977–8: Saint-Quentin-en-Yvelines (*th*) 28 April; Munich (*big top*) 8–11 May; Stuttgart (*big top*) 13–14 May; Münster (*th*) 16–17 May; Berlin (*big top*) 19–24 May; La Chaux-de-Fonds (*th*) 27 May; Brussels (*factory*) 30 May–1 June; Lyon (*th*) 5–10 June; Cergy-Pontoise (*w*) 17 June; Saintes (*out*) 5–8 July; Caracas (*g*) 12–17 July; San José (Costa Rica) (*big top*) 21–22 July; Mexico City (*th*) 25–30 July; London (*th*) 17–30 September; Rome (*w*) 3–7 October

Measure for Measure, 1978–1979

Théâtre des Bouffes du Nord: 27 October–31 December 1978; 2 January–3 February 1979

Measure for Measure and Ubu

On tour 18 February–22 April 1979: Louvain-la-Neuve (*th in farm*); Zurich (*w*); Nice (*th*); Geneva (*th*); Marseille (*th*); Milan (*th*)

Certificat et L'Os and The Conference of the Birds, 1979–1980

Creation: Avignon (*cloister*) 15–26 July 1980

First tour 1979: Berlin (*temporary th*) 8–16 September; Rome (*out*) 19–26 September; Saint-Quentin-en-Yvelines (*th*) 29 September

Théâtre des Bouffes du Nord: 6 October–17 November 1979; 23 October–31 December 1980

Further tour 1979: Villeneuve d'Asq (*th*) 21–23 November; Douai (*w*) 24 November; Mantes-la-Jolie (*th*) 27 November; Épernay (*th*) 28 November; Strasbourg (*university hall*) 29–30 November; Mulhouse (*th*) 1 December; Basle (*th*) 3–7 December; Monthey (*incinerator*) 9 December; Thonon (*gymnasium*) 10–11 December; Dijon (*exhibition hall*) 14 December; Montbéliard (*th*) 15 December; Saint-Étienne (*th*) 17–21 December

Further tour 1980: Arles (*village hall*) 8 January; Châteauvallon (*th*) 9 January; Aix-en-Provence (*th*) 10 January; Istres (*cold store*) 11 January; Carcassonne (*market*) 12–13 January; Perpignan (*w*) 15 January; Pau (*th*) 17 January; Tarbes (*th*) 18 January; Bordeaux (*th*) 18 January, (*gymnasium*) 19 January; Angoulême (*w*) 21–22 January; La Rochelle (*exhibition hall*) 23 January; Niort (*gymnasium*) 24 January; Orléans (*w*) 25–26 January; Angers (*w*) 27–28 January; Tours (*university hall*) 29–30 January; Saint-Lô (*th*) 10 February; Lisbon (*cloister*) 13–19 October

Certificat et L'Os, Ubu, The Ik and The Conference of the Birds, 1980

On tour: Adelaide (*q*) 18–29 March; Melbourne (*th*) 30 March–5 April; Sydney (*th*) 8–19 April; New York (*th* La MaMa) 30 April–15 June

The Cherry Orchard, 1981, 1983

Théâtre des Bouffes du Nord: 5 March–10 May 1981; 23 May–27 June 1981; 12 March–28 May 1983

La tragédie de Carmen, 1981–1982

Théâtre des Bouffes du Nord: 6 November 1981–30 April 1982; 26 October–31 December 1982

Ta Da Da
Théâtre des Bouffes du Nord: 25–26 December 1982

La tragédie de Carmen, 1983 (two tours at the same
time)
1st tour, in France: Annemasse (*th*) 15–19 February;
Grenoble (*th*) 22–26 February; Saint-Étienne (*th*)
1–5 March; Arles (*rice silo*) 8–13 March; Bordeaux
(*w*) 15–19 March; La Rochelle (*th*) 22–26 March;
Amiens (*th*) 29–31 March; Rouen (*th*) 1–2 April;
Strasbourg (*exhibition hall*) 6–9 April; Douai
(*church*) 12–13 April; Saint-Quentin-en-Yvelines
(*th*) 15–17 April; Villeurbanne (*th*) 19–24 April;
Bourges (*th*) 26–30 April
2nd tour: Barcelona (*w*) 28 February –9 March;
Hamburg (*w*) 25 March–9 April; Zurich (*exhibition hall*) 19–26 April; Stockholm (*theatre circus*)
25–28 May; Copenhagen (*gas container*) 31 May–5
June; New York (*th*) 24 October–28 April 1984

La tragédie de Carmen, 1984
Amsterdam (*theatre circus*) 7 February

The Mahabharata, 1985–1986
Théâtre des Bouffes du Nord: 17 April–13 June 1985,
8 November–31 December 1985, 10 January–24
May 1986
On tour 1985: Avignon (*q*, Boulbon) 2–31 July;
Athens (*q*) 12–14 September; Prato (*w*) 18–22
September; Frankfurt (*tram depot*) 1–5 October;
Madrid (*film studio*) 8–12 October; Barcelona
(*w*) 15–19 October; Villeurbanne (*th*) 22–30
October

La tragédie de Carmen, 1986–1987
On tour 1986: Pompeii (*Roman th*) 3–7 September;
Cagliari (*Roman amphitheatre*) 10–14 September;
Rome (*th*) 17–26 September; Düsseldorf (*train
depot*) 30 September–11 October; Frankfurt (*tram
depot*) 14–18 October; Munich (*studio cinema*)
21–25 October; Palermo (*th*) 29 October–1
November; Bari (*th*) 5–8 November; Milan (*th*)
12–20 November
On tour 1987: Tokyo (*th*) 2 March–26 April;
Jerusalem (*th*) 6–14 June; Athens (*q*) 17–23 June

The Mahabharata (English version) 1987–1988
Théâtre des Bouffes du Nord: 26 July–2 August 1987
On tour: Zurich (*boathouse*) 15–22 August 1987; Los
Angeles (*studio cinema*) 1 September–3 October
1987; New York (Brooklyn) (*th*) 13 October 1987–3
January 1988; Perth (*q*) 2–13 February 1988; Ade-
laide (*q*) 20 February–4 March 1988; Copenhagen
(*gas container*) 13–30 March 1988; Glasgow (*tram
depot*) 13 April–17 May 1988; Tokyo (*th*) 29
May–22 July 1988

The Cherry Orchard, 1988
English version: New York (Brooklyn) at the Majestic Theatre (BAM) 18 January–April

La tragédie de Carmen, 1988
On tour: Calgary (*th*) 12–24 February

The Cherry Orchard, 1989
English version on tour: Moscow (*th*) 6–14 March;

Tbilisi (*th*) 18–20 March; Leningrad (St Petersburg) (*th*) 25–28 March; Tokyo (*th*) 10–26 April

La tragédie de Carmen, 1989
On tour: Perth (*th*) 6–19 February; Glasgow (*tram
depot*) 10–30 April

Woza Albert, 1989–1990
Théâtre des Bouffes du Nord: 28 November–31
December 1989
On tour 1990: Seville (*th*) 10–11 February; Valencia
(*th*) 13–18 February; Bilbao (*th*) 20–21 February;
Grenoble (*th*) 1–4 March; Madrid (*th*) 9–11
March; Oviedo (*th*) 14–15 March; Frankfurt (*th*)
20–25 March; Dortmund (*th*) 27 March; Berlin
(*conference hall*) 29–31 March; Hamburg (*w*) 6–8
April; Brussels (*th in school*) 11–12 April; Caracas
(*th*) 15–16 April; Fort-de-France (*th*) 19–21 April;
Pointe-à-Pitre (*th*) 24 April; Prato (*w*) 27–9 April;
Milan (*th*) 2–5 May

La Tempête (*The Tempest*), 1990–1991
Creation: Zurich (*m*) 14–22 September 1990
Théâtre des Bouffes du Nord: 27 September–25
October 1990, 15 November 1990–2 March 1991
On tour 1990: Glasgow (*tram depot*) 30 October–3
November; Braunschweig (*th on stage*) 7–11
November
On tour 1991: Tokyo (*th*) 21 March–21 April; Frank-
furt (*exhibition hall*) 30 April–8 May; Hamburg
(*w*) 11–18 May; Vienna (*stock-exchange hall*) 22–26
May; Antwerp (*th*) 18–22 June; Milan (*th*) 25–30
June; Verona (*garden*) 4–7 July; Avignon (*q*) 11–31
July

Woza Albert, 1991
On tour: Lisbon (*th*) 31 May–2 June; Prague (*th*) 6–8
June; Bucharest (*th*) 12–14 June; Basle (*w*) 29
August–1 September; Vienna (*stock-exchange hall*)
3–6 September

Impressions de Pelléas, 1992–1993
Théâtre des Bouffes du Nord: 3 November 1992–23
January 1993
On tour 1992: Madrid (*th*) 21–27 December
On tour 1993: Zurich (*m*) 2–6 February; Hamburg
(*th*) 9–20 February; Glasgow (*tram depot*) 23–27
February; Barcelona (*w*) 3–7 March; Lisbon (*clois-
ter*) 9–13 March; Vienna (*m*) 16–21 March; Berlin
(*film studio*) 23–27 March; Frankfurt (*tram depot*)
30 March–3 April

L'homme qui, 1993–1994
Théâtre des Bouffes du Nord: 3 March–29 May 1993,
12 October–13 November 1993
On tour 1993: Munich (*m*) 12–20 June; Montpellier
(*w*) 25 June–5 July; Berlin (*th*) 30 August–9
September; Liège (*th*) 14–23 September; Villeurbanne (*th*) 28 September–8 October; Rennes (*th*)
17 November–20 December
On tour 1994: Lausanne (*th*) 11–29 January

The Man Who, 1994–1995
On tour 1994: Zurich (*m*) 18–26 February; Hamburg
(*w*) 2–12 March; Manchester (*th*) 18–26 March;

Newcastle (*th*) 30 March–9 April; Glasgow (*tram depot*) 13–24 April; Nottingham (*th*) 27–30 April; London (*th*) 6–21 May; Recklinghausen (*w*) 2–11 June; Stuttgart (*th*) 14–18 June; Amsterdam (*th*) 22–28 June; Vienna (*stock-exchange hall*) 2–5 July
On tour 1995: New York (*th*) 11 March–9 April; London (*th*) 19 April–6 May; Munich (*m*) 11–20 May; Jerusalem (*th*) 25 May–2 June

Who is there?, 1995–1996
Théâtre des Bouffes du Nord: 6 December 1995–23 March 1996
On tour 1996: Rennes (*th*) 1 April–4 May; Berlin (*th*) 11–24 May; Zurich (*m*) 29 May–8 June; Lausanne (*th*) 15 June–6 July

L'homme qui, 1997–1998
Théâtre des Bouffes du Nord: 25 October–31 December 1997
On tour 1998: Dijon (*th in church*) 13–17 January; Bordeaux (*th*) 20–25 January

Je suis un phénomène, 1998
Théâtre des Bouffes du Nord: 24 March–30 May
On tour 1998: Weimar (*w*) 3–14 June; Barcelona (*w*) 29 June–2 July; Lisbon (*th*) 8–12 July; Santiago de Compostela (*cinema*) 17–21 August; Zurich (*m*) 28 August–6 September; Lausanne (*th*) 9–19 September; Liège (*th*) 25 September–3 October; Milan (*th*) 7–22 October; Madrid (*th*) 27 October–1 November

The Man Who, 1999
On tour: Johannesburg (*th in a market*) 7–11 September; Buenos Aires (*th*) 16–23 September; Otsu (Kyoto) (*th*) 1–3 October; Tokyo (*th*) 7–16 October

Je suis un phénomène, 1999
On tour: Strasbourg (*th*) 5–30 January; Bordeaux (*th*) 5–13 February; Lille (*th*) 23–7 February; Montpellier (*th*) 2–7 March

Le Costume, 1999–2000
Théâtre des Bouffes du Nord: 16 December 1999–29 January 2000
On tour 2000: Lausanne (*th*) 3–20 February; Dijon (*th in a church*) 25 February–4 March; Chambéry (*th*) 7–10 March; Villeurbanne (*th*) 21–26 March; Taormina (Messina) (*th*) 6–7 April; Bologna (*th*) 11–16 April; Modena (*th*) 18–19 April; Toronto (*th*) 27–29 April; Montreal (*th*) 3–6 May; Basle (*w*) 10–13 May; Zurich (*m*) 18–20 May; Liège (*th*) 24–27 May; Hanover (*orangery*) 8–12 June; Recklinghausen (*conference hall*) 16–23 June; Frankfurt (*th on stage*) 28–30 June; Helsinki (*th*) 3–4 September; Stockholm (*th*) 12–13 September; Pôrto Alegre (*th*) 19–24 September; Berlin (*th on stage*) 3–7 October; Milan (*th*) 12–22 October; Turin (*th*) 25–29 October; Neufchâtel (*th*) 3–5 November; Gerona (*th*) 10–11 November; Narbonne (*th*) 14–15 November; Tarbes (*th*) 17–18 November; Toulouse (*th*) 22 November–9 December; La Rochelle (*th*) 13–16 November; Sète (*th*) 20–21 November

The Tragedy of Hamlet, 2000–2001
Théâtre des Bouffes du Nord: 21 November 2000–12 January 2001

Le Costume, 2001
On tour: Strasbourg (*th*) 5–13 January; Colmar (*th*) 17–18 January; London (*th*) 24 January–3 February; Coventry (*th*) 6 February; Nevers (*th*) 12–13 February; Compiègne (*th*) 15–16 February; Vire (*th*) 18–19 February; Caen (*th*) 22–24 February; Villefranche (*th*) 1–2 March; Châteauvallon (*th*) 8–9 March; Montpellier (*th*) 12–17 March; Sartrouville (*th*) 20–24 March; Vienna (*th*) 1–15 June; Dunlin (*th*), Manchester (*th*), Leeds (*th*), Brighton (*th*) October
Théâtre des Bouffes du Nord: 28 March–26 May

The Tragedy of Hamlet, 2001
On tour: Strasbourg (*th*) 17–27 January; Seattle (*gymnasium*) 6–19 April; New York (*th*) 24 April–6 May; Chicago (*th*) 10 May–2 June; Vienna (*m*) 8–17 June; Tokyo (*th*) 22 June–3 July; Otsu (Kyoto) (*th*) 7–8 July; Shizuoka (*th*) 11 July; Berlin (*th on stage*) 24–28 July; Basle (*w*) 3–5 August; London (*th*) 12 August–7 September

L'homme Qui, 2002
Théâtre des Bouffes du Nord: 28 November –22 December

Far Away, 2001-2002
Théâtre des Bouffes du Nord: 22 January 2001–30 March 2002

The Tragedy of Hamlet, 2002
On tour: Zurich (*m*), Saarbrucken (*w*), Venice (*w*), Sao Paulo (*th*), Rio de Janeiro (*th*), Barcelona (*w*), Aix en Provence (*out*), Warsaw (*th on stage*), Gdansk (*th*), Geneva (*th*), Milan (*th*), Lyon (*th*), Orléans (*th*), Annecy (*th*), Corbeil Essonnes (*th*), Cergy-Pontoise (*th*), Bourges (*th*), Nantes (*w*)

Le Costume, 2002
On tour: Elancourt (*th*), Lisbon (*th*), Reims (*th*), Forbach (*th*), Bourges (*th*) January; Ouagadougou (*out*), Bobo Dioulasso (*out*), Bamako (*th*), Dakar (*out*), Abidjan (*th*) February; Le Mans (*th*), Chicago (*th*), Bogotá (*th*), Caracas (*th*), Mexico (*th*), Naples (*w*), Bergen (*th*), Wroclaw (*th*), Hong kong (*th*), Singapore (*th*)

La Mort de Krishna, 2002–2003
Théâtre des Bouffes du Nord: 26–29 December 2002, 11–27 January 2003

La Tragédie de Hamlet, 2003
Théâtre des Bouffes du Nord: 7 January–13 April 2003
On tour: Bordeaux (*th*), Valencia (*w*), Chalon-sur-Saône (*th*), Ferrara (*th*), Antwerp (*th*), Coventry (*th*), Lisbon (*th*), Dubrovnik (*th*)

Places Visited by the International Centre

Abidjan (*th*), Adelaide (*q*), Aix-en-Provence (*th*), Amiens (*th*), Amsterdam (*th, theatre circus*), Angers (*w*), Angoulême (*w*), Annecy (*th*), Annemasse (*th*), Antwerp (*th1, th2*), Arles (*rice silo, village hall*), Athens (*q*), Avignon (*cloister, q1, q2*), Bamako (*th*), Barcelona (*w*), Bari (*th*), Basle (*th, w1, w2*), Belgrade (*unfinished cinema*), Bergen (*th*), Berkeley (*th*), Berlin (*big top, film studio, TV studio, temporary th, th on stage1, th on stage2, th1, th2, th3*), Bilbao (*th*), Bobo Dioulasso (*out*), Bogotá (*th*), Bologna (*th*), Bordeaux (*w1, w2, th1, th2, gymnasium*), Bourges (*th*), Braunschweig (*th on stage*), Brighton (*th*), Brussels (*factory, th in school, th*), Bucharest (*th*), Buenos Aires (*th*), Caen (*th1, th2*), Cagliari (*out*), Calgary (*th*), Caracas (*g, th1, th2*), Carcassonne (*market*), Cergy-Pontoise (*w, th*), Chalon-sur-Saône (*th*), Chambéry (*th*), Châteauvallon (*th*), Chicago (*gymnasium, th*), Colmar (*th*), Compiègne (*th*), Copenhagen (*gas container*), Corbeil Essonnes (*th*), Coventry (*th*), Dakar (*out*), Dijon (*exhibition hall, th in church*), Dortmund (*th*), Douai (*church, w*), Dublin (*th*), Dubrovnik (*th*), Düsseldorf (*train depot*), Elancourt (*th*), Épernay (*th*), Évry, Fort-de-France (*th*), Ferrara (*th*), Forbach (*th*), Frankfurt (*th, exhibition hall, th on stage, tram depot*), Gdansk (*th*), Geneva (*th1, th2*), Gerona (*th*), Glasgow (*tram depot*), Grenoble (*th*), Hamburg (*th, w*), Hanover (*orangery*), Helsinki (*th*), Hong Kong (*th*), Houston (*th*), Istres (*cold store*), Jerusalem (*th*), Johannesburg (*th in a market*), La Chaux-de-Fonds (*th*), La Rochelle (*th, exhibition hall*), Lausanne (*th*), Le Havre, Le Mans (*th*), Leeds (*th*), Leningrad (St Petersburg) (*th*), Liège (*th*), Lille (*th*), Lisbon (*cloister, th1, th2, th3*), London (*th1, th2, th3, th4, the Round House*), Los Angeles (*UCLA cinema studio, Hollywood cinema studio*), Louvain-la-Neuve (*th in farm*), Lyon (*th1, th2*), Mâcon, Madrid (*th1, th2, film studio*), Manchester (*th*), Mantes-la-Jolie (*th*), Marseille (*th*), Melbourne (*th*), Mexico City (*th*), Milan (*th1, th2, th3*), Minneapolis (*th*), Modena (*th*), Montbéliard (*th*), Monthey (*incinerator*), Montpellier (*th, w*), Montreal (*th*), Moscow (*th*), Mulhouse (*th*), Munich (*studio cinema, big top, m1, m2*), Münster (*th*), Nantes (*w*), Naples (*w*), Narbonne (*th*), Neufchâtel (*th*), Nevers (*th*), New York (Brooklyn) (*th*), New York (*Beaumont th, La MaMa th*), New-

castle (*th*), Nice (*th*), Niort (*gymnasium*), Nottingham (*th*), Orléans (*w, th*), Otsu (Kyoto) (*th*), Ouagadougou (*out*), Oviedo (*th*), Palermo (*th*), Pau (*th*), Perpignan (*w*), Perth (*q, th*), Philadelphia (*th on stage*), Pointe-à-Pitre (*th*), Pompeii (*Roman th*), Pôrto Alegre (*th*), Prague (*th*), Prato (*w*), Recklinghausen (*conference hall, w*), Reims (*th*), Rennes (*th*), Rio de Janeiro (*th*), Rome (*out, th, w*), Rouen (*th*), Saarbrucken (*w*), Saint-Étienne (*th1, th2*), Saint-Lô (*th*), Saint-Quentin-en-Yvelines (*th*), Saintes (*out*), San José (Costa Rica) (*big top*), Santiago de Compostela (*cinema*), Sao Paulo (*th*), Sartrouville (*th*), Seattle (*gymnasium*), Sète (*th*), Seville (*th*), Shizuoka (*th*), Singapore (*th*), Stockholm (*th, theatre circus*), Strasbourg (*th, university hall, exhibition hall*), Stuttgart (*big top, th*), Sydney (*th*), Taormina (Messina) (*th*), Tarbes (*th*), Tbilisi (*th*), Thonon (*g, gymnasium*), Tokyo (*th1, th2*), Toronto (*th*), Toulouse (*th*), Tours (*university hall*), Turin (*th*), Valencia (*th, w*), Venice (*cloister, Campo, w*), Verona (*garden*), Vienna (*m, stock-exchange hall, slaughterhouse, th1, th2*), Villefranche (*th*), Villeneuve d'Asq (*th*), Villeurbanne (*th*), Vire (*th*), Warsaw (*th on stage*), Washington (*th*), Weimar (*w*), Wroclaw (*th*), Zurich (*exhibition hall, m, w1, w2*).

Index